INCLUSIVE ETHNOGRAPHY

Caitlin Procter
Branwen Spector

INCLUSIVE ETHNOGRAPHY

Making Fieldwork Safer,
Healthier & More Ethical

1 Oliver's Yard
55 City Road
London EC1Y 1SP

2455 Teller Road
Thousand Oaks, California 91320

Unit No 323-333, Third Floor, F-Block
International Trade Tower Nehru Place
New Delhi – 110 019

8 Marina View Suite 43-053
Asia Square Tower 1
Singapore 018960

Editor: Charlotte Bush
Editorial Assistant: Rhiannon Holt
Production Editor: Gourav Kumar
Copyeditor: Joy Tucker
Proofreader: Caroline Hallworth
Indexer: KnowledgeWorks Global Ltd
Marketing Manager: Ben Sherwood
Cover Design: Shaun Mercier
Typeset by KnowledgeWorks Global Ltd

Editorial Arrangement © Caitlin Procter and Branwen Spector, 2024
Chapter 1 © Isobel Gibbin, 2024
Chapter 2 © Elena Butti, 2024
Chapter 3 © James Shires, 2024
Chapter 4 © Isabel Bredenbröker and Tajinder Kaur, 2024
Chapter 5 © Elsemieke van Osch and Sharon Louise Smith, 2024
Chapter 6 © Sandra Fernandez, 2024
Chapter 7 © Shannon Philip, 2024
Chapter 8 © Hareem Khan, 2024
Chapter 9 © Branwen Spector and Theodora Sutton, 2024
Chapter 10 © Caitlin Procter, 2024
Chapter 11 © Emma Louise Backe and Alex Fitzpatrick, 2024
Chapter 12 © Anne E. Pfister, 2024
Chapter 13 © Ezgi Güler, 2024
Conclusion © Caitlin Procter and Branwen Spector, 2024

Apart from any fair dealing for the purposes of research, private study, or criticism or review, as permitted under the Copyright, Designs and Patents Act, 1988, this publication may not be reproduced, stored or transmitted in any form, or by any means, without the prior permission in writing of the publisher, or in the case of reprographic reproduction, in accordance with the terms of licences issued by the Copyright Licensing Agency. Enquiries concerning reproduction outside those terms should be sent to the publisher.

Library of Congress Control Number: 2023946099

British Library Cataloguing in Publication data

A catalogue record for this book is available from the British Library

ISBN 978-1-5296-2003-0
ISBN 978-1-5296-2002-3 (pbk)

Contents

About the editors and contributors	vii
Acknowledgements	xiii
Introduction	xiv

PART 1   PREPARING FOR FIELDWORK

1   Ethnographic skills to keep you sane   2
    Isobel Gibbin

2   Safe and ethical ethnography: Looking inwards   18
    Elena Butti

3   Cybersecurity and ethnography   33
    James Shires

PART 2   DIVERSE IDENTITIES

4   Giving, taking and receiving care: Dis_ability and fieldwork   48
    Isabel Bredenbröker and Tajinder Kaur

5   Reflexive ethnography in intimate spaces: Motherhood and care work
    in and outside the field   63
    Elsemieke van Osch and Sharon Louise Smith

6   Fieldwork as a coded-as-Black woman   78
    Sandra Fernandez

7   Sex, sexuality and the ethnographer in the field   92
    Shannon Philip

PART 3 WORKING WITH INTERLOCUTORS

8   Betraying loyalty: Managing dis/trust as ethical feminist praxis   104
    Hareem Khan

9   Social media as method   118
    Branwen Spector and Theodora Sutton

10 Doing fieldwork in and on contexts of violence and instability   134
    Caitlin Procter

11 Fieldwork and feeled-work: Addressing mental health in ethnography   148
    Emma Louise Backe and Alex Fitzpatrick

PART 4 INCLUSIVITY IN ETHNOGRAPHIC WRITING

12 Participatory ethnographic methods: Collaborative data production,
    analysis and ethnographic representation   166
    Anne E. Pfister

13 Going against the grain in writing ethnography   182
    Ezgi Güler

Concluding recommendations for educators   197
    Branwen Spector and Caitlin Procter

Index   199

About the editors and contributors

Editors

Caitlin Procter is a part-time Professor at the Migration Policy Centre at the European University Institute, and a Marie Skłodowska-Curie Research Fellow at the Centre on Conflict, Development and Peacebuilding at the Geneva Graduate Institute (IHEID). Her work examines the experiences of children and youth in contexts of conflict and forced displacement, with a regional focus on Palestine, Jordan, Syria and Tunisia. She teaches on research methods and ethics and is a co-founder of The New Ethnographer.

Branwen Spector is a Lecturer in Social Anthropology at University College London. She conducts research on occupation, mobility and infrastructure in the Occupied Palestinian West Bank, Ukraine and Lebanon. She teaches on research methods, ethics, social media and decolonisation and is a co-founder of The New Ethnographer.

The New Ethnographer

The New Ethnographer is a project that addresses the challenges inherent in undertaking ethnographic research through teaching, training and writing, with a view to improving inclusivity and support for academics conducting fieldwork. For more information about our work, visit www.thenewethnographer.com

Contributors

Emma Louise Backe is a PhD candidate in Anthropology at the George Washington University (GWU). She also holds an MA and an MPhil in Medical Anthropology from GWU, a Certificate in Global Gender Policy and a BA in Anthropology from Vassar College. Her research deals with the politics of mental health, response and care for survivors of gender-based violence (GBV) in the US and South Africa. In her free time, she manages The Geek Anthropologist, a blog dedicated to the intersection of geek culture and anthropology.

Isabel Bredenbröker is a social and cultural anthropologist whose work focuses on material, sonic and visual culture, specifically the anthropology of death, afterlives of colonialism, synthetic materials, art and museums, queer theory and intersectionality. As Deutsche Forschungsgemeinschaft (DFG) Walter Benjamin Postdoctoral Researcher, they work between the Centre for Anthropological Research on Museums and Heritage and the Hermann von Helmholtz-Zentrum für Kulturtechnik at Humboldt Universität zu Berlin. They have co-curated public platforms and shown work in contemporary art contexts, produced collaborative films and presented work in ethnological museums.

Elena Butti is a Research Fellow at the Centre on Conflict, Development and Peacebuilding of the Geneva Graduate Institute (IHEID), and holds a PhD from the University of Oxford. Her research interests revolve around youth, drugs, crime, and migration at the urban margins in Latin America. Her current book project *We Are the Nobodies: Youth, violence and drug-dealing in contemporary Colombia* is an ethnographic exploration of adolescents' first steps into drug-related crime in Colombia. She regularly collaborates with international organisations on matters related to the Youth, Peace and Security agenda. She is also an amateur film-maker, using participatory film as a research methodology. More on www.elenabutti.com.

Sandra Fernandez has a PhD in Social Anthropology from the University of St Andrews. Her research examined the creation of safe spaces by anti sexual harassment groups in Cairo following the 2011 revolution. Sandra's interests focus on the body via construction/projection of masculinities/femininities, the impact of race and gender in research, gendered violence and potential solutions, social movements and NGOs. Sandra is currently exploring the potential applications of digital technologies in combatting sexual violence, and investigating how the construction of certain masculinities reinforces racist ideologies. Sandra is currently part of a Romania-based research group revisiting/reinterpreting the 2020 Ditro/Ditrau xenophobic incident.

Alex Fitzpatrick is currently Research Fellow in Digital Participation at the Science Museum in London. Originally trained as a zooarchaeologist specialising in later prehistoric funerary and ritual archaeology in Britain, Dr Fitzpatrick has since refocused her research on participation in heritage, with emphasis on inclusive and decolonial approaches to interpretation and engagement. She currently acts as Research Officer for the Enabled Archaeology Foundation.

Isobel Gibbin did their doctorate in Social and Cultural Anthropology at UCL. Their thesis explained the persistence of social inequalities in the UK's cultural sector using the anthropology of value, ritual, language and space. This was a based on a year's full-time fieldwork with the Barbican Centre in London. Izzy is a trained facilitator in dialectical behavioural therapy and worked in mental health crisis care after they graduated.

Ezgiv Güler is a Postdoctoral Researcher at Sabancı University in Istanbul. She is currently working at the intersection of migration and urban ethnography. Ezgi received her PhD degree from the European University Institute (Italy), where she studied the collective practices of transfeminine sex workers in urban Turkey. Her research interests include gender and sexuality, urban struggles, structural violence, sex work, migration and ethnographic research methods.

Tajinder Kaur is a PhD student at the Department of Anthropology, University of Delhi. She obtained her MSc and MPhil in Anthropology from the Department of Anthropology, University of Delhi. Her research interests include anthropology and disability, gender and disability, and visual documentation of the lived experiences of people with disabilities. She has published research articles and book reviews on disability and adoption, and the daily life experiences of people with physical disabilities during the COVID-19 crisis in India. She has also been involved with various NGOs working in the field of disability.

Hareem Khan is Assistant Professor of Anthropology and Ethnic Studies at California State University, San Bernardino. Her research has been published in American Studies Journal, Ethnicities, Journal of Asian American Studies, Wear Your Voice digital magazine, The New Ethnographer digital blog, and an anthology on global raciality organised by the University of California Center for New Racial Studies (Routledge). She is currently working on her first book project, which examines the burgeoning South Asian beauty and wellness industries focusing on the entanglements of race, labour, and the commodification of transnational aesthetic practices under neoliberal multiculturalism.

Elsemieke Van Osch is a PhD researcher in Social and Cultural Anthropology, at KU Leuven, and affiliated with the Centre for the Social Study of Migration and Refugees, Ghent University. She holds an interdisciplinary MA in International Migration and Human Rights Law *(Distinction)* from the University of Kent. Her PhD research is based on a follow-along ethnography of families' trajectories through the volatile, unpredictable asylum regime in Belgium, analysing how families navigate and contest manifestations of repressive asylum policies in their private lives, as well as how normative understandings of 'family' become entangled in bordering processes.

Anne E. Pfister is an applied, medical anthropologist and sociolinguistic anthropologist. Dr Pfister's research explores the experience of deafness from the perspectives of deaf youth and their families in Mexico City, Mexico. Her research interests include deafness and sign languages, language socialisation, medicalisation, health in social and cultural context, participatory and multi-modal ethnographic research methods, and the digital humanities. Her work has been published in *Ethos; Visual Anthropology Review; Behavioral and Brain Sciences; Collaborative Anthropologies* and *Medical Anthropology.*

Shannon Philip is a Lecturer (Assistant Professor) in Sociology at the University of East Anglia and a Research Associate at the University of Johannesburg. He recently published his first monograph, *Becoming Young Men in a New India: Masculinities, Gender Relations and Violence in the Postcolony* (Cambridge University Press, 2022). His current research comparatively explores youth, masculinities, sexualities, urban transformations and gender relations in South Africa and India.

James Shires is a Senior Research Fellow in Cyber Policy at Chatham House. He is a co-founder and trustee of the European Cyber Conflict Research Initiative (ECCRI), and a non-resident Associate Fellow with the Hague Program for International Cybersecurity at Leiden University. He speaks regularly and has written extensively on cybersecurity and global politics. His book *The Politics of Cybersecurity in the Middle East* (Hurst/Oxford University Press, 2021) is partly based on his ethnographically inspired doctoral research on cybersecurity expert communities in Egypt and the Gulf states. A full list of publications is available at www.jamesshires.com/research

Sharon Louise Smith is a final-year PhD researcher in the School of Education at the University of Birmingham. Her research, undertaken with fellow mothers of disabled children, explores educational inclusion and exclusion. Drawing on feminist new materialist theories and posthumanism, the enquiry explores parental subjectivity as becoming, in an attempt to move away from binary representations or static identity descriptions, such as 'warrior mum'. She also uses creative research techniques including collage and poetry for both analysis and dissemination purposes. Her work and research interests are influenced by her own experience as a mother of a disabled child.

Theodora Sutton is a digital anthropologist who completed her PhD at the Oxford Internet Institute in 2021. Her research focused on a technology-free retreat in California, USA, where she explored how attendees blended New Age beliefs with Western notions of mental health, and conjured visions of ancient tribal life among the redwoods. She is interested in ethnographic methods, a redirected focus towards researcher wellbeing, and our relationship with the natural world.

Acknowledgements

The idea behind this textbook is the result of discussions, teaching and writing within the New Ethnographer project, which started out as a blog for doctoral students and early career researchers in 2017 to write about challenges faced during fieldwork. The project has evolved into fieldwork training workshops and direct work with universities to develop better standards of fieldwork training and support for students doing ethnography: and now, into this textbook.

We would not have been able to conduct any of our work without the kindness, time and compassion of our many contributors, collaborators and supportive friends, family and colleagues along the way. We would like to begin by thanking the original contributors to our blog, started in 2017, who shared their time and expertise and, most importantly, their sentiments with us. The popularity of their contributions gave us the confidence to proceed with this project, and led us to prioritising methods training through our own careers.

We would particularly like to thank our colleagues who gave up their time and expertise to help us translate ideas from the blog into fieldwork training workshops, in particular to Luisa Enria, Shannon Philip, Sandra Fernandez, Isobel Gibbin and Maureen Freed.

We are grateful to the ASA, AAA, EASA, BRISMES and ICCG conferences which have hosted our panels and workshops on ethics, safety, health and mental health during fieldwork over the years, giving us the space to build our networks and open this conversation to international audiences. We also thank the University of Lisbon, the University of Geneva and the University of Oslo for investing in our ideas for better ways to teach ethnography, and exploring some of the content of this textbook with their staff and students.

At Sage, we would like to thank Charlotte Bush and Rhiannon Holt for their support and guidance in the latter stages of developing the book. We are also grateful to Jai Seaman, who not only saw and understood what we wanted to achieve through this book from its inception, but encouraged us to think bigger.

This project began from difficult experiences, which we could not have got through without the extensive personal support of friends and family. Our heartfelt thanks go to our parents, who listened to us, supported us, encouraged us, worked with us and cared for us to help transform those experiences into positive change.

Finally, our deepest thanks go to the contributing authors to this volume. We are incredibly grateful that you see the value in this book and gave your time to writing it with us.

Introduction

Two PhD students met at a research institution in the country where they were doing ethnographic fieldwork. After getting through the initial posturing required of such encounters (What are you working on? Which university are you based at? Who is your supervisor?), they quickly disclosed to each other that they felt extremely isolated in their field research, and as if they were making it up as they went along. In the neophytic stages of the famed 'rite of passage' of ethnographic fieldwork, both students felt they were duty-bound to experience this form of hardship, but had not been trained to deal with it. Both students were doing research in deeply complex community settings that at times were dominated by violence. Are you living there? With a family? How do you keep track of what's going on? They agreed on how useful Facebook could be as a source of information in the community; how well taken care of they were by the families they knew the best; and how useless formal channels of government advice that their universities had advised them to draw on had been. What did you tell your university about your fieldwork? Did they insure you to be here? How are you meeting people and getting them to talk to you? Are you volunteering? Are you working somewhere? Have you managed to make friends in the community? Do you think people trust you? It is all going to be OK, though, right?

They agreed to meet up in a café to debrief with each other as regularly as they could over the coming months. The more their respective fieldwork progressed, the more they encountered situations that they felt utterly untrained and unprepared to handle. Both faced issues navigating access to their research sites and accessing enough funding to adequately support their research. The question when they met became not 'How are you?' but 'How are you managing?', a subtle shift from recognising that working in their respective fieldsites was not something that could be answered with 'Fine', and an implicit recognition of the challenges they knew the other faced. Both of these students faced circumstances during their fieldwork that seriously threatened their own physical safety and their ability to carry out their research. Both during and after fieldwork, they found their institutions unprepared and sometimes unwilling to support them in the wake of their experiences.

This textbook is the product of the five years of work we have developed with The New Ethnographer, the project we founded that sought to try and improve ethnographic research methods training as a result of the conditions and experiences described above. It is a book that we wish we had read as graduate students, and one that we hope will help bring about positive change in enabling many different kinds of ethnographers to recognise themselves and the challenges they may face throughout the process of developing research. This book is about making equality, diversity and inclusion central to both teaching about and doing ethnographic fieldwork in practice. For students and junior researchers of colour, diverse sexual orientation and gendered identity, varying levels of physical ability, or living with mental illness there is little space within the academy to discuss how these core aspects of their identity interacted with the realities of doing ethnographic fieldwork. Similarly, there is little opportunity for others to learn from their challenges to inform their own practice. Neither is it common practice for researchers to own the mistakes they make in doing ethnographic fieldwork (often with limited training) along the way. This book focuses on the core challenges repeatedly raised by ethnographers – particularly those doing long-term fieldwork for the first time. In so doing, it seeks to contribute both to changing the way that ethnography is taught and changing the way we think about fieldwork.

By centring equality, diversity and inclusion in the training and practice of ethnography, we mean acknowledging the wide range of experience of researchers, learning from each other's experiences and approaches, and celebrating how our differences inform knowledge production. Having been educated in a period during which the importance of decolonising knowledge became central, we attend to the racist histories of both ethnography as a methodology and Western academia more broadly, taking as a starting point the need to understand and learn from past errors. We begin with the notion that decolonisation is both a necessary and intellectual process, and as such we aim to decentre Euro-American knowledge production. We acknowledge the power imbalances and structural barriers to inclusion present in our own settings and backgrounds. It is from this perspective that we make the case for an inclusive ethnographic practice.

By providing methods texts authored by scholars that might resonate with a wider and more diverse audience, we hope to engage junior scholars in candid discussions around what can go wrong in doing ethnography, and provide concrete and tangible guidance on ways of doing fieldwork which are safer, healthier and more ethical. In developing the book, the editors and chapter authors had the same question in mind: what do you wish you had read or been told before you started fieldwork, and what would you like to pass on to future researchers? The book brings together contributors to The New Ethnographer project who have shared our vision and helped us write and teach towards safer, healthier and more ethical fieldwork by creating our own training programmes and blog. We made our goal at The New Ethnographer to lobby for major institutional change in the way that students and junior scholars are prepared for field research. Part of this preparedness lies in recognising the diversity of those who undertake ethnographic research, and the kinds of challenges they may face, and working together to build and share a new vision and attitude.

The authors contributing to this textbook are all ethnographers who have conducted fieldwork within the last five years. The chapters walk the reader through the process of doing ethnography – from planning, to fieldwork, to analysis and writing up. We deliberately do not offer a traditional theoretical approach to conducting ethnography. Instead, this textbook centres the practicality and diversity of this kind of research to propose inclusivity and compassion as the framework for successful ethnography. In response to what we know, and also what we have learned from others (Procter, Spector and Freed 2024), we agree that methods training is often too theoretical at the expense of practical advice for the diversity of experiences in conducting ethnography. The intention of this book is to provide an intimate, vulnerable and confessional account of the challenges of ethnographic research. We therefore offer personal reflections on the kinds of challenges we faced during our own ethnographic research and share recommendations of ways of thinking ahead. This is not to put readers off the potential pitfalls and challenges of research, but to support the reader to feel confident, prepared and able to locate the support needed in completing their research. To this end, this book is a practical guide for early career researchers and established academics alike, to thinking afresh about the kinds of challenges fieldwork can entail and about centring equality, diversity and inclusivity in ethnographic practice.

We need to talk about doing ethnography

This poster, distributed around PhD common rooms at a UK university, represents the specific institutional and cultural attitudes to fieldwork we seek to challenge. In fact, this poster was distributed after one of us had lobbied their department to take fieldwork preparedness more

Figure 1.1 Poster displayed in an elite UK institution social science department. Photo by Spector, 2019

seriously. While we acknowledge it is an improvement on earlier approaches, this superficial nod to the safety and wellbeing of researchers is unfortunately commonplace. Reading the poster, one might assume that ticking these boxes would prepare oneself adequately for fieldwork. Yet there is no further information offered for each item on the checklist or even a contact address with whom preparing fieldworkers might contact to address these issues. It places the responsibility on the individual researcher to tick off such diverse subjects as ethical review board approval, travel safety training and mental health as things that can be completed, resolved and put aside.

This kind of messaging also reinforces an impression that fieldwork is something done 'elsewhere', conducted in a space and time vacuum in which you are removed from your otherwise everyday life. Over the course of the many fieldwork training workshops we have facilitated over the past five years through The New Ethnographer, students and early career researchers have often described the pressure they feel to boast 'exotic' and 'difficult' research topics and locations to set them apart from competing candidates on today's neoliberal academic job market. Similarly, conferences and symposia are often established specifically to address fieldwork in 'dangerous' or 'extreme' environments. With notable exceptions (for instance, the Advancing Research on Conflict flagship summer programme), these events often replicate power dynamics between junior and senior scholars, or simply offer an opportunity for researchers to present their own experiences with little space for dialogue or practical training. Whether researchers are conducting fieldwork in contexts of conflict and violence, or in spaces that might be conventionally considered as 'safe', they are liable to experience trauma, depression, anxiety, loss, financial hardship, or other kinds of challenging experiences. As women, we know we cannot guarantee our safety in any location. Why, then, should ethnographers identifying in other ways be asked to do the same? The impact that long-term research in the field can have on the health and wellbeing of those conducting fieldwork has led to concern over university preparedness for fieldwork, to which this book offers a response. It is surprising to us that, as a human-centred discipline, anthropology has been slow to engage with these issues and it is high time these attitudes that inhibit and obstruct conversations around the impact of ethnography on ethnographers were changed.

Why now?

The chapters in this book reflect on and respond to slowly changing circumstances in academia. In the years leading up to its publication, the COVID-19 pandemic; waves of industrial unrest across the UK and US higher education sector; and the high-profile cases of the death and torture of PhD students from Western institutions conducting research elsewhere have contributed to the acknowledgement that the relationship between researchers and institutions is unwell. This book is part of our response to this unwellness. It encourages its readers to place their wellbeing at the centre of their fieldwork experience as a contribution to resisting the increasingly neoliberal academy.

In 2009 Amy Pollard's often-referenced study 'Field of screams' demonstrated that experiences of violence, trauma and unsafety were ubiquitous among those returning from periods of ethnographic fieldwork. Fifteen years later, we note that little has changed. For those of us remaining in academia, and particularly those staying in anthropology, our first fieldwork experience is unlikely to be our last, and yet updated training is rarely provided. For this reason, we believe it is important and, unfortunately, radical to encourage first-time fieldworkers to shape fieldwork that works for them, in an open and supported environment. We founded The New Ethnographer as PhD students who were angry and reacting against their own (lack of) training, experiences of isolation and lack of support in the field. In the process, we found allies and like-minded educators, with whom we collaborated to design training that taught the skills we believe are necessary. Now, as educators ourselves, that anger has subsided into a desire and ability to work from inside universities to enact change.

We can enact this change owing to two broader developments in higher education over the past decade. The first is the mainstreaming of knowledge and information about mental health that has normalised an acknowledgement of the impact higher education can take on us, which at present is largely directed to undergraduate students. There remains, however, both an institutional discomfort and a lack of knowledge about how to address it. For research students, this combines with a lack of responsibility for considering the impact that extended fieldwork may have. The second change is in the creation of space to discuss difficult dynamics in fieldwork, usually in symposia and conferences on so-called 'dangerous' work. A thriving subgenre of methodological guides and edited volumes on experiences of danger and crisis in fieldwork have added to this development. While events and literature create a space, they remain marginalised as just that – a subgenre, deemed irrelevant to those not working in so-called dangerous spaces, and only the beginning of a solution to changing practice.

This textbook is only part of our contribution to the changing environment and attitudes in academia. The New Ethnographer was founded as a future-oriented project intended to eventually become defunct. We should not need to continue to publish books or host training workshops because our ideas about how methods are taught will, we hope, become naturalised as we continue to decolonise our practices. We also acknowledge that reforming the way methods training and fieldwork preparedness are taught is not the end of the road; these issues emerge from structural and cultural forces that generate and maintain inequality. This book is part of a wider movement towards enacting change that we encourage you, our readers – both staff and students – to take up in your own institutions, including encouraging adapting an ethos of compassion from research supervisors, funding bodies and universities.

This book began its journey as an edited volume and eventually became a textbook because of our commitment to moving beyond creating a space for voices, and towards changing the way ethnography is taught. As two white women, we certainly do not claim to be the face of inclusivity, but believe in centring a diverse range of experiences that we have learned from and value. This book is designed to reflect what we have learned from contributors, conversations and our own changing circumstances as carers, managing new and old illnesses, and precarity. Fundamentally, we centre the need to learn from everyone's experience, regardless of if we think it is relevant to our work.

Towards an inclusive ethnography

Ethnography is a series of research techniques requiring a holistic and often immersive approach. This book will not tell you how to put into use the different approaches encompassed under the term 'ethnography' – in-depth interviews, participant observation and other means of attempting to understand things from your research participants' points of view. It will, however, guide you through the practical implications of this immersive way of conducting research.

Our approach builds on the work of the reflexive turn of the 1980s, in which anthropologists were asked to reflect thoughtfully on their subjectivity and how it impacted their fieldsites and interlocutors. This led to a boom in an 'emotionally literate' anthropology, taking on the findings of feminist, identity politics and post-colonial scholarship. Anthropologists are now commonly trained in considering their subjectivities in their research, yet we have found that this is often simply a box-ticking exercise in training, or a simple reference in a methodology section; 'I am a white woman of a different class background to my interlocutors', for example, is often considered a sufficient engagement with the subject of reflexivity in the field. Meeting other scholars who agreed with us that such superficial engagement with the differences between ourselves and those we worked with, we shaped The New Ethnographer around the questions of 'how we impact our fieldsites, and how our fieldsites impact us'. Despite the wide body of work that has drawn from and built upon the reflexive turn of the 1980s (Clifford and Marcus, 1986; Rosaldo,1989; Tedlock, 1991), there remains a need for greater empathy and compassion for what it means to face challenges in ethnographic research that cannot be limited to a simple recognition of one's background and politics.

Centring inclusivity in ethnography attends to the wellbeing of both the researcher and their interlocutors. In so doing, it makes explicit and transparent not only the way our fieldwork impacts the places where we work, but also the ways fieldwork impacts researchers. What does doing ethnography look like if you are, for example, mentally ill, a person of colour, not able-bodied, or have caring responsibilities? These are not special or unusual cases and traits among ethnographers, and neither are they only relevant to those who identify similarly or share experiences. This book begins with the notion that nobody is the ideal type so often represented in training curricula, and instead invites its readers to consider how to centre their uniqueness in their research design and consider what they might learn from someone who does or doesn't share their way of experiencing the world. In doing this we emphasise the importance of wellbeing, which we relate to our health, mental health, attention to power dynamics of gender, sexual identity, class, race, ability, ethnicity and other markers of subjective identities. However, we also draw attention to additional themes that emerge for many ethnographers, including risk, deception and, perhaps most importantly, a sense of compassionate care. With these factors in mind, we return to the literal meaning of 'wellbeing': are we as researchers and those we work with being well as a result of our work?

It is therefore a central tenet of this book that we should only design and conduct research that works for our specific needs, and that keeps us well and safe. Our identities, illnesses, abilities and responsibilities should not be framed as barriers or limitations to conducting research, but instead as unique ways of understanding the world that can allow us to build better and healthier relationships with our research participants and produce nuanced and revolutionary knowledge. We invite our readers to push back against standards and expectations that ask you to set aside the things that make you unique. Ethnographic research is not a checklist to be completed, but an opportunity to celebrate our and others' diversity.

To this end, we believe ethnographers should be encouraged to detail their personal experiences relevant to their research, and move away from historical attempts to separate 'emotion' from 'data' in what Foley calls 'a somewhat schizophrenic manner' (2002, p. 474). This includes the emotions embedded in their own lives and relationships in the field. Many of the contributing authors to our project have referenced the importance of self-care in their work, especially in light of often hostile or disinterested institutional responses to challenges faced in the field or upon their return. Attitudes that place care for the self and care for those we work with as the responsibility of the researcher alone create a weighty intellectual and emotional burden.

When we talk about inclusivity, then, we centre compassion. We do this by celebrating the ways that people who do ethnography are diverse. We encourage compassion for what these differences entail for the practice of ethnography. This enables an openness to engagement with all these experiences to strengthen our own understanding and work. Compassionate practice acknowledges and seeks to understand the myriad experiences and responsibilities we share as colleagues, cohorts, allies and members of an academic and professional community. Compassionate inclusive practice would draw attention to these thought processes, actions and adjustments to methodology with the intention of raising attention towards managing this burden. It is one thing to have discussions about the importance of equality, diversity and inclusion, but compassion helps us put these values into practice.

Inclusive ethnography seeks to undo structural inequalities surrounding ethnographic research methods training, and to reform training and support across institutions. The book responds to the often-asked questions 'but what can we possibly do to bring about this change?' Through the following chapters, authors reiterate that genuine inclusivity requires both intellectual and practical work, but does not frame it in abstracted terms or naive hope of a suddenly 'un-neoliberal' university. The chapters draw directly from the ethnographic experience of the authors, seeing opportunities for compassion in the texts and practices we have studied. In so doing we do not accuse others of misconduct, but rather invite our discipline to notice and respond to structural challenges facing our work environment today, as we are forced to do in our research. We are no longer angry: we are hopeful. It is our intention that *inclusive ethnography* can represent a new cohort of scholars, open to all, who recognise the ways in which ethnographic practice has – indeed must – continue to grow.

Outline of the textbook

This textbook is divided into three sections, designed to walk the reader through the different stages of conducting an ethnography. In Part One we invite you to consider how you might prepare for fieldwork beyond permissions, buying tickets and negotiating visas, instead thinking about the core skills, aptitudes and attitudes ethnographers require to do their work. Part Two explores the diverse identities of people conducting fieldwork and what we can learn from them. In Part Three, we explore challenges in working with interlocutors, Finally, Part Four responds to the challenges of turning ethnographic fieldwork into academic content in data analysis and writing.

Each of the 13 chapters has been written by an ethnographer who has faced challenges to their physical or emotional safety, health or mental health, or serious ethical dilemmas. The chapters include deeply personal reflections from the authors on their own experiences while remaining practical in their approach. In order to reflect the fact that ethnography is not prescriptive, we gave autonomy to each author to use text boxes to highlight case studies, key terms and personal reflections as they saw fit. The chapters then conclude with recommendations for the reader to take forward in considering their own ethnographic practice. As such, this book will enable students and scholars to engage in the complex realities of doing ethnographic research, and to challenge our assumptions of what it means to produce knowledge by conducting fieldwork. It is intended for both qualitative research methods courses and fieldwork preparation courses and aimed towards all researchers from undergraduate, postgraduate, doctoral, postdoctoral and professional backgrounds.

Opening the discussion on preparing for fieldwork and the early stages of any ethnography, in Chapter 1 Gibbin engages in a radical discussion on the core capabilities of fieldwork: what personal qualities does it take to be an ethnographer? Many of these skills are taken for granted and rarely discussed in ethnographic education. In this chapter, the emotional, interpersonal and cognitive demands of field research are made explicit, and are situated in a broader discussion about the relationship between mental health and ethnography. In Chapter 2 Butti reflects on complex moments where researchers may be tempted to consciously cross ethical and safety lines with the aim of gathering data. Through this lens, she discusses risks related to the context, the topic and the researcher's positionality in the field, as well as the ethics of relationships with one's informants. Concluding this section, in Chapter 3, Shires provides an overview of cybersecurity considerations and the implications of moving ethnographic data around the world. After introducing the topic with several stark examples of why cybersecurity is an important and difficult topic to navigate for ethnographers, the chapter provides an overview of different kinds of cybersecurity threats in general, and then more specific threats likely to be relevant to ethnographers.

Part Two of the textbook engages with diverse subjective identities and the implications they may have for doing ethnography, focusing on the topics of ableism, care responsibilities, race, gender and sexuality. In Chapter 4, Bredenbröker and Kaur write about care, and against ableist conceptions in fieldwork from the perspectives of ethnographers from the Global South and the Global North, one of whom works on disability and the other who is a person with a 'dis_ability' due to chronic illness. They highlight how dis_ability and fieldwork can go together and what experiences they may entail. Critically, they argue that ableism is something that concerns every bodymind facing ethnographic field research.

In Chapter 5, Van Osch and Smith pick up the discussion of care, turning to the personal, intellectual and emotional challenges of balancing ethnographic fieldwork with care responsibilities at home. They unpack some of the strategies and tools employed to reconcile their roles and responsibilities at home – as a mother/carer – with those as an engaged ethnographer/researcher. Rather than seeing these responsibilities as shortcomings, they suggest that the frictions and synergies in the field arising out of diverse aspects related to the ethnographer's social background (including family relations and care responsibilities) should instead be understood as enriching analytical tools that enable different ways of approaching knowledge production.

Continuing the discussion around gender, in Chapter 6 Fernandez explores the way ethnographers might be perceived on the basis of the values placed upon skin colour combined with the gender roles they are expected to inhabit. She demonstrates how skin colour and gender can be both the source of varying degrees of discrimination, but can also be advantageous in navigating certain contexts. Going beyond a reflexive discussion of positionality, the chapter develops a framework for ethnographers to prepare themselves for the potential differences in how they may be treated, regardless of how they self-identify, offering a starting point in mapping out the choices they make that impact gathering data, maintaining their own safety and halting unwanted behaviour.

In Chapter 7, Philip takes forward discussions on harassment to address the important role of sexuality within different stages of ethnographic research. Understanding the sexual politics of the fieldsites, he suggests, can allow ethnographers a deeper insight into the social dynamics therein. This chapter provides tools to explore the sexual politics of fieldsites and focuses on the sexuality of research participants as well as the sexuality of the researcher. It also provides some useful strategies and methods to approach safe and effective ethnographic fieldwork with sexual politics in mind.

Part Three then turns to reflections on the ways ethnographers work with interlocutors and the impact this has on everyone involved. In Chapter 8, Khan leads a discussion on loyalty and betrayal in working with interlocutors. This chapter emphasises central questions of how trust and distrust is mediated by the raced, gendered, classed and religious identities of those involved in ethnographic encounters, and the ways through which dis/trust shapes how we carry out our methods as observers and interviewers. In Chapter 9, Spector and Sutton expand on this discussion to consider ways of working ethnographically with interlocutors online. Addressing relationship management, boundary setting and consent, they confront the way ethnographic research is increasingly entangled with social media, regardless of the method or topic of the research, and the importance of considering how this can impact both researchers and interlocutors' safety and wellbeing. In Chapter 10, Procter addresses the challenges of doing ethnography either in contexts of violence or on subjects related to violence. She moves away from the assumption that 'violent fieldwork' only happens in specifically 'violent places', instead discussing the ways that violence can interfere with building trusting relationships with interlocutors; the challenges of exiting from these fieldwork relationships when violence continues in the lives of your interlocutors; and the need to centre compassion for yourself and those you work with throughout this process. Concluding this section, in Chapter 11, Backe and Fitzpatrick consider the implications of such challenges by addressing the impact on mental health that challenging ethnographic subjects can take. The chapter is informed by a survey that was circulated globally to anthropologists at various stages of their careers and highlights the ubiquity of mental health concerns that still implicitly inform ethnographic fieldwork, as well as the absence of adequate support mechanisms.

Part Four engages with inclusivity in ethnographic analysis and writing. In Chapter 12, Pfister puts forward ideas for involving participants as collaborators in decision-making throughout the research process, from the understanding that inclusive ethnography means moving towards more parity between researcher and participants. The chapter explores how participatory analysis can help anthropologists dissolve the limitations of more 'traditional' ethnographic methods, while being more inclusive through attention to context and community-specific strengths and needs – including language and language modality. In Chapter 13, Güler discusses tension between pondering the ethics and politics of ethnographic representation and neoliberal and objectivist expectations in trying to write inclusive ethnography. She highlights the importance of emotionally engaged reflections, complex, dynamic and varied depictions of lived experience, and the incorporation of political commitments and critical analysis in ethnographic writing. Although the 13 chapters of this text book are written with students and early career researchers in mind, the book's conclusion is directed towards educators and research supervisors. Here we draw from the main lessons of the book to highlight the work to be done at an institutional level to ensure that a new generation of ethnographers are guided towards ways of doing research that are safer, healthier, ethical and fundamentally more inclusive.

References

Abu-Lughod, L. 1986. *Veiled Sentiments: Honour and Poetry in a Bedouin Society*. Berkeley: University of California Press.

Behar, R. 1996. *The Vulnerable Observer: Anthropology that Breaks the Heart*. Boston: Beacon Press.

Berry, M.J., Chávez Argüelles, C., Cordis, S., Ihmoud, S. and Velásquez, E.E. 2017. Toward a fugitive anthropology: Gender, race and violence in the field. *Cultural Anthropology*, 32, 4.

Clifford, J. and Marcus, G. (Eds.) 1986. *Writing Culture: The Poetics and Politics of Ethnography*. Berkeley: University of California Press.

Coley, A. 1999. *The Ethnographic Self: Fieldwork and the Representation of Identity*. London: Sage.

Cook, J.C. 2010. Ascetic practice and participant observation, or, the gift of doubt and incompletion in field experience. In Davies, J. and Spencer, D. (Eds.), *Emotions in the Field: The Psychology and Anthropology of Fieldwork Experience*. Stanford: Stanford University Press. pp. 239–66.

Foley, D.E. 2002. Critical ethnography: The reflexive turn. *International Journal of Qualitative Studies in Education*, 15(4), 469–90.

Humphrey, C. 1989. Perestroika and the pastoralists: The example of Mongun-Taiga in Tuva ASSR. *Anthropology Today*, 5(3), 6–10.

Lorimer, F. 2010. Using emotion as a form of knowledge in a psychiatric fieldwork setting. In Davies, J. and Spencer, D. (Eds.), *Emotions in the Field: The Psychology and Anthropology of Fieldwork Experience*. Stanford: Stanford University Press. pp. 98–126.

Marcus, G. 1994. What comes (just) after 'post'! The case of ethnography. In Lincoln, Y. and Denzin, N. (Eds.), *Handbook of Qualitative Research*. Thousand Oaks, CA: Sage. pp. 563–73.

Newton, E. 1993. My best informant's dress: The erotic equation in fieldwork. *Cultural Anthropology*, 8(1), 3–23.

Nicholson, L. 1982. Comment on Rosaldo's 'The Use and Abuse of Anthropology'. *Signs*, 7(3), 732–5.

Pollard, A. 2009. Field of screams: Difficulty and ethnographic fieldwork. *Anthropology Matters*, 11(2), 4–24.

Procter, C., Spector, B. and Freed, M. (forthcoming 2024). Field of screams revisited: Contending with trauma in ethnographic fieldwork. *Teaching Anthropology*.

Rosaldo, R. 1989. *Culture and Truth: The Remaking of Social Analysis*. London: Routledge. pp. 1–24.

Rosaldo, M. and Lamphere, L. (Eds.) 1974. *Woman, Culture and Society*. Stanford: Stanford University Press.

Scheper-Hughes, N. 1995. The primacy of the ethical: Propositions for a militant anthropology. *Current Anthropology*, 36(3), 409–40.

Song, H. 2017. James Clifford and the ethical turn in anthropology. *Cultural Critique*, 97, 176–200.

Taussig, M. 2004. *My Cocaine Museum*. Chicago: University of Chicago Press.

Tedlock, B. 1991. From participant observation to the observation of participation: The emergence of narrative ethnography. *Journal of Anthropological Research*, 47(1), 69–94.

PART 1

PREPARING FOR FIELDWORK

1

ETHNOGRAPHIC SKILLS TO KEEP YOU SANE

Isobel Gibbin

Summary

This chapter argues that in the context of a rising mental health crisis in academia, enabling fieldworkers to thrive requires *both* greater attention to pre-field skill development, and an expanded understanding of what is required to do 'good' ethnography. Here, I explore the core social, emotional and cognitive demands of fieldwork, and the skills needed to meet them effectively. Many of these skills are taken for granted and rarely discussed in ethnographic education, leaving students poorly prepared for the realities of fieldwork. I argue that this omission belies a tension between fieldwork capabilities as inherent features of our personality and as skills that can be acquired. This tension is keenly felt when talking about how mental illness and neurodevelopmental difference relate to our ability to perform fieldwork. However, by engaging with ethnographers writing from this vantage point, we can imagine a more compassionate future for our discipline.

Table of contents

Introduction 3
Why fieldwork skills are hard to talk about 4
Skills for fieldworkers 5

Mental health and the future of ethnography 11
Conclusion 14
Recommendations 15
Further reading 15
References 16

Introduction

What are the social, emotional, and cognitive skills crucial to doing good ethnography? And how are they affected by the experience of mental illness and neurodivergence?

As a young ethnographer trying to formulate my research proposal, I was anxious to answer these questions. I had a new diagnosis that described the way I interacted with people and the things I needed to stay well, and I felt certain that this would affect my work as an ethnographer. I was eager to discuss this likelihood with my teachers. However, there seemed to be no channel for doing so. There were no seminars about mental health and fieldwork, and certainly no productive conversations resulting from my attempts to raise the subject with experienced academics. It was only through talking privately to my peers and reading the New Ethnographer blog that I found my anxieties being openly addressed.

The time for discussions like this could hardly be riper. Researchers have described a rising 'mental health crisis' in academia (Evans et al., 2018), with graduate academics over six times as likely to experience anxiety and depression than the general population. The authors speculate that precarious working conditions, poor advisory relationships and overwork may contribute to this phenomenon. For fieldworkers, the risk seems particularly heightened. 'Taken-for-granted' fieldwork practices, such as seeking out dangerous fieldsites or minimising discussion of challenges, cause needless stress and suffering among practitioners (Tucker and Horton, 2019; Pollard, 2009).

This chapter explores some possible reasons why social scientists may find it hard to talk about the relationship between mental health and fieldwork readiness. The reflexive turn of the 1980s encouraged fieldworkers to explore how their position in the field affected their work. It is now customary for fieldworkers to view their gender, class, caste, ethnicity and nationality as important dimensions of their methodological approach. However, the epistemological relevance of our deepest 'selves' – our emotions, personality traits and psychological wellbeing – is comparatively underexplored. Indeed, the seemingly essentialist concepts offered up by diagnostic psychology may cause some awkwardness in social science disciplines, running headlong into our commitment to revealing social structures and questioning entrenched categories.

This squeamishness is compounded by the enduring stigma that mental health conditions continue to face, especially in academic institutions. As Baz Lecocq noted on their return from fieldwork in Mali, such problems form 'hidden discourses' about the realities of fieldwork: 'It is only in an informal setting, usually the pub, that some dare to speak of the danger, nuisance, despair, and general convenience of it all' (Lecocq, 2002, p. 273). It is hard to imagine an environment in which personal needs are openly addressed as part of the fieldwork preparation process when the current climate is so prohibitive of admitting weakness.

And yet, if we are to tackle this crisis head on, we must enable frank discussion of how fieldwork relates to the vulnerabilities that shape us, and the strengths that will enable us. In so doing it may help us to adopt Cerwonka and Malkki's understanding of fieldwork not as a set of defined tasks but as a 'sensibility' (Cerwonka and Malkki, 2007). The word 'sensibility' implies *both* an inherent disposition relating deeply to our personhood *and* a set of knowledges and skills that can be developed over time. The dual character of this word cites the tension between fieldwork readiness as a feature of one's personality, and something to be acquired in fieldwork education. I embrace this tension as a productive one, enabling us to make ethnography a more compassionate practice in two counterbalancing directions. First, by compelling us to make the social, emotional and cognitive demands of fieldwork explicit, and to develop the skills needed to face them in pre-fieldwork training. Second, by admitting that we all have characteristics that we consider unshakeable, and that some of these – such as the experience of longstanding mental illness or neurodivergence – will shape our ability to do fieldwork as it is traditionally understood. In the final section of this chapter I engage with the work of ethnographers writing from this vantage point, showing how their work imagines a much-expanded future for ethnography.

Why fieldwork skills are hard to talk about

'Methods training' is where students will receive their first insight into the practicalities of field research. A standard anthropology or sociology curriculum will cover mainstays like proposal writing, field notes, recording methods and risk assessment. Nevertheless, it is an 'open secret' that most students feel unprepared for their fieldwork (Lake and Parkinson, 2017), especially when it comes to the practical matters of getting along with participants, staying well in the field, responding to obstacles and addressing ethical quandaries that arise. In departments like linguistics or political science the fieldwork experience may be even more peripheral to the course and discussed very little. There is much that slips through the cracks, relegated either to the sphere of things that we 'naturally' already know and do, or things that cannot possibly be planned for or put into words. Novices in the field are mostly left to figure out many aspects of fieldwork by listening to the stories told by their peers or supervisors, if at all.

Fieldwork skills are often difficult to describe because they rely on the same impossible-to-define instincts that so frustrate us in everyday life. Most people are doing an informal kind of ethnography every time they find themselves trying to fit into a new social group, visiting a faraway place, or participating in an unfamiliar activity. That is, they are making use of their interpersonal and interpretive skills to figure out the underlying rules of a new situation. How do these people relate to one another and what do they think is normal? How can I best imitate them or assert my difference? How will I interpret this event later? Is this situation OK for me? Some people may feel they are good at answering these questions, others may feel out of their depth much of the time. Their differences in social competency are explained by a complex mix of luck, cultural influence, mental health, longstanding personality traits, cognitive traits and acquired skills that prepare us for such situations. Our ability to participate in demanding social situations is therefore determined by some things we cannot change, such as our genes, and things we might change with conscious effort, like our confidence in approaching strangers. The hard part is telling the difference: understanding if and how 'shy' or 'anxious' might become 'charismatic' or 'confident'. Indeed, the difficulty of linking causes to effects is the reason why endless speculation on the mysteries of social life persists – and keeps fieldworkers in business!

The institutional bracketing of these arcane secrets as 'ethnography', usually as part of a university degree in anthropology, sociology, or another social science, is at least tacitly premised upon the idea that you can teach people how to do fieldwork and – since admission to these courses is selective – that some people might be better suited to it than others. However, ethnographers would probably agree that this is one of the vaguer aspects of recruitment to the discipline. Prospective ethnographers (unlike, for example, therapists or social workers) are not selected for their resilience or their social skills but their written interest in the subject and the qualifications they have already attained. These might be adequate measures of academic suitability, but give few clues as to people's ability to undergo the unique emotional and interpersonal challenges that fieldwork will present. Therefore ethnographic education somewhat paradoxically proceeds on the assumption that its principles belong to a hidden realm of human intuition with which its students are already gifted.

The value placed on ethnography by the academy is mostly a measure of the skills employed after one returns from the field, when the researcher sets about interpreting, abstracting and writing up conclusions. We admire the arguments made and the author's contribution to general theory. We notice the quality of the prose, and the richness of the author's interpretations. We look for the ways that theoretical arguments are substantiated or critiqued. Social scientists recognise good ethnography when they *read* it. But of the galactic constellation of choices and actions that led to the final product – the 'fieldwork process' – relatively little is known. Researchers are rarely accompanied to the field by their peers, so their decisions are unlikely to come under much scrutiny. Despite the increasing availability of behind-the-scenes narratives, it is still rare to catch a glimpse of the primary materials (field notes or interview transcripts) from which they are drawn. The 'stuff' of fieldwork remains between the fieldworker and their notebooks. It is hard, therefore, to know what good ethnography looks like when you are doing it.

Skills for fieldworkers

Improvisation

Fieldwork, as a method that relies on social interaction and direct experience, is subject to the messy contingencies of both. The main job of the ethnographer is to respond to the social action as it unfolds, allowing the field to guide the research. The practical implications of such unpredictable research are numerous. Researchers might find that even the most basic components of their daily life are determined by others: when and what you eat, how you dress, how you socialise, when you will go to bed. Bureaucratic obstacles or relationship breakdowns might mean that fieldwork no longer becomes tenable in a particular institution or location. Research questions will often change partway through fieldwork, sometimes dramatically. And a great many of our successes and failures may be left completely up to chance: opportunities that arise as a result of being in the right place at the right time. It follows that 'how one has learned to cope with all the other exigencies to be confronted in the course of everyday life surely has more predictive power for fieldwork success than how many courses one has taken, manuals one has read, or ethnographers one has known' (Wolcott, 1995, p. 146).

Many social science departments have adopted the view that it is impossible to train researchers for uncertain environments (Law, 2004). The implication, as in Wolcott's statement, is that students should know already how to 'cope' with contingency, and that the most successful ethnographers will be the best at improvising their responses to the field. My own experience of pre-fieldwork preparation was heavy on the magic of risk-taking, trial and error, carpe diem and gut instinct. It was light on the machinery behind the magic: supportive mentors, learning from ethnographers that have been through it before and effective contingency planning. Indeed, the need for discussion of the likelihood of failure and requisite coping skills was so great that students took it on themselves to organise their own training day around these topics. Stories emerged of students' unanticipated dramas, from developing scurvy to facing vital informants withdrawing from study. I inherited wisdom from my more experienced peers; their stories gave me the confidence to step back from my PhD when health problems arose, increased the care with which I treated key informants and equipped me with workarounds that can only truly be understood in the context of real-life examples.

Drawing an analogy between ethnography and jazz musicianship, Cerwonka and Malkki show that the ability to improvise is itself the result of extensive training; 'To get to the point of improvising well, the ethnographer, like the jazz musician, must have devoted countless hours to practice and preparation of various kinds' (Cerwonka and Malkki, 2007, p. 182). Sometimes taken as an endorsement of ethnography as one long process of 'winging it', this metaphor actually proves the opposite. The authors insist on the role that informal networks, story-sharing and mentorship play in preparing to improvise; through these interactions with more experienced ethnographers students develop a 'second sense' for ways of responding to the field.

Improvisation also requires the acceptance of mistakes, and comfort with non-linear structure that modulates between the familiar and the unexpected, progress and failure. These are abilities that will expand through the experience of fieldwork, but can also be formed through the culture of the department before students leave. For instance, the development of a fully formed 'research proposal', such that many departments require before getting clearance to begin fieldwork, might be better supplanted with multiple pilot studies and experimenting with different options early on in what is currently called the 'pre-fieldwork year', before committing to a long-term fieldsite. Another option might be the aided development of strong peer support networks within departments, through which experiences and skills can be readily shared.

However, I would caution against the widespread view that radical uncertainty is inevitable in fieldwork. It is possible to design a project that allows for personal routines to be maintained (such as choosing a fieldsite near one's current place of residence), for relatively predictable and structured interactions to occur (like interview work within an organisation), or for pre-existing relationships to guide research (such as through activist networks). Indeed, doing so may be necessary for people that require greater stability and routine, such as autistic people, people with illnesses that require reliable access to treatment, disabled people, or people suffering from pre-existing traumas. However, facilitating these changes requires posing a challenge to ethnography 'as a total immersion in search of a holistic understanding' (Howell, 2017, p. 15) that requires 'a sense of adventure to undertake long-term fieldwork in faraway places; to go out to confront the radically unknown and come to grips with it' (p. 18). It requires the knotty work of proving the value of an ethnography motivated not by a sense of adventure but by a sense of compassion.

Attention

All fieldwork – whether online or in person, close to home or far from it – requires a high level of attention to subtle social information. Our data is a constantly shifting terrain of conversations, actions, emotions and relationships that most everyone else in the environment considers routine. This makes it difficult to sort the important from the mundane, especially at an early stage of research when most things we encounter are new. The novice ethnographer observes indiscriminately, assigning significance to almost everything to get an overall picture. Later, one builds up patterns of expectation, establishing connections between the things we observe – this thing is an effect of that, this thing is often described in those terms etc. Fieldworkers will often have to maintain this level of focus for long stretches of time – hours or even days. Openly taking field notes might be inappropriate for the situation – a dinner or a church service, for instance – so ethnographers must memorise as much salient information as possible for writing up later. Take alongside this the added pressure, common to ethnographers working abroad, of interpreting this information in a new language and we see that fieldwork is an extremely cognitively demanding activity.

Ethnographers are not unique in taking human interaction as their main medium. Psychotherapists and counsellors, for instance, also spend a large part of their working life in highly attuned dialogue, paying focused attention to what the other party is saying and subtle changes in atmosphere. It is understood that this skill can only partially be gained from academic study and that the bulk of it comes from experience. Trainees can therefore expect to spend several years in supervised practice building up the abilities and intuitions that form the foundation of their career. 'Active listening' is one example, describing the therapist's ability to stay present in the interaction, pick out important information from what the client says, and reflect it back accurately. While it is possible to mimic the appearance of listening intently, maintaining genuine focus through a long conversation requires the development of sensorial and cognitive faculties that can only come from repeated practice. It is regrettable that no parallel educational system exists for ethnographers. While some departments might offer one or two interview roleplays, it is more likely that the graduate ethnographer will spend their first year with their head bent over a book in the kind of academic solace they are unlikely to find in fieldwork. This is a great loss because, for most people, attention is a skill that can be developed over time and through practice.

It would also benefit ethnographers-in-training to gain a better understanding of 'how the sausage is made' by demystifying the process of capturing field data. Every researcher will develop their own style of recording field data, tailored to their preference for processing information and the circumstances of fieldwork. For instance, I know of several ethnographers that could not record interviews – either because of the circumstances of the field or because they found transcribing impossible – and would instead rely on voice notes recorded immediately after finishing a conversation outlining all the subjects discussed. This approach requires an iron focus throughout conversation so as not to misrepresent the other party's words. Others take only brief notes during participant observation but use memory devices to aid their ability to remember salient details. And still more find that they must rely heavily on being able to write everything down in minute detail before too much time has passed, which means building time and space into the fieldwork process to do so. Talking about these differences in data capture allows students to design projects, develop skills and procure equipment appropriate to the demands of their field and their own limitations.

Resilience

Resilience describes the ability to weather difficult situations without causing damage to our long-term health or self-image. It is vital to secure a bedrock of resilience throughout fieldwork because the challenges faced there can be many. This is the case whether you are conducting research in a conflict zone, or in the vegetable market ten minutes down the road from your house. Fieldworkers might experience profoundly limited access to home comforts, familiar routines, or social networks. They may find themselves socially isolated, subject to high levels of scrutiny and mistrust; or else socially saturated, and unable to get a moment's privacy. They may be exposed to newfound risks, sometimes at a high level. Add to this the well-documented demands of academic life, such as isolation or financial precarity, and it becomes clear why ethnographic research can present significant stress alongside more positive emotions.

So far, discussions of the relationship between psychology and social research have been dominated by the perception that the psychological challenges of fieldwork are what make it uniquely virtuous. Wengle describes fieldwork as the dissolution of selfhood in which the researcher 'wakes up to find himself a stranger, and perhaps a little afraid, in a world he never made, a world that is totally perplexing, mysterious, and often difficult to penetrate' (1988, p. 153). It is this 'grand and romantic, almost heroic, idea of self-sacrifice for the sake of knowledge' (p. 169) that sets ethnography apart from other methods. Likewise Davies, who identifies the core characteristic of fieldwork as total immersion in an unfamiliar social space, describes disorientation, withdrawal, doubt and altered perception as predictable consequences of placing our 'familiar internal structures' under strain (2010b, p. 94). These influences change our 'perceptual apparatus' in overwhelming but positive ways, fostering a sense of connectedness with a new group and changes in beliefs and attitudes. The ethnographer is painted as an isolated figure in an unfamiliar cultural environment, and alienation itself is their method. Degrees of psychological martyrdom also underpin the tacit hierarchy constructed between fieldsites, with the most remote and dangerous fieldsites attracting the most prestige.

However, this splitting of fieldwork from the concerns of 'normal life' is increasingly inappropriate for a humane practice. Many researchers carry their pre-existing obligations and relationships with them into the field and will retain those of the field in their personal lives. Fieldwork is an inextricable part of one's life, not a discontinuation with it, and should therefore be treated with the same care for one's own wellbeing and respect for one's aspirations and values as we would exercise outside fieldwork. This might seem a basic point, but it is startling how many researchers abandon their expectations of basic psychological wellbeing on the assumption that suffering is what makes fieldwork important.[1]

We mostly receive information about the state of our mental health through the messages sent to us by our emotions. Scholars have understood the relationship between ethnographic knowledge and emotion in several ways. Some ethnographic disciplines have retained a traditional attachment to fieldwork as an instrument of empirical observation. To this end, ethnographic researchers must 'subjugate or even efface personality' and 'restrain sentiment' (Davies, 2010a, p. 8), on the understanding that too much emotion can prejudice the data. In contrast to this, Devereux (1967) made use of the psychoanalytic concept of countertransference to describe feelings of anxiety generated by research encounters. He was among the first to establish a connection between the researcher's emotions and the sort of data produced through ethnography. Since then, many have developed the idea of an epistemological value to emotion (Davies, 2010a), such as Lorimer's assertion that her experience of countertransference when conducting research in a psychiatric setting helped her understand depression as a 'sense of emptiness' (2010, p. 105).

Attention to one's emotions and those of others can greatly enrich our data. However, just as vital is our ability to manage our emotions, both as a way of allowing ethnographic encounters to proceed appropriately and to keep ourselves safe and well. Smith (2009) found that it was more useful to adopt a cool-headed, 'objective' research persona to avoid internalising the negative emotions aroused by her fieldwork.

> This epistemological approach of attempting to create some sort of distance between my emotions and my 'analytical perspective' – this Weberian approach to a 'passionate detachment' – did, in many ways, help, if only as a temporary remedy in struggles for power, feelings of homesickness, fear, anger and unhappiness ... My fieldwork could, at once, be done, be useful and be lived, if only by simply feeling that as a happy anthropologist, I could be a good anthropologist.
>
> (Smith, 2009, pp. 8–9)

This approach has been extended to researchers working with traumatised populations, as there are steps we can take to reduce the likelihood of developing secondary trauma as a result.

Resilience, crucially, does not mean that the fieldworker must accept all events that occur in the field and work only on managing their emotional reaction to them. In fact one of its most important tenets is an awareness of one's deepest requirements for good health, an awareness that therapists often describe as 'boundaries'. Those boundaries, so far as it is possible, should not be violated for the sake of good data. It is all too easy to abandon ourselves when the opportunity to do right by the field presents itself. We might find ourselves climbing into a stranger's car, accepting drink or drugs we don't want, or doing favours we cannot afford. However important these compromises might feel at the time, too many will inevitably deplete us beyond repair. It is therefore important to have a strong sense of lines that cannot be crossed, and to employ negotiation skills to confidently make or refuse requests that maintain those limits. Because fieldsites sometimes present a host of unfamiliar behavioural norms to which fieldworkers are strongly encouraged to conform, this may be very uncomfortable. Indeed, there may be other situations where setting these limits becomes impossible and your research must be changed to avoid illness or trauma.

Social skills

To get anywhere in the field, the ethnographer will have to earn the trust of at least one person. Most ethnographies depend on the goodwill of dozens of people, all of whom will have to like, respect, or trust you enough to consent to feature in data that – very often – they will gain no other benefit from. Therefore, approaching the field with some level of social skilfulness is vital, though its principles will likely be quite different to those outlined in the enormous literature on social skills in business or friendship. Since the diversity of human ways of relating to one another is the key subject of enquiry for social scientists, many ethnographers will select fieldsites with social conventions different to the ones they are used to. Moreover, even in fieldsites local to the ethnographer, most people will respond very differently to an outsider coming in to study their lives than they will to a colleague or community member with whom some level of recognition and fraternity is already established.

Without the advantage of pre-existing familiarity it becomes necessary for fieldworkers to establish trust and goodwill in the interactional here-and-now – a quality known as 'rapport'. Rapport is different to friendship in that it establishes a relationship in the context of other goals. However, the distinction between friendship and rapport can be extremely murky. Researchers – especially feminist researchers – emphasise compassion, humour, empathy and mutual disclosure as the essential features of building rapport (Finch, 1984), contrasting this approach with early depictions of ethnographers as authoritative, detached figures. Presenting oneself as trustworthy and likable is central to fieldwork. This is best conveyed not through the structured interactions (like interviews) in which researchers are trained, but in the everyday tasks of hanging out and making small talk, which are almost never reflected upon.

The ability to interact smoothly with others is an unspoken prerequisite for ethnographic research, but it does not come naturally to everyone. Scott et al. (2012) characterise themselves as 'reluctant researchers'; that is, while they felt comfortable with the interpretive and written aspects of ethnography, their self-identified shyness held them back from its 'performative' aspects. By this they mean those parts of fieldwork that require 'high levels of performance, improvisation and interactional contingency' (p. 715) such as cold-calling and approaching strangers to ask them to feature in research. The pressure to present a convincing public persona (that may be very different to how we feel inside), as well as the heightened risk of rejection and embarrassment, led the authors to procrastinate or avoid those activities to the detriment of their work. Less socially demanding tasks like organising meetings by email or observational work could be performed much more readily. The authors show how, through discussing their struggles with fellow 'shy' researchers, they co-developed ways of coping with their feelings of embarrassment, and to reduce their anxiety surrounding social interaction.

The few frank accounts of the social labours that go into fieldwork highlight the unspoken assumptions made about the 'ideal researcher's' capabilities, many of which persist simply because it is embarrassing and taboo to suggest that someone might be socially lacking. Driessen and Jansen admit that 'some people have more social graces than others' (2013, p. 258), but are optimistic that it is possible to train ethnographers in social skills. They suggest that prospective fieldworkers are encouraged to practise approaching strangers, maintain alertness in conversations and to develop 'courtesy, politeness, attentive and disciplined listening, patience, honesty and openness, reciprocity, and respectful curiosity' (p. 258).

Mental health and the future of ethnography

The skills I have described above are those that I consider important to doing ethnography of any sort. All four work in harmony, each aiding the other. Taken together they will go a long way to keeping you well, to guiding your intuitions and to forging productive relationships in the field.

I have described them as 'skills' and not qualities or attributes because, for most people, these are elements of our character that can be developed over time. While we might have a sense of some fundamental and unshakeable features of our personality, the ability to improve focus or shore up resilience is generally felt to belong to the realm of conscious self-development. Indeed, going by the principle that practice makes perfect, these skills are often sharpened by the very experience of fieldwork. Many ethnographers feel that their ability to talk to strangers, to respond calmly to uncertain conditions, or to approach others with compassion improves the longer they engage with the field. These are capabilities that will not only benefit them in their professional lives, but in every aspect of life; in this sense, the experience of fieldwork can be said to be a profoundly enriching one for both the fieldworker and the people surrounding them.

I would now like to introduce two complications to this approach. To begin with, we must avoid the implication that fieldwork is somehow a test of character, and that it is down to the researcher to develop the fortitude to respond to whatever the field throws at them. On the contrary, awareness of the necessity of these complex skills only highlights the need to ensure that projects are designed within the limits of students' abilities, and that they are encouraged as much as possible during training and throughout fieldwork. It is for this reason that many of my recommendations focus on cautious project design rather than field coping skills. Not every fieldsite is appropriate to every student, and a large fraction of ethnographers find that the unanticipated demands of the field deplete the skills and resources they have arrived with beyond repair. As Nancy Howell puts it:

> To minimize the distress, we can recognize that mental stress can be very great in the field, and that we will vary as individuals and at different times in our lives in our ability to accept and cope with these stresses. We need to entertain the possibilities of our own limits in deciding what fieldwork we can and cannot do. There is an endless array of researchable problems ... 'Know thyself,' we are advised, and that seems to be particularly wise advice in the case of someone planning fieldwork.
> (Howell, 1990, quoted in Macaulay, 2004, p. 205)

Departments are implicated in this duty of care. As Amy Pollard's (2009) survey of returning fieldworkers confirms, many feel that their training did not prepare them for the extent of isolation, precarity, risk, or difficulty to which they were exposed. They report feelings of profound hopelessness and anxiety about their perceived ability to simply improvise in response to these conditions. These feelings increased the risk of developing mental health problems that seriously compromised their fieldwork. Researchers may feel too anxious to approach others, too depressed to participate in activities. Sometimes, these problems develop into crises that result in an early termination of research and a scorched relationship with academia.

Wellbeing is not external to good ethnography; it is a vitally constituent part of it, since what is at stake in its absence is our very means of research. Social science disciplines will therefore find themselves greatly impoverished by their overreliance on methods that exhaust, overwhelm and demoralise their practitioners. As Backe and Fitzpatrick will demonstrate later in this collection, this fact provides ethical impetus for academic institutions to better support the health and safety of students conducting research. The authors offer compelling suggestions for the provision of care in fieldwork-based departments, including trauma-informed training for supervisors and support for mutual aid work among students. To this I would add the importance of frank conversation about the challenges fieldworkers typically face that go beyond gaining access or securing interviews, that extend into the most essential parts of our selves. Though these are becoming increasingly available online and in published volumes, there is no substitute for hearing them from scholars in our own departments on whose example we depend.

However, the focus on preservation of wellbeing also throws up difficult questions for those entering fieldwork with challenges that run deeper than adequate training and preparation can account for. I am talking about the many fieldworkers living with longstanding mental health problems that structure their social, emotional and attentive capacities. For example, students with borderline personality disorder (BPD) or bipolar disorder may find it exceedingly challenging to regulate their emotions, while those suffering from anxiety disorders or depression could find social encounters demanding to the point of being intolerable. Mental suffering of any kind can affect our ability to face moral quandaries, tolerate uncertainty, maintain focus, regulate emotions, or coordinate with others. In some instances, these difficulties might be felt to be temporary or contingent, manageable with the appropriate care. In others, they might be understood as a longstanding and essential part of the self, through which interactions with the world are refracted.

This is especially the case in neurodevelopmental disorders such as attention deficit hyperactivity disorder (ADHD) and autism. Because pervasive from a young age, with significant genetic components and limited treatment options, these conditions are increasingly viewed not as diseases to be managed but as another kind of fundamental human difference. This reframing happens under the heading of 'neurodiversity', which seeks to provide a social model for cognitive deviation from the population average. As with the social model of physical disability, which seeks normalisation and societal support rather than an eradication of a condition, proponents of neurodiversity argue that differences in cognition should be accepted. This does not mean that neurodivergent people should not have access to treatment options; rather, that we should encourage awareness of the social accommodations and situations that allow neurodivergent people to thrive.

Ethnography may be one of the most important tools we have to offer to this new framework. Indeed, some of the most compelling arguments for acceptance of neurodiversity have been a result of prolonged ethnographic fieldwork rather than clinical case studies. Ochs and Solomon (2010), for instance, use the concept of 'sociality' to describe the modes of behavioural and social action available to autistic children. In so doing they make visible the fundamental, taken-for-granted components of social life – maintaining attention, attuning to emotions, reacting to stimuli, using gesture, engaging in dialogue. They show how variations in coordination between these activities, such as talking without being face-to-face or creating 'pockets of orderliness' in time, allow for maximum social coordination between autistic and non-autistic people.

Speaking to conditions that are usually unproblematically considered 'mental illnesses', several researchers have used their own position as patients to shed light on the effects of cognitive categorisation. Emily Martin, who is bipolar and has conducted fieldwork with mental health support groups in which she is also a participant, tells us how she was advised that 'students with those kinds of serious mental problems would simply not be able to function in the intellectually demanding environment at Princeton'. 'In this social setting,' she concludes, 'if you say you have manic depression, you may well be categorized as a nonfunctional person, as a less than a fully rational person' (Martin, 2009, p. xvii). Through her fieldwork she shows how elements of mania and depression – both of which are used to designate bipolar people as radically different – are shot through all aspects of American culture. By weakening the distinction between the biological and the cultural, Martin makes a powerful argument for the benefits of ethnographic study of what she calls 'insanity'. 'I am not saying that we are all alike,' she writes, 'or that some of us are not disabled by our craziness. I am saying that there could be friendly recognition across the sometimes arbitrary line between rational and irrational acts and thoughts' (2009, p. 83).

These studies show us how valuable ethnography can be to bettering our understanding of the diversity of human minds. Methodologically speaking, the simple, empathetic act of 'being together' that ethnographers undertake yields compassionate insight into the social worlds created by cognitive difference. Meanwhile the theoretical interrogation of cultural categories that characterises the social sciences allows us to problematise the biological essentialising of such experiences. However, it is also necessary to use these insights in a reciprocal way, to interrogate the forms of social cognition implicit in how ethnography itself is conducted. Anthropologist Dawn Eddings Prince, who is autistic, describes in her early academic training:

> putting the natural way I experienced and talked about the world aside. Of course, one of the first things I learned as a student of formal anthropology was that scientific objectivity was the only valid platform from which to see the world and the people in it.
>
> (2010, p. 58)

By contrast she has characterised her engagement with the natural world as profoundly connected and boundaryless, a feeling related to the sensory overload of the environment. Once unable to meaningfully communicate with other humans, and therefore struggling to finish a doctorate in anthropology, Prince began conducting fieldwork with gorillas in Seattle's Woodland Park Zoo (Prince-Hughes, 2004). Through her mute engagement with the gorillas, whom she shows to be models of care, protectiveness and love, Prince has come to reflect ethnographically on similar aspects of human sociality. Her work shows us the possibilities of ethnography even in the absence of any of its traditionally identifying features.

Conclusion

This chapter has argued that, while characteristics like gender or class are increasingly explored as part of our ongoing commitment to reflexivity, cognitive aspects of the researcher's positionality are likely to go uninspected. That the core competencies on which doing ethnography depends are so little talked about allows us the comforting fiction that anyone with the price of admission can engage in this methodological approach, without having to do any work to ensure that that is actually the case. This begs the question of how far we must conceive of a 'favoured psychology' (Davies, 2010b, p. 94) for ethnography: one that responds well to the challenges of fieldwork and is readily equipped with the resources I have described above.

We can take important lessons from mentally ill and neurodivergent researchers that have written candidly about their experience of doing research. These accounts do a great service to ethnography, taking seriously its remit to document and understand human difference. They allow us to understand the benefits of an ethnographic practice that is compassionate and ethically engaged. Reciprocally, by staking out a claim for researchers that do not fit the bill for traditional ethnography they engage directly with its epistemic limitations. If we are to continue developing our interrogation of ethnographic positionality, it is time to reduce our fear of using the language of cognition, emotion, neurodiversity, mental illness and personality to describe the core competencies of our discipline. We must use this language to ensure that students are adequately prepared for the challenges they will face, to encourage a culture of care and compassion in the social sciences and to reduce the likelihood of trauma in the field. Through these insights we can foster true epistemic inclusion in our practice.

Recommendations

1 **Pay attention to how you respond to uncertainty now.** When unexpected events occur, do you take it in your stride? Or do you find uncertainty difficult to cope with, and mitigate against it as much as you can? Use these insights to formulate your research proposal.
2 **Find opportunities to strengthen your powers of attention.** Techniques like mindfulness meditation have been proven to enhance our ability to focus, and – as always – having the basics of sleep, food and water down is crucial as well. An ethnographer can't do research if they are chronically exhausted!
3 **If you have a mental or physical health condition, think carefully about how you will manage this during your fieldwork.** If you do not have access to the same level of healthcare as you are used to, it is imperative that you formulate a plan to protect your wellbeing.
4 **Think about the kinds of social situations you currently gravitate towards.** Are you comfortable approaching strangers, interacting with large groups? What is your tolerance for approaching strangers and asking for help? Do you cope with rejection well? Allow this insight to guide your project design.
5 **Gain a sense for the social requirements of your fieldsite and how well-practised you are in these requirements.** For instance, if you are conducting research in a public space, you will probably have to get very good at just 'hanging out' with strangers. By contrast someone that is working in an institutional setting will make use of a more formal style of interaction.

Note

1 www.thenewethnographer.com/the-new-ethnographer/2018/04/22/competitive-hardship-ethnographic-guilt-and-early-career-pressure-to-conduct-authentic-fieldwork

Further reading

Cerwonka, A. and Malkki, L. 2007. *Improvising Theory: Process and Temporality in Ethnographic Fieldwork*. Chicago: University of Chicago.

Insightful look at the subtle intuition required in fieldwork through the email exchanges of a graduate researcher and her ethnographic mentor.

De Laine, M. 2000. *Fieldwork, Participation, and Practice: Ethics and Dilemmas in Qualitative Research*. London: Sage.

Deep dive into the ethics of field research, with extensive comparison of the possible approaches to ethical dilemmas.

Scott, S., Hinton-Smith, T., Härmä, V. and Broome, K. 2012. The reluctant researcher: Shyness in the field. *Qualitative Research*, 12(6), 715–34.

Fun and relatable article about the less-discussed performative aspects of fieldwork and the difficulty of doing 'cringe' things in research. Includes a challenge to the idea of the 'ideal researcher' and various techniques for coping with shyness in the field.

References

Cerwonka, A. and Malkki, L. 2007. *Improvising Theory: Process and Temporality in Ethnographic Fieldwork*. Chicago: University of Chicago.

Davies, J. 2010a. Introduction: Emotions in the field. In Davies, J. and Spencer, D. (Eds.), *Emotions in the Field: The Psychology and Anthropology of Fieldwork Experience*. Stanford: Stanford University Press. pp. 1–34.

Davies, J. 2010b. Disorientation, dissonance and altered perception in the field. In Davies, J. and Spencer, D. (Eds.), *Emotions in the Field: The Psychology and Anthropology of Fieldwork Experience*. Stanford: Stanford University Press. pp. 79–97.

Devereux, G. 1967. *From Anxiety to Method in the Behavioral Sciences*. Berlin and Boston: De Gruyter Mouton.

Driessen, H. and Jansen, W. 2013. The hard work of small talk in ethnographic fieldwork. *Journal of Anthropological Research*, 69(2), 249–63.

Evans, T., Bira, L., Gastelum, J., Weiss, L. and Vanderford, N. 2018. Evidence for a mental health crisis in graduate education. *Nature Biotechnology*, 36(3), 282–4.

Finch, J. 1984. 'It's great to have someone to talk to': The ethics and politics of interviewing women. In Bell, C. and Roberts, H. (Eds.), *Social Researching: Politics, Problems, Practice*. London: Routledge and Kegan Paul. pp. 70–87.

Howell, S. 2017. Two or three things I love about ethnography. *HAU: Journal of Ethnographic Theory*, 7(1), 15–20.

Lake, M. and Parkinson, S. 2017. 'The Ethics of Fieldwork Preparedness,' Political Violence @ a Glance.

Law, J. 2004. *After Method: Mess in Social Science Research*. Oxford: Routledge.

Lecocq, B. 2002. Fieldwork ain't always fun: Public and hidden discourses on fieldwork. *History in Africa* 29, 273–82.

Lorimer, F. 2010. Using emotion as a form of knowledge in a psychiatric research setting. In Davies, J. and Spencer, D. (Eds.), *Emotions in the Field: The Psychology and Anthropology of Fieldwork Experience*. Stanford: Stanford University Press. pp. 98–128.

Macaulay, M. 2004. Training linguistics students for the realities of fieldwork. *Anthropological Linguistics*, 46(2), 194–209. http://www.jstor.org/stable/30029028

Martin, E. 2009. *Bipolar Expeditions: Mania and Depression in American Culture*. Princeton, NJ: Princeton University Press.

Ochs, E. and Solomon, O. 2010. Autistic sociality. *Ethos*, 38(1), 69–92.

Pollard, A. 2009. Field of screams: Difficulty and ethnographic fieldwork. *Anthropology Matters*, 11(2), 1–24.

Prince, D. 2010. An exceptional path: An ethnographic narrative reflecting on autistic parenthood from evolutionary, cultural, and spiritual perspectives. *Ethos*, 38(1), 56–68.

Prince-Hughes, D. 2004. *Songs of a Gorilla Nation: My Journey Through Autism*. New York: Harmony.

Scott, S., Hinton-Smith, T., Härmä, V. and Broome, K. 2012. The reluctant researcher: Shyness in the field. *Qualitative Research*, 12(6), 715–34.

Smith, K.L. 2009. Is a happy anthropologist a good anthropologist? *Anthropology Matters*, 11, 1–11.

Tucker, F. and Horton, J. 2019. 'The show must go on!' Fieldwork, mental health, and wellbeing in geography, earth and environmental sciences. *Area 51*, 84–93.

Wengle, J.L. 1988. *Ethnographers in the Field: The Psychology of Research*. Tuscaloosa, AL: University of Alabama Press.

Wolcott, H.F. 1995. *The Art of Fieldwork*. Walnut Creek, Calif.: AltaMira Press

2

SAFE AND ETHICAL ETHNOGRAPHY: LOOKING INWARDS

Elena Butti

Summary

This chapter reflects on the inner, subjective dimensions of safety and ethics dilemmas when conducting ethnographic research. It argues that, in a context of increasing pressure on early-career researchers, first-time ethnographers may be tempted to cross ethical and safety boundaries under pressure. Drawing on long-term ethnographic fieldwork with adolescents engaged in criminal narco-gangs in Colombia's urban peripheries, I reflect on those complex moments when I felt compelled to go beyond what I felt was safe or ethical with the aim of gathering data. I argue for the need for deeper inner work and for more structural support systems to be built into doctoral programmes for researchers to be better prepared to face the unexpected inner challenges fieldwork will present them with.

Table of contents

Introduction 19
Academic pressure, fieldwork fatigue and data anxiety 19
Safety dilemmas 21

Ethical dilemmas 25
Conclusion 29
Recommendations 30
Further reading 30
References 31

Introduction

It is more and more common – though not yet universal – for academic institutions to require doctoral students to undergo ethics approval processes and complete risk assessments before embarking on fieldwork. Safety and ethics considerations also increasingly feature in postgraduate trainings and are an essential prerequisite to secure funding. This does not necessarily or automatically result in more ethical and safer ethnographic research, however. In a context of increasing pressure and job insecurity for young scholars, rather than being taken as meaningful opportunities to reflect, these procedures are often seen by students as bureaucratic hurdles that stand between them and their data.

In this chapter, I reflect on the ethical and safety dilemmas I encountered in my own fieldwork with adolescents involved at the low ends of criminal narco-gangs in and around Medellín, Colombia's second biggest city. I look at these challenges through the lens of a shifting academic labour market, in which increasing competition, job precarity and the liberalisation of the research endeavour place unprecedented pressures on researchers to gather data and publish results quickly. This pressure can, I argue, push even well-trained early-career ethnographers to cross ethical and safety boundaries when conducting research in challenging contexts. I do not provide an exhaustive review of all possible ethical and safety challenges one may encounter in the field. Rather, I draw attention to the inner, more subjective dimensions of ethics and safety, and offer ideas on how first-time ethnographers may deal with them and on how institutions may support them better.

Academic pressure, fieldwork fatigue and data anxiety

I have always been a very diligent student. In the year that preceded my fieldwork in Colombia, I did everything I could to prepare. I participated in both mandatory and optional trainings offered by my university, and I diligently compiled my risk assessment and ethical review forms – a time-consuming process with several rounds of assessment.

These procedures prepared me well for the factual risks I could expect to encounter in my fieldsite. I was aware of the risks of being kidnapped, robbed or assaulted, and I took extensive precautions to minimise these. I was, however, a lot less prepared to navigate the more subjective dimensions of safety – those complex moments in which researchers may allow themselves to take risks with the aim of gathering exciting and unique data. Similarly, while I was ready to navigate foreseeable ethical issues such as obtaining informed consent, it proved a lot harder to face those instances when I found myself wondering whether my behaviour was ethical, but allowed myself to engage in it nonetheless. In other words, I did not expect that it would have at times been *me* – rather than external factors – to push myself into possibly risky and unethical situations.

This happened as a response to the increasing pressure that I – like many other early-career academics – have been facing in recent years. From the day I began my doctoral training, I was continuously reminded that the academic career is extremely demanding and that, if I wanted to make it, I had to gather data that was new and unique, and I had to publish quickly and well. At the same time, I was told that it was paramount for an ethnographer to spend extensive time conducting fieldwork, understanding local dynamics and building deep relationships of trust with informants. What was I to prioritise?

As many young ethnographers, I found myself trying to do it all. The feeling of having to prove myself, coupled with the need to escape loneliness, led me to work non-stop (cf. Watts, 2008; Caretta and Joniken, 2017). During the first months of my fieldwork, data-gathering, note-writing, analysing, thinking and reading about my research topic literally took all of my time. I would wake up in the morning and get ready to get out as I listened to local news. I would go to a café in the hope of meeting someone with whom I could talk about local events. I wrote field notes about the morning events while eating lunch. I then met my main informants and spent the whole afternoon and a large part of the evening with them. I would get home at some point between 9pm and 12pm, extremely tired, and write down what I could remember from my conversations in some disorganised jottings, which I would then convert into more organised notes early the following morning, before going out again.

I stuck to this routine every single day of the week, including weekends and holidays. I declined all invitations from my local host family – who were my only support network during those early days of research – to do something fun and relaxing with them. I was haunted by what Baird (2018, p. 356) called 'data anxiety' – the constant feeling that I was not gathering enough or good enough data. I could not accept my limits; I wanted to see it all, understand it all and do it quickly. At the time, however, I did not recognise this routine as stressful. It is often easy for ethnographers to sweep into a heavy working rhythm without even realising it. After all, our fieldwork consists of hanging out, having interesting conversations with people, participating in social gatherings and writing about it – all of which can feel relaxing and even fun. Who could think of a better job?

After several weeks of holding this rhythm and having no break, I started not to sleep well. The stories of violence, crime and marginalisation I heard from my informants started to sweep into my dreams (some have characterised this as a form of 'secondary trauma', see Wood, 2006, p. 384). Luckily, I recognised this as a signal that something was not going well. I left my fieldwork location for a few days to go visit some friends in the capital city, and for the first time in months I properly relaxed.

From that point on, I forced myself to actively build sports, hobbies and relaxation time into my routine. This meant reducing the time I was gathering data and dedicating more time to focused note-taking. I stopped taking detailed notes of every single thing I witnessed and started to narrow down my thematic interests, which helpfully reduced my writing time. I also accepted the fact that, if I wanted to be well, I had to reduce the amount of time I spent data-gathering and consequently the amount of information I gathered. I had to allow some things to escape my attention; I could not take it all in.

These experiences of fieldwork fatigue and data anxiety – which are not in any way unique to me – can seriously hider first-time ethnographers' ability to conduct research in a safe and ethical manner. Before fieldwork you think you are stronger and stricter than that, but when in the field, feeling fatigued and fragile, the boundaries between what is safe and ethical and what is not become increasingly blurred, and it is much easier to give in to your data-anxious self. In what follows, I describe a few instances in which this happened to me and how I dealt with them; based on this I propose a few ways forward.

Safety dilemmas

EXAMPLE 2.1

A few weeks after arriving in my fieldwork location, I ask Juan, a 15-year-old I met in my first days there, if he'd be willing to take me to visit the neighbourhood where he grew up, in the close-by city of Medellín. He readily agrees, on the caveat that I'd pay the bus ticket for him and we set on a date a few days later.

Once we get to the city, however, I am unsure on how to proceed. While Juan seems happy to show me around, he doesn't seem willing to tell me much about his past life. Rather than focusing on talking with me, he keeps making up different excuses to go to his uncle's house: 'Let's go hang up there,' he says. Or: 'I need to go get the dog.' Or: 'I need to make some food.' Clearly, I am hesitant to enter a house I don't know, in a neighbourhood I don't know, with an adolescent whom I have just recently met. I gently refuse a few times, but I am also afraid that if I show too much mistrust, Juan may get offended and this may prejudice the delicate relationship of trust I am starting to build with him.

I start thinking: 'What can happen to you, he's only an adolescent,' or 'The neighbourhood looks OK, I'm sure nothing bad will happen.' In the end I try to come to a clumsy compromise: 'OK, let's go and sit on the stairs in front of the house,' I tell him. 'But I won't come inside.'

The stairs were not a very comfortable place to sit and chat, however. More easily than I'd thought, we find ourselves in the apartment. He takes the keys and almost locks the door. 'Don't do it,' I say. 'I have to close, we can't leave the door open,' he says. And there we are, despite of all my precautionary thinking, locked in an empty apartment of which he has the keys. I send a WhatsApp message to my safety contacts to tell them about the situation and inform them of my whereabouts. Surprisingly, I feel relatively tranquil. Although my rational voice tells me I am doing something imprudent, my instinct tells me everything will be fine.

Almost as soon as we are locked in, Juan relaxes a lot. He starts inhaling some poppers (the popular name for alkyl nitrites, a drug which produces a profound relaxation and that the youths in my network used frequently). He takes out a big vodka bottle and asks me if I want a sip. I say no and ask him to please not drink. He asks why and laughs, but eventually he doesn't drink. In this new situation, the conversation flows much more smoothly. Suddenly Juan starts opening up and tells me a lot of things about his past life. After a while he adds: 'Do you have anything else to ask me? You can ask me anything, I will answer you. That's why I take this,' he says, hinting at the poppers. 'Because it helps me to relax.' We chat for a bit longer, then we say goodbye and I head home.

While the situation with Juan[1] eventually turned out fine, it was clearly a risky one that I allowed to get myself into. I was afraid that showing mistrust would upset Juan and prejudice our relationship and I was keen to get to know his story, afraid that I wouldn't have another opportunity. This led me to push my boundaries more than I'd have done if I had thought about it with a lucid mind. My gut told me that a situation was not risky after all, while clearly it could have led to much more dire consequences.

Situations like this were not uncommon during my fieldwork time, and they raise important questions about the researcher's ability to stick to the safety rules one has set for oneself in advance. How much is it possible to lucidly recognise and stay away from risks while in the midst of conducting research that one considers exciting and important? How does the narrative we construct on our research work influence the way we are seen in the field? And what role do our gender and positionality play in shaping research-related risks and our ability to mitigate them?

Context-related risks

For anyone conducting research in places affected by violence, some level of context-related risks will be unavoidable. In my case, these risks were linked to the possibility of me being the target of violent robberies or sexual assault, or of my presence upsetting the local gang and making me the target of violence as a result.

I adopted a number of strategies to mitigate these risks, such as always carrying two cell phones and wallets on me (in case one of them got stolen), always being accompanied by a local when I entered a new location and avoiding, as much as possible, finding myself in unknown locations where I had no escape route, being alone with unknown people or alone at night. I set up a network of safety contacts (my local host family and a few close friends), explaining to them in detail the kind of research I was doing and asking them to be reachable when I was engaged in situations like the one with Juan. I agreed to inform them of my whereabouts around every hour; if they didn't hear from me for longer and couldn't reach me, they'd call the police.

While I generally stuck to these strategies, there were instances in which I allowed myself to bend my own rules – such as when I followed Juan into his uncle's house. Why did I do that? As Hanson and Richards (2017, p. 595) note, it is common for ethnographers to 'los[e] perspective and engag[e] in behaviours that they wouldn't in their everyday lives'. Usually I did that because I felt safe enough – without appreciating that *feeling* safe doesn't equate to *being* safe.

A better approach would have been to ask myself if it was really necessary to put myself in a certain situation for the sake of gathering data. In most cases, the answer would have been no.

While I did gather a lot of interesting data by allowing myself to take risks, I also gathered as much interesting material in relatively safe environments. While researchers may be tempted to break their own safety rules for the sake of gathering data, this is not necessary and, most importantly, it is not worth it. Thanks to the long nature of ethnographic fieldwork, there will always be other opportunities to gather similar data further down the line. Researchers should trust the process and not give in to their data-anxious selves.

Of course, conducting ethnography on certain topics would be unrealistic if one shut oneself in a hotel room and only conducted interviews in public places and broad daylight. We all know the power of penetrating people's lives, homes and private spaces is an essential component of ethnography, especially when studying certain topics. Acquiring what Baird (2018, p. 344) calls an 'intuitive feeling of danger' takes *a lot* of time. What is dangerous in one context may enhance safety in another; and the only way to know this is to spend enough time in that context, rather than following a list of decontextualised safety tips. When we are unsure, better to take a step back, even if that comes at the expense of rapport-building or quick data-gathering.

Topic-related risks

Risks can also arise in relation to the specific object of the research. In my case, asking questions about how adolescents enter narco-gangs, what the strategies are for recruitment and what role they play in them was something to handle with care, which could potentially pose risks both to myself and to my informants.

A key way to protect myself and those involved was to construct a 'non-threatening narrative' of the research topic. The requirement of complete transparency enshrined in many ethical guidelines can be problematic from a safety perspective. As Kovats-Bernat (2002, p. 215) puts it, '[t]here are instances when I found it necessary to misrepresent myself, not to conduct the research clandestinely but, rather, to protect or safeguard my own well-being'. I adopted a similar strategy during my own fieldwork, describing myself in general terms as 'someone interested in the lives of young people in contexts of violence' rather than going into the specifics of my research interests into gangs and the drugs business, which could have been perceived as too sensitive.

However, I rarely posed any limits to what my informants wanted to share with me. I would tell myself that if the youths were willing to talk about something then it was fine for me to listen. When I felt that my young informants were sharing sensitive details of their entanglement in crime and violence – for example, the name of a gang chief or a confidential issue regarding a transaction – I never stopped them, but rather I simply avoided recording this information in a written note.

My direct informants knew I was never questioning them on aspects of their lives which were too delicate or risky. However, I lacked control on how I was seen by the broader criminal network; the fact that people saw me speaking to many young people involved in criminal activities gave rise to some unwanted suspicion. In one instance, one of my young informants told me that his chief had asked him whether I was a spy of some sort. This question made me very concerned, not only for my safety but also for the safety of those talking to me. I left that location for several days, and returned only once I had confirmed with other contacts that it was safe to do so.

In hindsight, I wish I had more firmly stopped the youth's disclosure of sensitive information towards me, which did not prove to be very useful in the final write-up, as I could not write about it. I also wish I had reiterated more often and publicly the 'non-threatening narrative' of my role and intents as a researcher in that context.

Positionality-related risks

Yet another set of risks relates to how our identity interacts with the dynamics of the field we study. In my case, this entailed reflecting on what being a young, middle-class, foreign woman meant for conducting research with Colombian, lower-class and predominantly male adolescents.

In contrast to male ethnographers of gangs (cf. Rodgers, 2007; Baird, 2018), I did not make efforts to display bravado, nor did I try to be seen as 'one of the guys'. Rather, I retained a feminine identity and typically related to the youths as an older sister and confidant, which allowed them, I believe, to be more vulnerable in their conversations with me. In this sense, my gender and positionality shaped rather than hindered my data-gathering process, insofar as being a woman allowed me to uncover more intimate, doubtful and vulnerable narratives than a male ethnographer may have.

In general, I always felt safe with my young informants: despite our differences, we came to be very close. Making such closeness explicit helped us to demystify the somewhat unusual nature of our relationship. 'You must think we could rob you any moment,' 15-year-old Pablo once said, laughing. 'But how would I ever rob a *parcera* [buddy, friend]?'

Still, the fact that I did retain a feminine persona and did not try to be 'one of the guys' also meant that sexual and romantic interest were not automatically ruled out of the relationship. When men in the field – not only my close informants, but other boys and men as well – acted flirtatiously towards me and occasionally expressed appreciation towards me, as it was culturally appropriate to do in the local context, I often faced an inner dilemma. Who was I to tell them to stop? By doing so, would I have appeared as a stiff, rigid and ethnocentric European, and thus prejudiced the fluidity of my relationships with them. These reflexive concerns about potentially misjudging local attitudes, as well as the fear of prejudicing a carefully built rapport with my informants, meant that I would gently resist, rather than explicitly and firmly oppose, their initiatives. And while in most cases this approach turned out alright, there was one instance in which one of my informants misinterpreted my attitude, and I found myself in an ambiguous situation that could have resulted in a sexual assault.

This experience, while exceptional, functioned as a powerful reminder that I should always maintain boundaries. It also made me realise that intimacy with research participants does not always go hand in hand with trust and rapport. As Hanson and Richards (2017, p. 596) remark, while getting 'as close as possible' to one's research participants is often predicated as a good way of getting good ethnographic data, it may not be an advisable strategy for a lone researcher in a high-risk setting. As they note, '[w]hen intimacy – which implies the breaking down of barriers and boundaries – is the goal, other aspects of our research relationships, such as trust and rapport – which often hinge on the respect of boundaries – may become overlooked'. First-time ethnographers should regard guarding their boundaries as at least equally, if not more important than building relationships with research participants.

Ethical dilemmas

EXAMPLE 2.2

'Come, I'll show you around,' 19-year-old Sebastián tells me, heading towards the door of his house in a marginal Medellín neighbourhood. 'I took a day off work because you were coming,' he says as I step across the door. 'Oh, really?' I ask. 'What are you doing?' 'I'm working for the men up there,' he says, using a lower voice so that his mother does not hear. He refers to the local gang, which has its basis in the upper part of the neighbourhood.

We head out. Sebastián clearly knows his way around. He looks confident and relaxed. 'Come here, Mateo!' he shouts at some point, as he sees a younger boy on the other side of the street. 'He wants to work with us as well,' he murmurs to me as the boy crosses the street, 'but we're trying to see whether he's good enough.' He then turns to Mateo: 'I'll introduce you to a friend of mine from Italy,' he says.

We continue walking together. At some point, Mateo lights up a joint. 'Not here, brother,' Sebastián tells him, calmly at first. The gang has established specific (hidden) spaces in the neighbourhood where youngsters are allowed to consume drugs, and Mateo knows that. But maybe he feels self-assured, and he keeps walking with the joint in his hand, as if he had not heard Sebastián's remark. Sebastián quickly gets upset, steps in front of him and says, in a louder and resolute voice tone: 'Not here, I said, NOT HERE! Do you want to smoke?! Then go far away behind that corner, no problem! But not here where everyone sees you [...],' he continues, hinting at me. 'Do you want our visitor to think that this place is full of filthy junkies?!' Mateo is clearly intimidated.

Sebastián takes a deep breath, then asks, more calmly: 'How old are you?' 'Fifteen,' whispers Mateo. 'In a couple of years, you can hang out with us,' says Sebastián. 'Or even earlier, perhaps. But you have to be serious, brother. I was like you, a dirty junkie, a street kid. But up there, they taught me to be serious. This is a serious business ... Do you want to see how we control crazy people?' he asks and then, in the fraction of a second, punches Mateo in the stomach. Mateo falls on the ground and Sebastián continues to kick him, laughing, while a few other boys come closer to watch. 'That's how we control crazy people, those who don't respect the law of the neighbourhood,' he concludes. 'Be serious, brother.'

In the following days, I kept thinking about what I had witnessed between Sebastián and Mateo. Sebastián's repeated reference to my presence during his exchange with Mateo made me reflect on the fact that things may have not unfolded in exactly the same way had I not been there. Clearly, Sebastián wanted to show something to Mateo – but he also wanted to show something to *me*. Maybe he wanted to impress me, or prove that the things he had told me about his new role in the gang and his growing importance in the neighbourhood were true.

This episode highlights various key ethical questions that I had to face in my research. How much does our manifested interest in certain (potentially problematic) behaviour encourage our participants' engagement in them? How much is it within our role, power and duty as researchers to try and steer our informants away from actions that we morally reject? And how much is it recommendable or even possible to participate in our informants' daily activities where these fall outside the realm of things we consider legal or moral? In what follows, I discuss these and other ethical matters, highlighting the distance between ethical guidelines and the real-world dilemmas that one encounters in the field.

The ethics of our research focus

The focus we choose for our research bears ethical implications, particularly when one's research interest revolves around stigmatised, immoral or illegal aspects of people's lives. This is because of the risk of further stigmatising the research population as well as the real risk of 'reducing' people's lives to just a small fraction of their 'problematic' behaviour.

In my case, I had to ask myself whether the way I was selecting, observing and asking questions to my informants could result in a skewed narrative that overrepresented crime and violence as opposed to other aspects of daily life. It can be tempting as first-time ethnographers to focus on the more sensationalistic aspects of our informants' lives. We may think this is likely to result in more attractive and 'unique' data which will be more easily publishable. I was certainly guilty of that, and when I started the research, I found myself overfocusing on sensationalistic events that – I later understood – failed to be fully representative of my young informants' lives. As Jones and Rodgers (2019, p. 302) note, there is a real danger for crime and violence to 'take over' the text – that is, to 'become more prominent on the page than may be the case materially on the ground'. Because much of the performance of violence and illegality is relational, the fact that I was there, observing, asking questions and manifesting interest in these matters made it more prominent in their narratives than it actually was in their lives.

As I noted above from a safety perspective, from an ethical perspective too it would have been better for me to avoid putting crime and violence at the centre of my research, and rather to focus on the more intimate, everyday dimensions of these young lives. I did gradually shift to this approach throughout my fieldwork and writing process, but I now wish that I had been cognisant of the power of my gaze from the start.

The ethics of participant observation

Some anthropologists consider that participation in their informants' activities is a prerequisite to fully understand their social reality even in borderline cases. For instance, Joseph and Donnelly (2012, p. 360), who have conducted research with habitual heavy drinkers, felt that consuming alcohol with their research participants was crucial in order to build rapport, gather data and genuinely represent the social milieu they were studying. I had to ask myself a similar question: could I ever fully understand the life experiences of young people for whom drug consumption constitutes a large part of life and socialisation without consuming drugs with them?

In my case, I chose never to consume any drugs with my research participants, as I considered that this would have hampered my ability to lucidly observe their social reality, and could have also excessively blurred the boundaries between research and friendship. At the same time, however, I always retained a non-judgemental attitude towards their use of addictive substances, marking a clear difference between me and other adults in the community.

I also decided never to raise this matter with my informants' caretakers, school teachers, or other institutions. Underlying this decision was a genuine commitment not to betray my young informants' trust and to protect our confidentiality agreement. Talking to their parents would have meant completely alienating them from me, the only adult to whom – they often said – they felt they could talk freely.

While I was satisfied with how I dealt with the drug consumption topic, a much more complex question arose when I became aware of my informants' engagement in violence towards others. This could go from mild forms of interpersonal violence, such as Sebastián beating younger Mateo, to more extreme instances in which my informants told me of having seriously harmed or even killed people. While I never witnessed concrete instances of heavy violence, which would have imposed on me a legal obligation to report, I often learned about these episodes in the youth's narratives.

The surprising thing for me was to notice how much my moral judgement suspended in these cases. Because I understood the structural causes which could lead young people to act in certain ways, actions that would seem unacceptable in principle started to make sense in particular situations. As Rodgers (2007, pp. 457–8) notes, '[m]aintaining a disapproval of violence can be difficult in practice'. When researching violent actors, we must be prepared to face ambivalent situations, where, as Theidon (2014, pp. 2–3) puts it: 'Some of [our informants] may appal us; others may become friends we care about very much. A sizeable segment will fall into both categories at different moments in time.'

Balancing empathy and distance with my young informants was both a challenge and a profound learning experience. While I initially decided to retain a non-judgemental attitude, I did, towards the end of my research, start to step out of these impartial shoes and tried to prompt my informants to reflect critically on what they were doing or sometimes pointing them to sources of help, as I would have done with a family member or friend. The more my fieldwork progressed, the more I felt I was becoming emotionally close to the youths I was studying. As much as I was interested in learning about my informants' lives, I started to recognise that I was also *in* their lives, which made me feel a certain degree of responsibility for helping, advising and supporting them.

Overall, I felt that the ethical balance between being impartial and being engaged was a difficult one to strike. At times empathy took the form of understanding why they were engaging in violence, at others it took the form of really wanting to help them get out of it. Avoiding any judgement and intervention may grant us easier rapport and is considered more ethical. Sometimes, however, this fully detached approach fails to appreciate that our informants may sometimes be embroiled in situations they themselves want to get out of, and turns a blind eye to our ability to help.

A better, more ethical approach is to stay flexible and adapt our degree of involvement to each individual situation, for some people may welcome help and intervention more than others. It is crucial to remain cognisant of the power we have to influence and help our closest informants and not shy away from taking a more active role in their lives if so they wish, even if this falls outside of the standard ethnographer's shoes.

Dealing with power imbalances

Additional ethical dilemmas emerge regarding power imbalances between oneself and one's research participants. While fieldwork trainings tend to emphasise the importance of forging bonds of trust and respect with our informants, much less attention is paid to how we ought to relate with, confront and denounce the larger structures of oppression and inequality within which such relationships are typically inscribed.

As ethnographers we can find ourselves building relationships of trust with people from structurally disadvantaged, stigmatised, or hard-to-reach populations. During fieldwork, we may find ourselves under the illusion of 'horizontality' with or even dependent on our informants – as they are often more knowledgeable and less vulnerable than us in the field. But in the broader horizon, when fieldwork is completed, the power hierarchy becomes all the more apparent. We go back to our universities, often based in first-world countries, with data to analyse, a sense of satisfaction and achievement for having completed the fieldwork and a challenging yet promising career in front of us. By contrast, our informants stay in the same place, with their situation unchanged and being further deprived of the presence of the researcher, who may have become, during the fieldwork, an important source of support. As Vanderstaay (2005, p. 399) admits, at the end of his fieldwork '[t]he balance sheet seemed egregious: I left the relationship with a dissertation, a PhD, and a job offer; [his informants] left the relationship jailed, drunk, and drug addicted'.

It is easy for first-time ethnographers to become blind to these imbalances and not even want to see them. Once we leave the field, we quickly become absorbed in the writing process, we start feeling the pressure of the academic job market and we are often too immersed in our own precarity to appreciate how privileged our situation is in comparison to those whose lives we have studied. We may find ourselves failing to return phone calls or answering their messages slowly – much more slowly than when we were in the field and our data depended solely on our informants' willingness to talk to us. For many, the geographical distance, cost of travel and heavy demands of the academic profession make it almost impossible to continue engaging with our informants as often as we did during fieldwork. Some would even argue that some degree of separation is epistemologically desirable, for good analysis requires 'taking distance' from the emotionally charged dynamics of the field. But what does 'taking distance' mean, in a context where we are actually distancing ourselves from individuals whose stories we are building a career on – while their lives and struggles continue unresolved?

While it's not in our power to fully resolve this tension, we should remain conscious of the fact that, as Irwin (2006, p. 169) puts it, we are always 'doing structure' in the field. Despite the best intentions, we cannot avoid re-enacting and reinforcing historically exploitative practices, relationships and power differentials – and we should, at the very least, acknowledge and write about it, and if possible take action to redress the situation.

At the end of my fieldwork, I did invest time to produce a series of advocacy and practice-oriented research outputs that did not necessarily advance my academic career but sought to generate a change in the life situation of these youths. At the time, I felt I did what I could in this sense – but, in hindsight, I wish I had considered these aspects more carefully from the start of the fieldwork, and prioritised advocacy and restitution work over my own academic career in a more ethically balanced manner.

Conclusion

Writing this chapter has been both a difficult and cathartic experience. It has made me see how alone I have been when facing these situations – and how little I actually sought out help. Why did I never reach out to my supervisor to discuss these matters? Why did I never seek out the advice of the university's research committee? Why didn't I even discuss these matters with peers, almost turning away from, rather than openly acknowledging, the tensions and dilemmas I was experiencing?

The reasons were probably many: a combination of fear of the consequences of disclosing my mistakes, a willingness to prove I could navigate these challenges alone, a lack of lucidity in actually seeing that I needed help, a sense of lack of time and data urgency. These feelings – not unique to me but, as I later learned, quite common among first-time ethnographers – not only led me to push my safety and ethical boundaries under stress, but also prevented me from seeking the help I needed. This is why building check-in moments structurally into supervisory relationships and ethical and safety procedures, rather than leaving these to the initiative of the researcher, is of paramount importance.

The practice of speaking and writing explicitly about these matters is also a key component of ethical research practice. Despite anthropology priding itself on being the most reflexive social science, it is remarkable how rarely we actually have the confidence to write about the mistakes we may have made in the field. While I was encouraged to thoroughly reflect about ethical issues *before* embarking on fieldwork, during the write-up process I often felt pressured to 'clean up' or 'simplify' the dilemmas I had experienced, and emphasise instead the ways I successfully negotiated and resolved any issues that I was faced with. Surely, this is an effective strategy to convince examiners that our work is unproblematic and that we deserve being awarded the PhD. But it often fails to reflect our fieldwork experience; and it does not help future researchers to prepare for fieldwork complexities beforehand. A more 'confessional inflicted ethnography', as Wolseth (2019, p. 356) calls it – one that openly discusses inner dilemmas, mistakes and lessons learned – would not only be more useful, but also more ethical when considering ethnography as a collaborative practice.

This is also what I have tried to do in this chapter. Confessional accounts are not easy to write – much less if one is still in the early stages of one's career and wonders, as I have, what implications this kind of transparency may have on one's academic future and ability to be taken seriously. However, I believe that by joining forces we can promote a more honest, transparent and self-critical account of the ethnographic experience. At the same time, we should make equal efforts to acknowledge, denounce and collectively change the structural conditions of fatigue and anxiety that lead especially early-career researchers to make not-well-thought-out choices under pressure.

Recommendations

1 **Approach ethics and safety assessments as a process, not as one-off bureaucratic hurdle.** Once you begin fieldwork, build your local safety net, and discuss safety and ethical concerns with them.
2 **Fight data anxiety.** Always think twice before doing anything during fieldwork. You will always have more data than you need in the end.
3 **Follow the opportunities that open up for you.** Do not struggle to get into places or scenes that seem inaccessible. Doing so may be more likely to put you in trouble.
4 **Find strategies to extend your time in your field location.** Generally, ethnographers are not granted enough time to do the work they need to do; this can lead to corner-cutting when it comes to making safe and ethical decisions. Explore the options available through your research to spend more time with your interlocutors – for example, through work or volunteer placements connected to your research, or applying for additional field research funding.
5 **Try to uphold the professional boundaries you set for yourself.** Before embarking onto fieldwork, ask yourself: Why are you doing this? What is your broader aim? What are the values and the boundaries you will not compromise on? Write down your answers and read them again when needed.

Note

1 All names are pseudonyms for the sake of anonymisation.

Further reading

Baird, A. 2018. Dancing with danger: Ethnographic safety, male bravado and gang research in Colombia. *Qualitative Research*, 18(3), 342–60.
An excellent reflection on how one can acquire ethnographic safety.

Bourgois, P. and Schonberg, J. 2009. Introduction. In *Righteous Dopefiend*. Berkeley: University of California Press. pp. 1–24.

An insightful discussion on the mismatch between ethical and safety requirements and the realities of the street.

Caretta, M.A. and Jokinen, J.C. 2017. Conflating privilege and vulnerability: A reflexive analysis of emotions and positionality in postgraduate fieldwork. *The Professional Geographer*, 69(2), 275–83.

This article is an open and reflexive discussion of the challenges encountered by first-time ethnographers.

Vanderstaay, S.L. 2005. One hundred dollars and a dead man: Ethical decision making in ethnographic fieldwork. *Journal of Contemporary Ethnography*, 34(4), 371–409.

Insightful discussion of the complexities of conducting fieldwork with drugs- and crime-involved informants.

Wolseth, J. 2019. Writing after betrayal: *Desahogarse*, street outreach, and ethnography. *Ethnography*, 20(3), 342–58.

Honest account of the limits of ethnographic representation and of the need for more confessional ethnographic writing.

References

Baird, A. 2018. Dancing with danger: Ethnographic safety, male bravado and gang research in Colombia. *Qualitative Research*, 18(3), 342–60.

Caretta, M.A. and Jokinen, J.C. 2017. Conflating privilege and vulnerability: A reflexive analysis of emotions and positionality in postgraduate fieldwork. *The Professional Geographer*, 69(2), 275–83.

Hanson, R. and Richards, P. 2017. Sexual harassment and the construction of ethnographic knowledge. *Sociological Forum*, 32(3), 587–609.

Irwin, K. 2006. Into the dark heart of ethnography: The lived ethics and inequality of intimate field relationships. *Qualitative Sociology*, 29(2), 155–75.

Jones, G.A. and Rodgers, D. 2019. Ethnographies and/of violence. *Ethnography*, 20(3), 297–319.

Joseph, J. and Donnelly, M.K. 2012. Reflections on ethnography, ethics and inebriation. *Leisure/Loisir*, 36(3–4), 357–72.

Kovats-Bernat, J.C. 2002. Negotiating dangerous fields: Pragmatic strategies for fieldwork amid violence and terror. *American Anthropologist*, 104(1), 208–22.

Rodgers, D. 2007. Joining the gang and becoming a broder: The violence of ethnography in contemporary Nicaragua. *Bulletin of Latin American Research*, 26(4), 444–61.

Theidon, K. 2014. 'How was your trip?' Self-care for researchers working and writing on violence. *Social Science Research Council Working Papers*, 2.

Vanderstaay, S.L. 2005. One hundred dollars and a dead man: Ethical decision making in ethnographic fieldwork. *Journal of Contemporary Ethnography*, 34(4), 371–409.

Van Maanen, J. 1988. *Tales of the Field: On Writing Ethnography*. Chicago: University of Chicago Press.

Watts, J.H. 2008. Emotion, empathy and exit: Reflections on doing ethnographic qualitative research on sensitive topics. *Medical Sociology*, 3(2), 13.

Wolseth, J. 2019. Writing after betrayal: *Desahogarse*, street outreach, and ethnography. *Ethnography*, 20(3), 342–58.

Wood, E.J. 2006. The ethical challenges of field research in conflict zones. *Qualitative Sociology*, 29, 373–86.

3

CYBERSECURITY AND ETHNOGRAPHY

James Shires

Summary

This chapter introduces ethnographers to cybersecurity. It first explains why ethnographers are among high-risk groups exceptionally vulnerable to and likely to be targeted by some cyber threats. This discussion includes examples drawn from the author's own experience of ethnographic interactions with cybersecurity professional and expert communities in the Middle East. It then details four categories of cybersecurity protection, focused on general risks and mitigations rather than specific technologies: identity, data protection, secure communication and internet access. It concludes with five recommendations that together constitute a basic process of cybersecurity risk assessment for ethnographers.

Table of contents

Introduction	34
Cyber threats to human security	35
Cyber threats to ethnographers	35
Cybersecurity protections	38
Conclusion	44
Recommendations	44
Further readings	45
References	45

Introduction

British academic Matthew Hedges was imprisoned by the UAE authorities on charges of espionage in May 2018, and sentenced to life imprisonment in November 2018. Following global publicity around his case and diplomatic pressure from the UK government (on whose behalf he was accused of spying), Hedges was pardoned immediately prior to the UAE National Day on 2 December 2018. He was subsequently deported and, in 2021, filed a case in the UK High Court claiming damages for torture experienced during his detention. A news conference given by the UAE government on Hedges' case featured a likely doctored video – not released publicly – in which Hedges purportedly confessed to spying, although official statements claimed that data obtained from Hedges' laptop and phone were equally important in their prosecution. Hedges himself surmised that his phone had been 'bugged from the moment he arrived' in the UAE (Parveen, 2018).

Other academics, dissidents and journalists working in the Middle East have not been so 'lucky'. Just as the Hedges case hit the global news cycle, international media outlets were focused on the murder of Saudi journalist Jamal Khashoggi by Saudi officials in the Saudi consulate in Istanbul in October 2018. The grisly details were gradually leaked by the state-directed Turkish media, leading to speculation (and, in 2021, an official assessment from the US Director of National Intelligence) that Crown Prince Muhammad Bin Salman had approved the murder. Investigations by the Canadian NGO Citizen Lab suggested that Khashoggi's contacts had used devices infected with Israeli-manufactured spyware bought by the Saudi government, revealing all conversations they had on these devices to Saudi intelligence agencies (Marczak et al., 2018).

Three years earlier, the Italian academic Giulio Regini was tortured and killed in Cairo. Following international condemnation and an extensive investigation hindered by their Egyptian counterparts, four individuals in the Egyptian Interior Ministry's National Security Agency were tried for the murder of Regini in Italy in absentia – although the trial collapsed in October 2021. Although there is no specific evidence that Regini was targeted by commercial or state-built spyware, the Egyptian government is a customer of several firms selling such software to governments around the world. Regini's laptop and phone were never released for examination by Italian investigators.

All three cases are devastatingly severe signals of a deterioration in freedom of expression in the above states. Hedges and Regini were conducting interviews on sensitive subjects (UAE military developments and Egyptian street workers' unions respectively), while Khashoggi was a columnist for the *Washington Post*. Among their many repercussions, the spyware and other digital elements of these cases highlight very real cybersecurity threats to ethnographers, who share many of the same characteristics as the individuals above from the point of view of a suspicious state.

I am a scholar of cybersecurity, who has used ethnographic methods to analyse professional cybersecurity communities in the Middle East (Shires, 2021). My experience suggests cybersecurity is not a standard part of ethnographic training, so ethnographers are often unaware of simple data protection measures they can take to mitigate cybersecurity risks they face in the field. Although these risks can never be fully prevented, countermeasures do exist. A more inclusive ethnography is one that thoroughly addresses cybersecurity risks, given the differential impact of such risks along gendered and other intersectional dimensions (Millar et al., 2021).

The chapter is structured as follows. It first provides an overview of a theoretical conception of human-centred cybersecurity; then examines cybersecurity issues specifically related to ethnography; then gives pointers to ways ethnographers can improve their cybersecurity posture; and, finally, contextualises these resources through a process of risk assessment. The concluding section is the most important, as using tools without knowing why or what limitations they have can be as dangerous as not protecting yourself in the first place.

Cyber threats to human security

Cybersecurity can be defined as the prevention and mitigation of malicious interference with digital devices and networks. Cybersecurity covers a vast range of threats and risks, expanding over time as digital technologies become ever more ubiquitous, and morphing into an integral thread of the fabric of everyday experience for millions around the world. Most treatments focus on national or commercial cybersecurity, considering risks to governments and state critical infrastructure, or to the operations and profitability of companies. These concepts of cybersecurity are not especially relevant for ethnographers, as they are not inclusive: they do not place at their heart the concerns of all individuals, including those in risky situations such as academics, journalists and dissidents.

Others have put forward a more inclusive concept of human-centred cybersecurity. Ron Deibert, director of the Citizen Lab mentioned above, explicitly ties cybersecurity to a broader movement of 'human security': to see what are usually cast as questions of national or international security as threats to individuals (Deibert, 2021). Theories of human security usually articulate these threats in reference to international human rights in two key ways: first, freedom from torture, mistreatment or arbitrary detention in connection to spyware or surveillance facilitating such actions; and, second, freedom of expression in connection to censorship and filtering. There are of course other human rights, including rights of development, political participation and non-discrimination, that are relevant to cybersecurity due to phenomena such as disinformation campaigns on social media, the manipulation of targeted advertisements and free or subsidised provision of essential services in exchange for personal data. Human-centred cybersecurity can adapt with the expansion of cybersecurity itself, keeping individual rights at the core of its protective mission.

Cyber threats to ethnographers

Within a broader concept of human-centred cybersecurity, there are specific cybersecurity issues relating to ethnography. Of course, it is problematic to generalise across all ethnographers as a single group, as their exposure to cyber threats varies depending on their background, focus and fieldsite(s). Internal and digital ethnographies especially will have different risk profiles to more traditional versions. Despite these differences, most ethnographers spend a substantial time in the field, seeking to participate as fully as possible in the activities of a particular community. In many cases, these communities are wholly or partly online – leading to the rise of 'digital ethnography' as a distinct methodology. As such, there are several cybersecurity risks specifically relevant to ethnographers, and an inclusive ethnography should approach these risks individually, taking into account each ethnographer's specific context. The emotional, time and other commitments made by ethnographers to their communities, including their interaction with and participation in behavioural norms that they might consider risky or unwise, mean that while some of these risks are also faced by academics and similar profiles, they are likely to be higher for ethnographers.

First, ethnographers should be aware that their academic identities could be exploited by cybersecurity threat actors. Some phishing emails (containing malicious links or attachments) sent by cybersecurity threat actors look very similar to emails I and many other academics send asking for interviews. The box below is an example of a phishing email addressed to a journalist working on technology and human rights in the Gulf, sent by a threat actor linked to the UAE government during my research in the region (Marczak and Scott-Railton, 2016).

EXAMPLE 3.1

From: andrew.dwight389@outlook.com
Subject: FW: Correspondence Request
Greetings Mr. Donaghy,

I have been trying to reach you for comment and I am hoping that this e-mail reaches the intended recipient. My name is Andrew Dwight and I am currently writing a book about my experiences in the Middle East. My focus is on human factors and rights issues in seemingly non-authoritarian regimes (that are, in reality, anything but). I was hoping that I might correspond with you and reference some of your work, specifically this piece ([MALICIOUS LINK]), for the book. I'm quite impressed with the way you articulate this complex issue for the masses, and hope to have a similar impact with my book.
Happy New Year,
Andrew

The link in the email above was intended to install malware on the device of the targeted individual. Although, to my knowledge, there is no Andrew Dwight conducting research on human rights in the Gulf, the same technique could be used to impersonate real academics and thereby install malware on the devices of ethnographers or their interlocutors. In my research, given that the cybersecurity community I worked with was unsurprisingly hyper-aware of phishing risks, I consciously sought to distinguish my communications from phishing emails by not asking for sensitive information via email, providing plenty of verifiable detail and not including links.

More broadly, the malicious adoption of academic personae demonstrates an important and well-known feature of the ethnographic fieldsite, updated for the digital age: namely, that potential interlocutors may already be suspicious of researcher approaches. As one interlocuter in my research mentioned, pointing out my university's connection to the UK intelligence community, 'they don't know who you are, you come from a country with a bad history in these things, they don't know what you will do with the information' (Shires, 2018). The cases of Matthew Hedges and Gulio Regini in the introduction highlight the perception of some states that ethnographic research is a cover for espionage, and the horrific consequences when such states act on these perceptions.

Unfortunately, this is sometimes true. While anthropological connections with colonial power – and more recently the US military – have been subject to sustained analysis within the discipline, one incident illustrates how similar connections continue in the field of cybersecurity. In 2018, Maria Butina, a Russian graduate student in the US, was arrested for using a college assignment to 'gather information on the cyberdefenses of US nonprofit organizations that champion media freedom and human rights' as part of a 'clandestine political influence campaign' (Butler, 2018). Here the identity of an academic researcher *in cybersecurity* seeking to engage with at-risk communities, especially NGOs, human rights groups and academic institutions, was likely exploited by actors associated with state intelligence agencies as a way to collect information about the cybersecurity weaknesses of those groups.

Cybersecurity advice intended for NGOs and academics has also been adapted by some of the very groups that pose a threat to them. In 2014, Kuwaiti cybersecurity company Cyberkov wrote a publicly available cybersecurity manual in Arabic, which they claimed was directed to 'journalists and activists (especially those working in war zones like Gaza)' (Al-Ali, 2015). Such resources are important for ethnographers and the communities they study, as most cybersecurity documents are written in English and there are well-documented problems with the Arabic language in core internet functions. However, this manual was later integrated into an ISIS operational security document. This incident points to a basic feature of human-centred cybersecurity: that the same tools that protect ethnographers also protect everyone else, and this knowledge is of use to many groups that do not have a purely academic motivation.

My ethnographic research was conducted at the intersection of these diverse cybersecurity issues. I was a white male researcher associated with a prestigious Western university, conducting research in a region with a complicated colonial history (specifically, Egypt and the Gulf states). The Gulf states, for various reasons, had an ambivalent relationship with colonialism, as British colonial policy in the Gulf was to preserve the ruling families while maintaining British influence. Egypt, in contrast, was far more overtly integrated into the British colonial project. In both cases, though imperial power has ended, coloniality continues to constitute security relations, including in cybersecurity (Mumford and Shires, 2023). As the opening examples show starkly, my profile in this region created personal safety risks for ethnographic research on any sensitive subject, as well as the cybersecurity risk that my identity could be used by malicious threat actors to gain access to their targets (like 'Andrew Dwight' above).

In addition, my research was on the topic of cybersecurity itself. On the one hand, as cybersecurity professionals, my interlocuters were hyper-aware of the risks created by our interaction, whether from suspicion of me directly or the risk that third parties could seek to access my data.

They would usually refuse digital recordings of interviews and other interactions and occasionally interrogated me on my data protection and cybersecurity measures from the perspective of an expert. On the other hand, their clear enthusiasm – and, in many cases, evangelism – for their subject meant that they saw assistance to research as a way to 'pay back' or advance the common good. Consequently, despite the significant security risks (and, in the field, a substantial dose of security theatre), they were also friendly, welcoming and sometimes surprisingly open. I cannot generalise their reasons for this here, but simply recognise this generosity and repay it through objective and thorough research.

Cybersecurity protections

This section introduces key cybersecurity protections and explains briefly why they work. As cybersecurity typically takes the form of a sociotechnical cat-and-mouse game between attackers and defenders – solutions are developed for existing attacks, new vulnerabilities are found in those solutions and so on – the exact route of this adversarial development is complex and difficult to predict. Consequently, this section aims to be technology-neutral as far as possible, but some dating is inevitable. To prevent the individual tools mentioned from being the focal point of this section, I group them into four broad categories that will hopefully remain more relevant: identity, data protection, secure messaging and internet access. It should be stressed that it is merely an introductory overview, and there are whole disciplinary debates about the benefits of certain actions within each category.

There is a general point that applies throughout this section. Individuals are generally tied to corporations through their digital devices and services. As much as corporations can be a cybersecurity threat to individuals, they also have significant commercial interest in protecting their customers' data, and Apple, Alphabet (Google), Microsoft, Facebook etc. have more resources and more people dedicated to this task than many states. When they provide new hardware and software, this is nearly always more secure than older versions. The old cybersecurity adage that the easiest and most important thing you can do is to download and install security updates is still relevant, although this choice has largely been taken away from most consumers and becomes partly a question of corporate relationships. For example, Apple IOS and Google Android devices are likely to receive the best service in terms of security, while others may not. The security of a device is closely related to its age, and here cybersecurity concerns conflict with questions of environmental sustainability and reuse.

Also, the relationship between cybersecurity protection and physical protection deserves emphasis. As the illustrative examples with which I began the chapter demonstrate, cybersecurity risks do not 'stay' online; cyber threats can be combined with or lead to physical threats in cases as varied as technology-facilitated intimate partner violence and state-sponsored assassination or arbitrary detention. Consequently, cybersecurity protections help to protect ethnographers and others offline as well as online; conversely, physical security (especially around devices) is a key part of cybersecurity.

Identity

The first aspect of cybersecurity for ethnographers is securing your digital identity. This includes all your digital accounts: email, social media, banking, university accounts and so on. This is the most basic form of cybersecurity, as many cyberattacks rely on some sort of identity compromise: masquerading as you in order to do something else. There are three main ways in which identities are protected:

1 **Passwords.** One of the first pieces of cybersecurity advice for individuals is to use strong passwords. Passwords can be weak in two ways: they can be easily guessed (like the word 'password'), or they can be 'brute forced': a program can cycle through all possible combinations until it finds the right one. Many websites require upper- and lower-case letters, numbers and special characters to increase the number of possible combinations, making a brute force attack more difficult. However, such passwords are difficult to remember, with the reuse of passwords increasing the risk of compromise, so passwords should be longer – but easy-to-remember – phrases. Accessible password recovery mechanisms can themselves be a point of vulnerability, as they rely on text messages or emails that can be spoofed. Alternatively, password managers remove the need to remember more than one password, but become a focal point for attackers, redistributing while reducing risk.

2 **Biometrics.** The second way of proving your identity is through biometric recognition: usually fingerprints, irises, or faces. This is increasingly common for personal devices, and removes password risks around memory and storage. Many biometric recognition features can be bypassed due to flaws in the underlying architecture, or even fooled using a fake finger/face. Although biometric recognition for personal devices is usually designed *not* to share the biometric details with even the software designer, this is not the case for other biometric systems, such as passports. As biometric systems grow in popularity the value of biometric details themselves increases, and it becomes a new area of vulnerability and protection. As an extra layer of security, to prevent unwanted photos of your face taken from your laptop webcam you can buy a privacy screen, uncovering the webcam only when required, or use some tape.

3 **Multifactor authentication.** Multifactor authentication is designed to mitigate attacks against any single factor system, whether biometric or password (credential) based, as very few adversaries have access to several means of authentication. For example, two-factor authentication is used by most banks, universities and large businesses, and is available on most free webmail accounts. Although the use of a physical token as a second factor is most secure, it is also most inconvenient, and other two-factor systems rely on a text or online notification to a separate device (e.g., a smartphone for laptop access). Again, this introduces new vulnerabilities, as these text messages can be intercepted or faked, or the apps used to provide two-factor authentication have their own vulnerabilities. Nonetheless, two-factor authentication is becoming a mainstream standard and should be adopted for key accounts by all ethnographers.

Data protection

The second aspect of cybersecurity for ethnographers is data protection. Like many other professions, ethnographers collect and hold often extremely sensitive data about themselves and many others. Ethnographers should secure this data to reduce their own risks and risks to their interlocutors – and to comply with relevant data protection laws. I highlight three aspects of data protection. Before doing so, it is worth mentioning a point that is not strictly a cybersecurity protection: it is a good idea, for many reasons, to *frequently back up all data*. The same data protection advice below then applies to both the data itself and its backup.

1. **Restriction.** The simplest form of data protection is to restrict the amount of data that you provide to others, through limiting access to datasets or reducing the constant stream of data from your personal devices. Here, data protection can clash with academic norms of transparency in research design. The balance between sensitivity and transparency in academia is not a new debate, and only becomes a cybersecurity issue because it is much easier to copy datasets and drafts to a much wider audience using digital technologies. Also, locking down devices is inconvenient: for example, disabling location services makes it much harder for companies (and adversaries) to track you, but also means that apps may not function properly. Careful use of social media is another example of deliberate data restriction. Most obviously, opinions and activities can be read directly from social media content, but the metadata of social media (location, timestamp, device, responses, friends, contacts, etc.) also provides a rich source of information for malicious actors. It is a good habit to reflect on the implications of specific posts, tweets, or images before sending them, and investigate carefully the privacy settings of online services. Finally, even the physical transfer of data presents significant cybersecurity risks, as USB sticks are a well-known threat vector for both nation-state and cybercriminal malware (and the prevalence of USB charging at airports and other locations – which can permit data transfer – makes this risk far more common).

2. **Encryption.** It is very easy to encrypt data stored on a personal device, and this makes it significantly more difficult to access for an adversary. Programs such as VeraCrypt are free and easy to use, allowing you to work with encrypted data as you would normally. They are also flexible depending on your risk profile, allowing you to encrypt your device as a whole, or to encrypt specific files and folders on that device. Some offer 'hidden' options, allowing you to display a 'dummy' encrypted section depending on the password entered, which is designed to prevent even adversaries who forcibly obtain a password from you (e.g., in a police interview) from accessing or being aware that the sensitive data exists. For all encryption systems, incorrect use merely provides a false sense of security, or prevents you from accessing your data.

3. **Cloud.** The other main way of protecting your data is to outsource the responsibility. Cloud services mobilise the resources of large companies to protect your data. This is not perfect, as such companies have suffered comparably massive data breaches of usernames and passwords, but it is a useful first step. The main risks then lie in controlling the

permissions to share access to various documents in your online accounts, and in increasing reliance on a single company. There are free alternatives to corporate cloud services, such as MEGA. Finally, cloud services rely on fast and reliable internet access, something that cannot be guaranteed for many ethnographers in the field.

Secure communication

The third aspect of cybersecurity for ethnographers is secure communication.

1. **Email.** Email, as the default means of communication for most academics, is a focal point for attackers in several ways. First, emails are still the primary means of delivery for 'phishing' attacks, where users are tricked into downloading attachments or clicking on links that deliver malicious software or take them to a fake login site to harvest their credentials. Although spam filters increasingly remove such emails from users' daily experience, phishing remains the most reliable means of compromise for attackers from low-level cybercriminals to advanced states. Emails also contain much sensitive data, available to the company providing the email service and any state that obtains or convinces them to share it (nearly always without open acknowledgement). Some email providers, such as Protonmail, advertise higher privacy subscription services where data is not shared with advertisers or states. It is easy to encrypt email communication using standards such as PGP, and browser extensions such as Mailvelope integrate PGP encryption into most webmail accounts. As PGP uses asymmetric encryption (with both public and private keys) a public key (or shorter signature) must first be shared before communication. These services have easy online help for first-time users (Raicea, 2017).
2. **Apps.** Messaging apps are a ubiquitous alternative to email for both business and personal communication. These apps often advertise 'end-to-end' encryption, meaning that the message is encrypted on the sender's device and decrypted only by the receiver. Neither the company itself (in the case of WhatsApp, its parent company is Facebook) nor third parties should have access to the unencrypted message. This is not always the case: for example, in the UK messaging companies have come under pressure to provide an escrow solution (where they keep a copy of the encryption key) for governments to provide access. There are some open-source messaging apps with end-to-end encryption, such as Signal, that are less likely to cooperate with governments in this way. Such apps are blocked (either completely or partially) in many states. An adversary with network-level access can usually access communications through secure messaging apps due to flaws in implementation or targeted access to specific devices, rather than seeking a cryptographic solution. Some malicious actors have even built replicas of apps, including WhatsApp and Signal, that appear legitimate but send users' data to the adversary. Overall, apps with end-to-end encryption should be a default mode of communication, although they are not a panacea. For ethnographers, secure messaging raises new questions of storage and reference for academic purposes (e.g., through screenshots or periodic downloads of all chat data).

3. **Conferencing.** Since the COVID-19 pandemic, nearly all organisations use online conferencing software. Most is incorporated into wider business software, provided by large tech companies, although there are many reliable, free and open-source versions (such as Jitsi). Links to online events should be treated with caution, and their creators should take care in sharing links, especially in public.

Internet access

The fourth and final aspect of cybersecurity for ethnographers is internet access. Carefully controlling your internet access helps both to protect your privacy and act as a first line of defence against most forms of cyberattack. Web traffic travels between your device and the server hosting a particular website through various servers in different locations around the world, and website owners know a lot about your browsing activity due to cookies and other tracking software. In general, anti-tracking browser add-ons, along with high browser privacy settings that clear history regularly, are a good start. Browsers such as DuckDuckGo do not collect user data for advertising. It is not a good idea to connect to unsecured or poorly secured Wi-Fi networks or those that you do not trust.

1. **Virtual private networks (VPNs).** VPNs are encrypted 'tunnels' from a device to a web server: traffic from your device goes to this server first through the encrypted tunnel, and then to a website 'in the clear'. Unless an adversary or website owner has access to the intermediate VPN server, they are unable to identify the details of the individual using the VPN. VPNs enable users to circumvent organisational or national censorship, so an individual in China could use a VPN server in the US to access the Wikipedia page of the Tiananmen Square massacre. For this reason, VPN use for censorship circumvention is illegal in many states and some seek to block popular VPN providers. However, most universities provide remote access to their servers for restricted resources via a VPN, and these are rarely blocked by states. VPNs also allow users to connect securely to open and insecure Wi-Fi access points (such as cafés, airports or hotels), as the traffic is encrypted from the device so adversaries with access to the Wi-Fi network cannot inspect this traffic, although they can still see that it has occurred. Free VPN services are available for mobile devices, although these services often monetise the data passing through them. Many devices can be configured to only allow traffic through a VPN route and block all other traffic, which is recommended for high-risk areas.
2. **The Onion Router (Tor).** Tor is a technology originally developed by the US Navy for anonymous browsing. It works by routing traffic through several servers ('nodes'), and re-encrypting the traffic with another layer of encryption at each point. The website owner is thus aware that their site has been visited from a Tor node, although they do not know the details of the individual using Tor to visit it. The protocol relies partly on popularity, as the reason an individual's traffic cannot be identified is because there is a large amount of other Tor traffic through the same server. Although the Tor protocol is very secure, it is used by a wide range of people seeking to anonymise their traffic: critics claim it facilitates

child pornography, narcotics sales and terrorism. Tor nodes are thus a high priority target for many state security agencies. If the first Tor node you use is compromised, then your identity can be revealed, while compromises of multiple Tor nodes or their combination with extensive signals intelligence can enable the reconstruction of a complete browsing history (Schneier, 2013). Finally, although easy to install, Tor slows internet traffic generally.

3 **Virtual machines (VMs).** Virtual machines add another layer of security to internet access and handling suspicious files. Virtual machine software creates an almost entirely segregated system within your current operating system, which looks and feels like a different device, although it uses the same internet connection. Virtual machines do not anonymise internet traffic, but if the concern is that you might download something that could infect your computer, doing so in a virtual machine entirely removes this problem, as the virtual machine itself can be deleted following access. Free VM services such as VirtualBox are simple to use and have extensive online guidance. Finally, there is a VM version called Tails that combines several of the security features discussed so far: it is fully encrypted and booted from an external drive (e.g., a USB stick) with no persistent files on the device used, and always uses Tor for browsing. This is the most secure way of accessing the internet, although it requires some time investment and careful continued use.

To summarise this section: there are four main areas for improving human-centred cybersecurity: identity, data protection, secure messaging and internet access. They will likely remain the focal points for both threats and responses despite rapidly changing technologies. Within these four areas, there are a range of simple steps that ethnographers can take to improve their cybersecurity posture. However, the exact course taken depends on the risk faced in specific situations.

Finally, although there is not space to repeat my personal process of risk assessment, these are the following protections I decided on using or not using during my doctoral research. I adopted separate strong passwords, biometrics and two-factor authentication for key accounts. I stored research data offline and encrypted with a regular encrypted backup. I restricted the information publicly available on Twitter and LinkedIn to reflect the minimum necessary for academic ethics while not enabling avenues for social engineering, and revisited this decision regularly. I also reviewed social media posts carefully before publishing them. In some states, I used a separate phone (not bought new, but factory reset) and local SIM card, and kept all communications and contacts separate between devices. For non-local devices I used mandatory VPN routing (with free, paid and university VPNs at different points), and used encrypted messaging where possible. I did not use Tor or Tails regularly, although I did use VMs for browsing risky sites and downloading or inspecting suspicious documents. Finally, given that phishing is the most likely method of compromise, I carefully screened texts and emails. This did not mean my devices and communications could not be compromised, but, in my view, it lowered the risk to an acceptable level given my profile and patience.

Further information about risk assessment, and an online method with more resources than can be listed here, can be found at the two website recommendations listed in Further reading.

Searching for the names of the products mentioned in this section will bring up many articles and advice pages on their use. Crypto-parties or other community activities are a good place to begin implementation of security tools. More generally, one can use online resources such as Wired, TechCrunch, Schneier on Security and Motherboard, or national awareness campaigns like those run by the UK National Cybersecurity Centre, to learn more about cybersecurity developments.

Conclusion

It is never too late to reassess cybersecurity risks, although there is a significant advantage to doing it early on, as the ethnographer will not be accustomed to insecure software or risky digital practices and will not have to break such habits. The tools and resources in the previous section are not helpful unless accompanied by a process of risk assessment, as one could easily protect against the wrong threats or build in unnecessary delays and inconveniences to already limited research time. As stated in the second section of this chapter, the generalisations about ethnography are not meant to homogenise all ethnographies but act as a helpful guide; inclusive ethnography requires supplementing this general advice with tailored individual recommendations.

Recommendations

1 **Understand why you face specific cybersecurity threats (i.e., threat motivations).** Identify what it is about you and your ethnographic research that makes you a target. Are you researching a sensitive or controversial topic? For whom is this topic sensitive? Are you working in a country with a heightened threat to academia more generally? What aspects of your positionality increase your cybersecurity risk?
2 **Understand the threat actors you are likely to face.** Is it a state with high intelligence resources? A non-state actor with significant cyber capabilities? Or a state or other organisation with relatively low capabilities? Move beyond the 'who' to the 'how': how would these threat actors seek to use their capabilities?
3 **Identify resources or practices that counter your threats** to reduce the ability of your adversaries to achieve their aims, or increase the cost to them of doing so. Consider using different devices for different countries or phases of the research, or having separate accounts for different communities.
4 **Identify negative side-effects from these resources or practices.** In some cases, the negative side-effects of these mitigations will simply be the impact on your research, maybe making your research harder, or more costly in money or time. In others, these side-effects will be further inferences made by your adversaries due to the tools themselves – for example, if you have Tor and Tails installed on your device, does this make you more suspicious if found?

5 **Select a list of resources or practices for implementation that work for you.**
Not all resources or tools will necessarily be available for differently abled ethnographers. Take the implementation stage seriously, review it regularly, attempt to build the practices you select into a habit. If possible, stay in touch with cybersecurity developments.

Further reading

FrontlineDefenders (www.frontlinedefenders.org/)
Online resource providing (among much else) cybersecurity advice and guidance for human rights defenders.

Schneier, B. 2015. *Data and Goliath: The Hidden Battles to Collect Your Data and Control Your World.* London: W.W. Norton.
A classic post-Snowden account of the reasons for government surveillance, how it works and the role of corporations in enabling or permitting it.

Security Planner (securityplanner.consumerreports.org/recommendations)
General advice on online security, with recommendations categorised according to cost and effort.

Stevens, T. 2023. *What is Cybersecurity For?* Bristol: Bristol University Press.
Authoritative and accessible discussion of the need for a more inclusive and politically engaged cybersecurity.

Zuboff, S. 2019. *The Age of Surveillance Capitalism: The Fight for the Future at the New Frontier of Power.* London: Profile.
Highly influential – and much debated – work arguing that privacy violation is at the heart of the business models behind digital technologies.

References

Al-Ali, A. 2015. Statements. *Cyberkov* (blog), 23 November. Available at perma.cc/3CWH-H92K (accessed 25 September 2023).
Butler, D. 2018. Russian held as agent studied US groups' cyberdefenses. *AP News*, 29 October. Available at perma.cc/P38F-J4YS (accessed 25 September 2023).
Deibert, R.J. 2021. *Reset: Reclaiming the Internet for Civil Society.* Tewkesbury: September.
Marczak, B. and Scott-Railton, J. 2016. Keep calm and (don't) enable macros: A new threat actor targets UAE dissidents. *Citizen Lab*, 29 May. Available at citizenlab.ca/2016/05/stealth-falcon/#:~:text=Executive%20Summary,journalists%2C%20activists%2C%20and%20dissidents (accessed 25 September 2023).
Marczak, B., Scott-Railton, J., Senft, A., Deibert, R.J. and Razzak, B.A. 2018. The kingdom came to Canada: How Saudi-linked digital espionage reached Canadian soil. *Citizen Lab*, 1 October. Available at citizenlab.ca/2018/10/the-kingdom-came-to-canada-how-saudi-linked-digital-espionage-reached-canadian-soil/#:~:text=In%20this%20report%2C%20we%20describe,operator%20linked%20to%20Saudi%20Arabia (accessed 25 September 2023).

Millar, K.M., Shires, J. and Tropina, T. 2021. Gender approaches to cybersecurity: Design, defence and response. United Nations Institute for Disarmament Research (UNIDIR). Available at unidir.org/publication/gender-approaches-cybersecurity (accessed 25 September 2023).

Mumford, D. and Shires, J. (2023) Toward a Decolonial Cybersecurity: Interrogating the Racial-Epistemic Hierarchies That Constitute Cybersecurity Expertise, *Security Studies*, 32: 4–5, 622–652

Parveen, N. 2018. Matt Hedges: I feel no resentment to friend who reported me to UAE. *Guardian*, 29 December. Available at perma.cc/DH4D-KHTQ (accessed 25 September 2023).

Raicea, R. 2017. How Pretty Good Privacy Works, and how you can use it for secure communication. freeCodeCamp.org, 8 October. Available at perma.cc/J824-VEVV (accessed 25 September 2023).

Schneier, B. 2013. Attacking Tor: How the NSA targets users' online anonymity. *Guardian*, 4 October. Available at perma.cc/57RF-HYMW (accessed 25 September 2023).

Shires, J. 2018. Enacting expertise: Ritual and risk in cybersecurity. *Politics and Governance*, 6(2).

Shires, J. 2021. *The Politics of Cybersecurity in the Middle East*. London and Oxford: Hurst/Oxford University Press.

PART 2

DIVERSE IDENTITIES

4

GIVING, TAKING AND RECEIVING CARE: DIS_ABILITY AND FIELDWORK

Isabel Bredenbröker and Tajinder Kaur

Summary

Ableist conceptions are omnipresent and it is important to respond to them with care in field contexts and academia. This chapter delves into the political components of two researchers' narratives and fieldwork experiences and gives methodological advice for researchers with dis_ability and working on dis_ability. Emphasising societal and cultural factors that characterise dis_ability as opposed to medical or biological points, we discuss dis_ability as a category, the connections between dis_ability rights, academic and state structures, Global North–South divides and the use of language. Linking insights from literature, personal experience and the field, we propose responses to systemic discrimination.

Table of contents

Introduction 49
'Disability'? Categorisation, temporality and language 51

Doing fieldwork on disability in India 52
Doing fieldwork with multiple sclerosis 56
Conclusion 59
Recommendations 60
Further reading 61
References 61

Introduction

In this chapter, we suggest that thinking about dis_ability and ableism (see Box 4.1) is something that concerns every bodymind facing ethnographic field research. By this, we are not implying that everybody is dis_abled but suggesting that learning from dis_ability is something that every researcher in the field and academia benefits from. So even if you do not identify as a person living with a dis_ability or seek to do research with dis_abled interlocutors, we are convinced that our thoughts will be helpful for you – please read on! Also, once we let go of the negative idea of the 'disabled' as something one would not wish to represent, it becomes obvious that dis_ability and dis_abling structures are everywhere around us. They are part of our everyday lives.

This is a conversation about care and against ableist conceptions in fieldwork between a person from the Global South and a person from the Global North. To complicate matters, this is also a conversation between two people who were socialised and are socially perceived as female, one of whom identifies as non-binary and queer. It is also a conversation between a person working on disability and a person with a dis_ability due to chronic illness. Tajinder Kaur, an anthropologist from India, researches the lives of people with physical disabilities in Delhi, and Isabel Bredenbröker, an anthropologist from Germany, lives with multiple sclerosis and has done fieldwork in Germany, Ghana, Greece, Togo and South Africa. In this exchange, our respective backgrounds, experiences and perspectives – the intersectional traits that form part of who we are – help us to fill in the 'missing parts' when thinking about care and ability (or the supposed lack of it) in fieldwork. Here, intersectionality is not so much an analytical tool as it is part of the grain of our personal experiences, yielding a different perspective on dis_ability within the intersectional spectrum. German anti-ableist digital activist Mika Murstein remarks that ableism has many points of crossover with 'other forms of suppression, such as racism, (cis) sexism and classism which reinforce each other or rather join in an inseparable bond for multiple marginalised persons. The latter is what we call intersectionality'[1] (2022, p. 16). Coined by critical race theorist Kimberlé Crenshaw in the late 1980s, intersectionality has come to stand for an approach that considers various kinds of marginalising factors that define the position of a person in society and the empowering factors that they can rely on (Carbado et al., 2013). While the chapter cannot delve into all intersections of our personal and interlocutor's experiences, we want to stress that the conversation which you can follow here cuts across various intersectional categories. Mediated in writing and over distance, the constraints of digital space, language and difference of experience form part of this text. When thinking together despite these obstacles, intersectionality is also about simply making an exchange that includes intersecting points of difference and commonality possible in the first place.

Disability and ableism

BOX 4.1

By using the spelling dis_ability, we are following the queer-feminist disability discourse, represented among others by Mika Murstein (2022). Dis_ability highlights the fact that society is excluding dis_abled people from access on many levels, rather than it being a natural property of 'disabled' people that they cannot do those things. Ableism is a term that refers to this latter viewpoint and associated socially shared convictions. It defines an ideal of normality and projects this against its aberrations which are unwanted and need curing. Disability studies scholar and activist Fiona Kumari Campbell gives a neat definition of ableism:

> A network of beliefs, processes and practices that produces a particular kind of self and body (the corporeal standard) that is projected as the perfect, species-typical and therefore essential and fully human. Disability then is cast as a diminished state of being human.
> (Campbell, 2009, p. 5)

Based on our own experiences, we give methodological advice to other researchers doing ethnography on how to treat themselves and others in a non-ableist and empowering way. How do we overcome physical and mental challenges in the field and how can we become aware that the two are not separate? How do we treat those challenges in a caring way, meaning that we do not punish ourselves for not meeting expectations that are too harsh in that situation (whether these expectations are our own or others')? How do we develop a caring attitude towards the dis_abilities of interlocutors? And, finally, how can we flag and counteract viewpoints and structures (in academia, in conversation with colleagues or interlocutors) that apply ableist values? At the same time, fears around doing or saying wrong things about supposed 'Others' in fieldwork and with regards to one's own health and status are as much part and parcel of fieldwork per se as of interaction with non-ableist-conforming bodies and minds specifically. These experiences can become less daunting and, indeed, lead to more empowerment of oneself and interlocutors when considering the intersectional nature of disability. Making one's own perspective visible and giving interlocutors the space to speak in their own voice about issues that concern them are helpful tools towards giving, taking and receiving care in the field. Instead of reproducing an ableist kind of mindset when using anthropological methods, we are calling for different models of collaborative and supportive (auto)ethnographic research that leave ableist expectations behind.

'Disability'? Categorisation, temporality and language

We believe that the term disability, due to the ways in which it is quantified and qualified, should be regarded as a normative tool (see Box 4.2). In some circumstances, this category empowers those who are affected, while in others, it does not. Examining the various settings in which this term is used reveals the inner workings of power.

Disability as classificatory category

BOX 4.2

On a global scale, the World Health Organisation, established an International Classification for various types of 'disabilities' in 1980, distinguishing between impairments, disabilities and handicaps: 'any loss or aberration of psychological, physiological, or anatomical structure or function' is classified as impairment. A 'disability' is defined as any restriction or lack of ability (due to an impairment) to do an activity in the way or range regarded as 'normal' for a human being. A 'handicap' is a disadvantage for a certain individual that hinders or prevents them from fulfilling a 'typical' role. The above-mentioned terms are frequently used interchangeably. The 2006 United Nations Convention on the Rights of People with Disabilities recognises that disability is 'an evolving concept'.

In academic discourse, critical disability studies have emerged over the past 15 years and offer theoretical pathways towards understanding the categorisation of dis_abilities and their effects as socially produced. For an excellent overview, have a look at Melinda C. Hall's entry on 'Critical disability theory' in the *Stanford Encyclopedia of Philosophy* (Hall, 2019). By questioning the categories of ability and disability, critical disability studies have invited intersectional approaches from disciplines such as critical race studies, gender studies, feminist studies, queer studies and activist practice. When thinking about categorisations of abilities, 'disability' and dis_abilities in academic settings and in fieldwork-based research, the meanings of such categories concern us as researchers directly. If we have a dis_ability, be it visible or invisible, we may wonder how we can and want to make this known and talk about it to our interlocutors, supervisors and colleagues. Depending on your personality, you may wish to share less or more information relating to your dis_ability. There will be information that feels private, but your feelings towards sharing information about your dis_ability may change over time or depending on a specific situation. Yet, in order to have a chance of receiving support and not being met with ableist expectations, it might be necessary to communicate about a dis_ability. The tricky question is how, to whom and to what avail?

Depending on the country and academic structures that you work or study in, there may be different procedures, categorisations and support models in place, not all of which may be working in your favour. If these categories and structures affect your dis_abled interlocutors, you will want to gain an understanding of what they are and how they matter in their everyday lives as well as in interaction with you as a researcher. We will give you different examples of how we have dealt with the category of disability in its various connections to power, both at our places of work and study and in the field. We will speak about aspects that were challenging for us and responses that we have found to these challenges. Our discussion evolves around three areas: categorisation, temporality and language. Since we are two authors that represent countries from the Global South and the Global North, we would also like to point towards regional differences. In our fields and at our places of work or study, it is vital to be aware of implications that come with a state-recognised disability status. When doing fieldwork, working or studying in academic settings it is important to know of different systems of classification, support or exclusion and the implications that these have for dis_abled people. It is also important to be aware of inequalities between places and institutions on a global scale. Returning to our initial statement about taking an intersectional approach to dis_ability, we recommend openly communicating and considering one's own positionality with the 'ad_vantages' and 'dis_advantages' that it brings, in order to be able to explain to interlocutors or colleagues more transparently where one is speaking, thinking or writing from. This is not to compare factors that may be dis_abling and creating inequality, but to have better, more caring and more informed exchanges about these.

Doing fieldwork on disability in India

> Tajinder: I haven't had any interaction with disabled people, but I found them very *'special'*.
> Woman with physical disability: You found disabled people *'special'*?
> Tajinder: Yes, I really adore them.
> Woman with physical disability: We don't like the term 'special'. We don't need anyone's sympathy. We are also a part of this society. We don't need any *special* kind of treatment.

During fieldwork for ethnographic research on the lived experiences of women with physical disabilities in Delhi, India, this was my first interaction with an interlocutor. I never had, either practically or conceptually, worked with anyone with disabilities before. My lifelong curiosity about things that don't adhere to normative standards influenced my choice of research topic. But, during the course of research, my understanding of what qualifies as a 'disabled' individual was questioned, and the conversation above made my ableist perspective evident to me as an unconscious bias that I had picked up from growing up in an ableist society. During my fieldwork, I noticed that non-disabled individuals called people with disabilities 'patients', associating their wheelchairs with hospitals and a disempowering way of being cared for. "This section uses 'disabled' and 'disability' to refer to interlocutors' self-introductions and institutional categories.". When I asked one of the informants, 'There are so many terms associated with you, but which term would you prefer?', they responded: 'We have no problem with the term itself, but please don't judge our skills or abilities based on these terminologies.' Looking back, I'm still embarrassed about the fact that, at the start of the fieldwork, I made huge mistakes and had a perspective that I now view differently. It has worried me that this might have a long-term impact on my interactions with other disabled people. Initially, I was anxious to reveal my frame of perception, which was informed by an ableist perspective, which I was hoping to change through my research. I was very aware of the risk of reproducing a pattern in which disabled people are exotified through a non-disabled gaze or even a 'non-disabled stare' (Garland-Thomson, 2009). Notwithstanding historical advances and disabled people's movements, individuals with disabilities continue to feel marginalised in various ways. To define disability from an institutional or non-disabled point of view, therefore, still holds genuine power over disabled people and handles them as disciplined subjects. As I began the research, I knew that I did not want to fall into this trap and misrepresent my interlocutors.

This was a process that I aspired to throughout the research as I started out as a person who did not count as, or consider themselves, disabled. My ethnographic work focused on the perspectives of women with physical disabilities and their lived experiences with their caregivers. While accompanied by participant observation which also included carers, my main research tool was in-depth interviews with women with physical disabilities to amplify their narratives. Eventually, taking on this new perspective gave me an insight into the negotiation of delicate power relations that emerge during caregiving for physically impaired people by family members and the childlike dependency of adults with physical disabilities. In India, the physical and mental wellbeing of a person with a disability is dependent on the support provided by family members. I met different primary caregivers and women with physical disabilities who related to one another through care in the able-bodied environment of Delhi while also sharing kin-relations. I was particularly interested in the roles that the state and civil society play in this because there are no formally organised care systems in India, and people with disabilities, therefore, are mainly dependent on kinship ties to receive care. Auto-descriptive narratives of the women that I spoke to expressed feelings of guilt and shame in reaction to being called 'patient', based on the visibility of their disability and on their difficult interaction with the able-bodied environment. Helpfully, women with disabilities were more comfortable expressing their daily life experiences and vulnerabilities to me than men since I could understand their vulnerabilities as a woman, regardless of my role as a researcher.

Persons with disabilities are sometimes presented as 'Other', somehow distinct from those who are not regarded as having disabilities (Ablon, 1995). What shocked me initially was that there continue to be many aspects of the topic of disabilities that I was unaware of. Encounters in the field assisted me in reflecting on acquired assumptions shaped by an ableist society. With a caring approach, I could analyse and change my word choices during fieldwork to communicate without bias. I had what is undoubtedly a widely shared experience among ethnographers: I realised my frames of reference and their relativity, which changed how I interacted with my interlocutors. I became more aware of giving them space for their narratives and self-identification instead of classifying their disability. I became increasingly committed to engaged anthropology, becoming complicit with my interlocutors and considering methods to ameliorate their status.

In the Indian context, disability has different definitions and terminologies. The 2011 population census lists properties as 'markers' of disability:

Paralytic persons; those who crawl; those who can walk with aid; those who have acute and permanent problems of joints and muscles; those who have stiffness or tightness in movement or loose, involuntary movements or tremors of the body or fragile bones; those who have difficulty balancing and coordinating body movement; those who have lost body sensation due to paralysis, leprosy, or other physical health issues; and finally those who have a deformity of the body like hunchback or are dwarf.

(ORGCC, 2011, p. 15)

Use of the term '*divyang*' is poorly received by people with disabilities. During my fieldwork, they showed considerable scepticism about the meaning of the term '*divya*' which means supernatural. According to one of the responders, 'they [the Indian government] believe that we are something extraordinary, that our disability is something magical'. Many people with disabilities feel that by identifying them as *divyang* they are being pushed to the margins of society. The 2016 Indian Rights of People with Disabilities Act defines a 'person with disability' as someone with a long-term physical, mental, intellectual, or sensory impairment that, when combined with barriers, prohibits them from fully participating in society. It also denotes a medically verified person as experiencing at least 40 per cent impairment. Contrastingly, the 2006 United Nations Convention on the Rights of Persons with Disabilities suggests a shift from the medical to the social concept of disability (see Box 4.3).

Medical and social model of disability

BOX 4.3

According to the medical model, disability is inherent in the individual and is associated with activity limitations. According to the social model coined by disabled scholar and activist Michael Oliver, disability is caused by interactions between individuals and society. Hence disability, is all the things that impose restrictions on disabled people, ranging from individual prejudice to institutional discrimination, from inaccessible public buildings to unusable transport systems, from segregated education to excluding work arrangements. It situates the definition of disability at the most fundamental level of activity or involvement in core domains, defined as the ability or inability to perform simple tasks such as walking, ascending stairs, lifting packages, seeing a friend across the room and so on.

In Indian institutions, persons with disabilities are still characterised using the medical model rather than the social model of disability. The application of the medical model is exclusively concerned with institutionalising the individual, with little regard for the perspectives of people with disabilities or their family members (see Box 4.4). Based on this, disabled people in India frequently experience challenges obtaining a disability certificate because there are no suitable evaluation tools or training for identifying an individual's specific disability. Therefore, norms and behaviours associated with dis_abled bodies further reinforce the medical model of disability that already prevails.

As I stated earlier, a researcher's social milieu may influence or reinforce their unconscious ableist bias. Herbert Blumer, an American sociologist, talks about the sense of group position (1958). He describes this as a normative function inherent to groups, where members absorb prevalent points of view. In the case of an ableist perspective on dis_ability, a sense of group position influences interactions between non-disabled and disabled persons, even if personal views differ significantly from the dominant group position. In Indian culture, people use slang terms such as *'apahij'* ('handicap'), *'kubda'* ('hunchback'), *'langda'* ('cripple'), *'aandha'* ('blind') and *'kaana'* ('wall-eyed') to make fun of others by associating them with a disabled person, revealing a complex and troubled relationship between non-disabled and disabled people. However, when speaking to a disabled individual directly, non-disabled people are also wary of possibly offending them. Therefore, it is imperative that we are cognisant of discriminatory experiences for dis_abled people and take care to avoid them in our fieldwork.

Experiencing classification: An amplification of interlocutor's voices

EXAMPLE 4.1

An interlocutor of mine experienced the absurdity of classifying a disabled body. The 44-year-old woman with a physical disability caused by polio lived in Delhi with her parents. When applying for a disability certificate, she had to undergo tests in the hospital. In conversation with me, she talked about the disagreement between her and the doctors about the functionality level of her body.

> When I visited AIIMS hospital for my disability certificate, doctors asked me to lay down on a hospital bed; when I lay down, I am almost like a 'dead body'. There is no movement in my hands; legs are always like this, whether I sit or lie on the bed or change sides by taking support from anyone that I cannot take by myself, the lower portion of my body is dead. After sitting, I can move my hands properly. Actually, above my neck area, it is OK, but below, it is dead. So, according to them, 10 per cent remaining is functional. According to doctors, I cannot bathe, cannot eat. Senior doctors said this to me. There were three doctors, and all of them were saying you are lying when you say that you can do all these things. You cannot do anything at all. By chance, my brother was with me in the hospital. He convinced them that his sister is not lying; she does all her work alone; bathing and wearing clothes. They think that I am doing it on purpose.

Cultural anthropology has focused on the perspective of the outsider with respect to how different cultures perceive 'otherness' and contributed to the discipline of disability studies by using ethnographic, phenomenological and cross-cultural methods which, according to

Reid-Cunningham, still have potential for expansion (2009). As a partial outsider in my field, interactions between dis_abled and non-dis_abled people revealed their difficult and complex relationships as well as a sense of vulnerability that both share. There is another interaction that I would like to highlight here. A sensitive situation arose during my engagement with a disabled person at an event sponsored by an organisation for which I volunteered. I had established some rapport with my informants by that point. One of the dis_abled women enquired about my disability: 'What type of disability do you have?' I was unprepared to respond to this query. She believed that I had some invisible disability. I responded, 'I do not have any disability. I am just here for volunteer work.' She nodded and left. When I tried to understand what had happened in this interaction, I found the work of American sociologist Erving Goffman helpful. He terms 'persons who are normal but whose special situation has made them intimately privy to the secret life of the stigmatized individual and sympathetic with it, and who find themselves accorded a measure of acceptance' as 'wise' (1963, p. 40). Becoming such a 'wise' person, I became intimately related to my primary informants through my research. However, my close proximity led some disabled people to believe that I was one of them or had some invisible disability.

My ethnographic research and my awareness of the subject of dis_ability from the standpoint of disabled people living among non-disabled people has been dramatically expanded due to research encounters. Throughout the course of my fieldwork, I was given the opportunity to reflect on ways in which I could enhance not only my capacity to communicate with dis_abled people but also the language that I use. Because of this shift in perspective, I was forced to re-evaluate and reject previously acquired norms, attitudes and assumptions that were founded on an ableist perspective. Isabel, however, has the experience of doing fieldwork with a dis_ability, while sharing many of the same insights that I have had by working in fields that require ethnographic sensibility and adaption to new contexts. Thus, while our perspectives may be different, they are not mutually exclusive.

Doing fieldwork with multiple sclerosis

Something that is always with me, Isabel – in the field or inside my university office – is multiple sclerosis (MS), a (so far 'incurable') chronic neurological illness. Here I reflect on preparing for and doing fieldwork with this condition, as well as on the systemic challenges and support (or lack thereof) when working with this (often invisible) dis_ability in German academia and at different fieldsites. Based on my experiences, I will give some suggestions on how a caring attitude towards yourself and your own needs may help you to be well, both in the field and at your place of work or study. I will address temporal aspects of planning, doing and processing fieldwork, the access to help if needed and ways in which communicating about one's own disability may be done to one's own advantage.

When planning my fieldwork, I have to consider my MS and will include emergency eventualities and institutional support. Often, though, planning for such emergencies has turned out to be unrealistic when plans needed to be implemented and there was little to no institutional support or a lack of flexible financial means. These are issues that result from the unpredictable nature of my condition and the classificatory structures around disability that are in place in Germany on a national and academic level – also connected to funding and employment. Our bodies and their dis_abilities should not be considered our 'private' concerns when it comes to working and studying. Yet, we all have our personal ways of relating to physical and mental challenges. I have had to develop a personal relationship to living with this kind of insecurity which has resulted in a more forgiving and gentle way of treating myself as a person who has work goals and ventures out into fieldsites with unknown challenges. This caring attitude needs to be paired with an unapologetic attitude towards personal needs and, if needed, a vocal way of making those known. A forgiving and careful way of treating oneself in the field and at university is a skillset that you can develop and personalise, leading to an empowered way of working and thinking.

At the beginning of 2023, I went to South Africa for six weeks of fieldwork. Since before my departure, and worsening after, I had been experiencing muscle spasms all over my body, numb hands and legs, a sensation of vibrating in my entire body, a stiff neck, tiredness, worse eyesight than usual and more. This turned out to be an MS 'attack' during fieldwork. Labelled 'the illness with a thousand faces', MS can have many effects. As of now, it remains unclear what causes MS and how it operates in the body. It is known that it involves an auto-immune attack on our nerves. This leads to inflammation and scarification, causing nerves to dysfunction. Effects can be impaired vision up to blindness, numbness, tingling, immobility or weakness of limbs, pains and aches, muscle spasms, bladder dysfunction, balance problems, cognitive issues, fatigue and depression. While active inflammations in nerves are considered 'attacks', the damage that has been done to the nerve means that symptoms can also reoccur. Causes can be psychological stress, temperature changes, illnesses and infections or even periods. Everyone with a dis_ability has a personal way of living with it, constantly working to be comfortable with discomfort. These ways differ and there is no right or wrong way of doing dis_ability. Yet, when it comes to responses from the outside world, as statements from Tajinder's interlocutors show, we are treated differently, for better or worse, depending on whether dis_abilities appear as visible.

Everyone with a dis_ability deserves to be given the support they need when working, studying and researching, which is why we need to be able to openly communicate our needs without compromising our interests. Hence, the legal status of having an acknowledged disability becomes important, something which is difficult to 'earn' when not permanently and visibly 'disabled' in a way that fits the medical model. Writer and poet Meghan O'Rourke gives personal insights into the world of invisible dis_ability and chronic illness (2022). In my case, chronic illness means that I can usually move around without assistance and look able-bodied. Reality is more complicated and I need 'evidence' in the form of a recognised disability status to claim support, such as postponing fieldwork in case of poor health, having more flexible work conditions on days when I am not well and giving my colleagues evidence that working differently is not being lazy. The expert knowledge and emotional resilience needed to endure the ensuing bureaucratic processes is often beyond what one may be capable of. My legal disability status is currently below the degree that is acknowledged as 'severely disabled' and the paper war of asking to be made equal in a work context has yielded perplexing conversations:

Legal aide at the German Employment Office: 'You may only receive equal status when you can prove that you have previously been treated unequally in a job interview.'
Isabel: 'How could I have revealed previously that I had a chronic condition in a job interview without the legal status? Do you expect me to self-sabotage?'

This shows how frustrating dealings with systems that have power over us can be. While my faceless pen pal here is a representative of the state, universities are also connected to this field of power. Fieldwork and the institutions that we hail from are not separate. Universities have a say in how we plan research, often by granting funding or withholding it, paying our salaries and deciding under what circumstances fieldwork may happen. This ties in with the circumstantial conditions that determine how the needs and requirements of dis_abled researchers are being met. Due to universities being underfunded and understaffed on all levels, there is often no way of being flexible. My trip to Cape Town, which I would have preferred to abort due to poor health, was funded by an internal body at a university. The money was granted under tight conditions and there were no means for an emergency return. Since I had paid for the journey upfront and was waiting to be reimbursed while on a precarious 50 per cent salary, I could not fund it either. These issues are systemic. What I can recommend for individual researchers is to be vocal about your needs, to always have an exit strategy and to make sure you do not give up getting the legal status you need in order to get access to proper support. Looking at insurance that may cover emergency events and finding out what universities offer in those instances is something that you need to think about. This kind of information, in maze-like institutions like universities, is often not readily available; you will have to search for it. Try to get support with this from someone who is in charge of access and dis_ability issues at your institution or ask a person you trust.

When I prepared for my PhD fieldwork in Ghana, I was taking a medication for my MS which repressed the functioning of my immune system. When planning the trip, I learned that I was not able to take a yellow fever vaccine, a live vaccine unfit for people with immune deficiencies. Yet, a vaccine certificate must be presented at the border, with the risk of being turned away otherwise. I was unsure what would await me in Ghana, as I had not been there before. I could not prepare sufficiently for such challenges because I was accepted for my PhD position at very short notice. German universities do not have a formal process of risk assessment before fieldwork; all I had was a conversation of disclosure with a supervisor. I was offered research in an archive in Germany, which would have seemed like defeat. I had conversations with medical professionals. From a medical perspective, it was difficult to get an informed opinion on the risk of taking the vaccine versus the risk of contracting yellow fever. In the end, it was only with great effort and creative measures that I was able to get an opinion that I could trust and acquire a document that let me pass the border.

When I was trying to figure this out, a concerned family member urged me to quit my funded PhD position because I was 'not able' to conduct this research. As I am writing this, I am aware that I have the privilege of access to medical care in Germany. In other countries (of the Global North and South), not only would I not have access to diagnostic measures or the medication I was on, I would also not be able to afford either, whereas in Germany my health insurance paid.

I also have the privilege of a German passport which allows me to travel. And, finally, I had funding and a salary to cover my trip. The struggles I had undergone and awareness of my privileges convinced me that it was important to reach my field in order to make the best possible use of all of this. I spent a total of eight months over three visits in Ghana, without reassurance that I would be safe in relation to my MS. I was careful to avoid possible contact with flies or mosquitoes and a heightened anxious awareness accompanied me. This has given me a specific experience of being in the field and also of relating to the environment I was moving in. My medication did not require special cooling facilities, as other medication that I had taken previously would have. But when thinking about additional support one may need, be it a person assisting or enough medication and stable temperatures for it, the impediments that one may be facing can look daunting. But they do not have to be and it is worth fighting for making the fieldwork you want to do possible.

Thinking about one's own abilities, dis_abilities, privileges and intersectional traits fits well with autoethnography. One's social yet individualised traits as a researcher form a key part of one's perspective when interpreting the findings of one's ethnographic work. When researching in Ghana, I was aware of the lurking dangers of 'Othering' and being 'Othered' by my interlocutors. This fear is justified and correlates to Tajinder's fear of misrepresenting her dis_abled interlocutors. With every new personal interaction, perspectives need to be recalibrated between those who are meeting. Taking a non-ableist perspective towards myself, also regarding the ways in which I make sense of my position in the field, has helped me to trust in the encounter that fieldwork is and in the multitude of different perspectives. As much as I was possibly referring to pre-fabricated and socially shaped ideas of my interlocutors, by simply not 'knowing' my field well in the beginning, my interlocutors were also projecting all kinds of ideas and assumptions onto me. This yields an interesting exchange. Being non-ableist here means that I trust and invest in the process of learning which is fieldwork, while I remain conscious of my perspective and the factors that I cannot change, meaning that I will not be able to represent every perspective at once and equally well. But, at least, I can clearly indicate where I am coming from to continue that conversation beyond the field and beyond the page.

Conclusion

By bringing together two different perspectives on dis_ability and fieldwork across intersectional lines, our chapter has looked at the inside and outside of dis_ability. As field researchers, we always contain both perspectives. Questions of positionality, belonging and projection, of reflecting on those insides and outsides, are part of what makes for good anthropological thought. Dis_ability is no different and also has its insides and outsides, just as much as it is always entangled with other factors of background and perspective, such as gender, status, class, racialisation, nationality and many more. By talking about some of our own experiences in the field while researching on and with dis_ability, we hope to have been able to shine a light on how dis_ability and fieldwork can go together and what experiences they may entail. When working in the field with a dis_ability, be prepared to think creatively, asking for all the support that you can get. Decide what your personal level of comfort in the face of risks is. Researchers working with interlocutors with dis_abilities will need to be aware that they, as in many other field settings, may feel different, out of place and insecure about how to behave sensibly, or they may find that interlocutors' ideas about them are incongruent with their own. By sharing the perspectives of people with dis_abilities through fieldwork, Tajinder gets a window into this experience which is also shared by Isabel as an anthropologist working with dis_ability in the field. From this exchange, we take a fundamental sense of being obliged to take care, both of ourselves and of others. Researchers going into the field may face what they experience as limitations or fear due to a multitude of factors. Informed by our individual experiences, we strongly believe that these must be taken seriously, addressed and supported in an academic and larger social context, be it through the university's counselling, supervision or state bodies and support structures. This goes beyond dis_ability.

Recommendations

1. **Insist on getting the factual information you need to make informed decisions and assess risks.** Think about what your personal position towards the situation is and do not rely on what other people think of as right or appropriate in relation to your dis_ability.
2. **Dealing with power and context at the university or in fieldwork.** Be aware of your own comfort level and needs when addressing your own dis_ability. Try to challenge your ingrained ableist perspective and reassess your field-specific interlocutory expectations.
3. **Dealing with categorisation.** Engage with critical discourse in the field of disability studies as an empowering tool and frame of reference. Listen to accounts of dis_abled people or those who work on dis_ability. Be familiar with the legal and medical implications of having a 'recognised disability status'. As a dis_abled researcher, insist on getting the formal categorisation that you need and inform yourself about what these categories do for you.
4. **Interaction with interlocutors and use of language.** Non-dis_abled researchers must learn how different classificatory models affect their interlocutors' daily lives before they can effectively speak about dis_ability and provide interlocutors with the opportunity to speak in their own voice. As a dis_abled person, think about whether you want to address needs that arise in relation to your dis_ability.
5. **Mental and physical wellbeing.** Reassure yourself that you have a right to being supported. Make sure you know what medical support you can receive in the field and have insurance that covers emergencies. Ensure that you develop a compassionate approach towards the obstacles and impairments of interlocutors and know how to detect ableist attitudes and structures.

Note

1 Translation from German original by Isabel Bredenbröker.

Further reading

Clare, E. 2017. *Brilliant Imperfection: Grappling with Cure*. Durham, NC, and London: Duke University Press.
Writing from a queer intersectional perspective, writer and activist-scholar Eli Clare uses personal recollections and critical discussion of theory to question the notion of cure as something that defines returning to a state of normality.

Hedva, J. 2020. Sick woman theory. *Mask Magazine*. https://topicalcream.org/features/sick-woman-theory/
Artist Johanna Hedva addresses dis_ability in her visual as well as written work. The essay 'Sick woman theory' is a feminist intersectional reflection on the artist's position as a person with a chronic condition that renders them dis_abled.

Lewnham, N. and LeBrecht, J. 2020. *Crip Camp: A Disability Revolution*. Netflix.
The award-winning documentary by Nicole Newnham and James LeBrecht tells the story of a summer camp for disabled teenagers in the US that became a driving force in the disability rights movement in the 1970s. Using contemporary and historic footage, it portrays dis_abled people as social, sexual, political and mobile beings.

Frank, G. 1986. *Venus on Wheels: Two Decades of Dialogue on Disability, Biography, and Being Female in America*. Berkeley, CA: University of California Press.
Diane DeVries, a woman with a physical disability, and Gelya Frank have divergent opinions on the subject of disability. This book is helpful for students and scholars who want to understand the political nature of personal narrative and how it can affect societal and cultural change.

Ghai, A. 2018. *Disability in South Asia: Knowledge and Experience*. London: Sage.
This book is an excellent resource for scholars as well as students interested in learning more about disability studies in South Asia. It also emphasises first-hand experiences of people with disabilities.

References

Ablon, J. 1995. 'The Elephant Man' as 'self' and 'other': the psycho-social costs of a misdiagnosis. *Social Science and Medicine* (1982), 40(11), 1481–9.
Blumer, H. 1958. Race prejudice as a sense of group position. *Pacific Sociological Review*, 1(1), 3–7.
Campbell, F.K. 2009. *Contours of Ableism: The Production of Disability and Ableness*. New York: Palgrave Macmillan.

Carbado, D.W., Crenshaw, K.W., Mays, V.M. and Tomlinson, B. 2013. Intersectionality: Mapping the movements of a theory. *Du Bois Review Social Science Research on Race*, 10(2), 303–12.

Garland-Thomson, R. 2009. *Staring: How We Look*. New York: Oxford University Press.

Goffman, E. 1963. *Stigma: Notes on the Management of Spoiled Identity*. New York: Touchstone.

Hall, M.C. 2019. Critical disability theory. In Zalta, E.N. (Ed.), *The Stanford Encyclopedia of Philosophy*. Available at https://plato.stanford.edu/archives/win2019/entries/disability-critical/ (accessed 25 September 2023).

Murstein, M. 2022. *I'm a Queer Feminist Cyborg, That's Okay: Gedankensammlung zu Anti/Ableismus*. Münster: edition assemblage.

Office of the Registrar General and Census Commissioner (ORGCC) 2011. *Census of India 2011: National Population Register and Socio-economic and Caste Census*. New Delhi: Ministry of Home Affairs. Available at https://censusindia.gov.in/nada/index.php/catalog/42619 (accessed 26 September 2023).

O'Rourke, M. 2022. *The Invisible Kingdom: Reimagining Chronic Illness*. New York: Riverhead.

Reid-Cunningham, A.R. 2009. Anthropological theories of disability. *Journal of Human Behavior in the Social Environment*, 19(1), 99–111.

World Health Organisation (1980) *International Classification of Impairments, Disabilities, and Handicaps*. Geneva: World Health Organisation. Available at https://unstats.un.org/unsd/disability/pdfs/ac.81-b4.pdf

5

REFLEXIVE ETHNOGRAPHY IN INTIMATE SPACES: MOTHERHOOD AND CARE WORK IN AND OUTSIDE THE FIELD

Elsemieke van Osch and Sharon Louise Smith

Summary

This chapter reflects on the personal, intellectual and emotional challenges of balancing ethnographic fieldwork with care responsibilities. Drawing on Smith's research with parents of disabled children and Van Osch's research with families going through asylum procedures, we explore our positionalities as mothers/carers and unpack the strategies and tools we employed as engaged ethnographers. We argue that the web of dependent relations and caretaking practices that form our daily lives profoundly shaped our enquiries and that the frictions and synergies in the field must be understood as enriching analytical tools that employ generative ways of approaching knowledge production.

Table of contents

Introduction 64
Care work and research: A feminist approach 66
Opportunities within research arising through an orientation of care and relationality 67
Entanglements and embodiments in/outside the field 70
Messy trajectories and institutional challenges 72
Conclusion 74
Recommendations 75
Further reading 76
References 76

Introduction

During fieldwork, we are expected to immerse ourselves in the complex webs of social relationships that our participants are part of and acknowledge that we are people who are emotionally, intellectually and physically embedded in the social fabric that makes up our participants' everyday lives. Additionally, during fieldwork we are not putting our private lives on hold. The spatial and temporal lines between ethnographic encounters in the field and our private relationships may become blurred, especially when doing 'fieldwork at home' – fieldwork in proximity to the webs of social relationships that make up our daily lives – or, when bringing family members along into the field. This is especially demanding when the emotional labour required for fieldwork and for intimate others coincide – for example, when caring for dependent children, disabled family members or other relatives.

In this chapter we reflect on the personal, intellectual and emotional challenges and opportunities we experienced when balancing ethnographic fieldwork with care responsibilities at home as mothers. Drawing on Smith's research with parents of disabled children who are navigating the education system, while being the primary carer for her disabled teenage daughter, and Van Osch's research with families that apply for asylum during pregnancy and while looking after young children, we unpack some strategies and tools we employed to reconcile our multiple roles and responsibilities as mothers and as engaged ethnographers. Attending to our experiences as mothers profoundly shaped our engagement with fieldwork, the knowledge/s we were able to co-create and how we subsequently approached data interpretation and analysis. We do not shy away from the emotions and care emerging within 'the field'; rather, we pay attention to the relationships that are forged when we, as mothers, spent time in the field developing meaningful connections with interlocutors (building on Palmer et al., 2022).

Drawing upon the idea of an 'ethics of care', feminist scholars (Noddings, 1986) have drawn attention to the ways humans are always in a mesh of social relationships with others, including in caring relations that are often wrongly perceived as confined to the private sphere. Scientific research is still imagined to be performed by a fully independent, autonomous and rational researcher. This idea of the detached objective researcher has been challenged by feminist philosophers and feminist anthropologists among others, who instead consider the ways periods of (full or partial) dependency (and, thus, the need for care) are fundamental to the human condition, and how we, as human beings, always stand in relationships of (inter)dependence (Kittay, 2020). Engaging with these critiques, we demonstrate the entanglements and continuation of our caring relations, from our homes, into our ethnographic practices and vice versa.

From our position as mothers of dependent children, we engage with these feminist critiques and call for a reflexivity into our social positions – in terms of gender, race, class or age, as well as family relations and care responsibilities – suggesting this has the potential to profoundly transform our idea of what fieldwork is. Looking back at our own 'messy trajectory' in the field as well as in our personal lives, we acknowledge that our own social realities might also be full of change, unexpected happenings and key moments that influence our engagement in the field and our subsequent theorising. We therefore strive to carve out a space for reflexivity that goes *beyond* the field and invite further discussion about how our changing social realities and caring responsibilities affect relationships we forge during fieldwork, while avoiding making our research 'about us'.

We draw on experiences of doing ethnographic fieldwork for our doctoral research. Smith's research involved relationships with mothers of disabled children who are navigating the UK education system. It is primarily mothers who take on this intensive advocacy role for their children. Her enquiry was designed as an ongoing conversation over an academic year, including several face-to-face meetings in mothers' homes or in their local communities, Zoom/telephone calls and email correspondence. Each mother was invited to start the 'conversation' by bringing an item they wanted to use as a prompt to start a discussion about their child's inclusion. Research as conversation enabled Smith to be an active participant, bringing her experiences as a fellow mother of a disabled daughter into the research encounter. This approach to research was also shaped by Smith's own experiences of being a research participant, having spent time reflecting on how it felt to be a participant in a range of studies since her daughter was born; Smith sought to introduce a more 'care-full' approach (Rogers, 2015; Barnacle, 2018).

Van Osch's research is a longitudinal, follow-along ethnography of families' trajectories through the asylum procedure in Belgium. As a young mother with care responsibilities in a bicultural family, experiencing pregnancy during fieldwork, her engagements with participating mothers provided access to unique knowledge/s. She started her fieldwork in a large-scale reception centre in a rural area in Flanders, Belgium, after which she was able to follow families into their new homes after they left the reception centre. In many encounters over the course of two years, she co-created knowledge/s through a diverse range of interactions that arose spontaneously out of mutual interests with participants: dialogical conversations, home visits, cooking and eating, assisting with paperwork and sociolinguistic brokering in a variety of settings related to the migration regime. A considerable number of her interactions were multilingual, including a large portion in Arabic, a secondary language to her that is also spoken in her home.

The first section of this chapter describes feminist scholarships on "ethics of care". The second section discusses the dialogical approaches in the field that arose as we enacted care in the field and at home. The third section explores how taking 'the personal' into 'the field' provided us with unexpected learning opportunities. Finally, the fourth section discusses the challenges of combining care work with expectations in academia. As we go on to elaborate, we use the term 'motherhood' to reflect on the particularities of our experiences *as mothers*, as well as those of our (predominantly) female interlocutors. We draw attention to the embodied dimensions of motherhood (i.e., pregnancy, intimate, embodied nature of care work) and to our gendered positions in broader societal structures, as well as in our respective fieldsites. We seek to use the term 'motherhood' in an open-ended, inclusive manner, acknowledging that these experiences resonate with those of all who identify as parents. Moreover, we include references to care *beyond* parenthood, to describe the specifics of these other forms of care – with potentially intensive or unexpected periods of caring for intimate others – for example, when caring for disabled family members, other relatives like elderly parents, or pets. We hope that ethnographers engaged in different forms of care and in any stage of their research may find inspiration and recognise themselves in the conversations and approaches that follow.

BOX 5.1

Mothering is a labour-intensive relationship that requires turning one's time and attention to keeping the child's body alive, safe, fed, bathed and emotionally well. This deep responsibility for liveliness of the child body is a relation of time, as it requires the mother to devote a great deal of time to the labour of parenting. The life of a scholar requires that one devotes time and attention towards teaching, research and writing, and orient towards the objects of these pursuits. 'For the mother-scholar time and attention become distributive, as the objects and actions of motherhood and scholarship are rarely aligned' (Childers, 2015, p. 121).

Care work and research: A feminist approach

Throughout our research we employ feminist scholarship on relational ethics or an ethics of care. We understand fieldwork to be formed through our relations to one another, arising out of a 'web of connections' (Noddings, 1986, pp. xiii–xiv) within encounters that are characterised by direct attention and response. With this idea in mind, we found that this required us to listen closely to the changing needs and preferences of our participants, adjust the forms of our engagement accordingly and respond positively to requests when possible. There was no 'care recipe' to follow. Rather, it became necessary to have a 'genuine openness' and 'attuned responsiveness' to research participants, to ascertain what an appropriate response might be (Noddings, 1986, in Barnacle, 2018, p. 82). This was not something that we had anticipated in advance of being in the field, as it was not discussed within our research training as new doctoral researchers. Instead, the training we received appeared to suggest a clear linear trajectory and that we could neatly plan out our research and monitor progress against our plan during our supervisory meetings. While this might work in some situations, the research we both undertook could not be approached in this manner.

As mothers and carers doing ethnography, we sometimes found ourselves Janus-like: providing care in two opposite directions, both at home and in the field. By incorporating our caring responsibilities at home into our research practice, we did not necessarily remove the tensions, but opened space for new opportunities and possibilities. We needed therefore to find our own strategies for navigating the entanglements between our home life and the lives of those who were taking part in our research.

Opportunities within research arising through an orientation of care and relationality

Sharing struggles of motherhood and care responsibilities

Elsemieke van Osch

I started my fieldwork in a large-scale reception centre hosting around 450 people in a rural area in Flanders, Belgium. From the beginning, I was aware of the particularities of my position in the field: a young mother with an Arab partner who also experienced the darkest side of the asylum procedure over little more than a decade ago. After engaging with families at the reception centre, relationships naturally expanded beyond this locality. I was, for example, asked to accompany mothers on visits to the hospital or to the municipality to renew residency documents, and was invited over to the new 'homes' that families moved into after leaving the centre. We would chat about the struggles and joys of mothering, pregnancy and care work that made up an important part of our daily realities that are otherwise very much characterised by power imbalances. I remember calling participants to cancel meetings because my children were sick, and vice versa. Although frustrated because I was 'missing out in the field', these happenings eventually proved to be useful when shared with participants: I showed them my vulnerabilities and expressed my appreciation for our relationship by speaking up and sharing. Moreover, families could relate to my experiences or were curious to know 'how these things work in Belgium'. They would offer me a word of comfort and blessing, sometimes provide me with advice. When it was the other way around, some mothers would request help getting a doctor's appointment (which often came with complex administrative procedures when families did not have legal residency) or seek my help for translation. The vignette below describes a scene in which I accompanied Imaan, a Palestinian mother, on a visit to the hospital.

EXAMPLE 5.1

'Do you have ANY official document of the child with his name and date of birth?' asks the lady behind the reception. I translate this question to Imaan, the Palestinian mother that I am accompanying to the hospital. Her two-month-old baby has a fever and she is worried. Since they only recently moved out of the reception centre, she is not yet familiar with seeking medical care. Imaan's situation is complicated by the difficulties she has in expressing herself in another than Arabic language and because the family is still awaiting a decision in their asylum procedure, so accessing medical care involves a complex administrative procedure with which not all caregivers are familiar.

Imaan pulls a few folded pieces of paper from her handbag and searches for the right one. She hands me a copy of the birth certificate of her son. The woman behind the counter nods and types in the computer. She says: 'You don't have insurance, so you have to pay a deposit of 150€.' I explain that the migration authorities are responsible for the payment. Meanwhile, Imaan takes the baby out of the stroller, comforting him in her arms. She looks puzzled at me, makes hand gestures as to ask me what is wrong. I keep discussing with the receptionist, she confuses me as a social worker working for the migration authorities and suggests that I sign a document, but I explain I am just an acquaintance of the mother, helping her with her administration. She then takes the phone and calls a colleague, after which she turns to me and confirms that we can take a seat in the waiting room and that the doctor will issue a 'certificate of urgency', as is done for persons without legal residency.

When we are sitting in the waiting room, the baby starts crying and Imaan takes him out of the stroller to feed him discretely under her hijab. We spend our time talking, about how our children are doing in their new schools, about her life in the reception centre and about their stay in Greece, where her second son was born. She compares her experiences with medical care in these different settings and explains how she had to walk through the entire camp on Chios to get a doctor, and how she scared she was giving birth there.

As described in this vignette, the sharing of struggles and joys of mothering, pregnancy and care work provided me with methodological, epistemological and ethical opportunities in the field. Methodologically, it offered a welcomed conversation topic that related to other aspects of these mothers' lives, giving me access to all kinds of knowledge/s that would otherwise remain out of reach. Ethically, sharing struggles, worries and coping mechanisms surrounding motherhood in a context of uncertainty, vulnerability, often also poverty, created a therapeutic, friendly atmosphere and enabled us to engage in a more horizontal relationship. I consider having provided a safe space for mothers who expressed the need to tell me their stories – both in the context of my research and in a confidential space beyond – one of the most valuable ways in which I was able to be there and *care* for them. This consisted of simple, much-appreciated acts: asking how their day was going, having a tea together, cancelling other meetings when participants had received 'bad news'. I was the outsider that did not judge, a friend to which they could speak in their mother tongue. The mothers and fathers that did not speak a secondary language were especially pleased to have somebody to talk to. Being open about my private life, including my vulnerabilities as a new mother – as sometimes unfamiliar with my family-in-law's cultural expectations in ways very similar to their struggles in a new country – helped in creating this safe environment.

Epistemologically, while tracing the changing social realities of my participants over the course of a two-year ethnographic engagement, I came to acknowledge the changing (shared) social realities of my participants, but also of myself as a person – as a mother – over the course of fieldwork. As our social lives evolved over time, our children grew older and, with it, their needs and our worries changed. We shared some important family milestones, including school transitions, family members arriving to Belgium, the joys of obtaining papers and the birth of new members into our families.

Performing care in the research encounter

Sharon Smith

As a mother of a disabled child undertaking research with mothers of disabled children, I knew that impartiality, objectivity and separation would be both unthinkable and undesirable. I wanted to bring motherhood and my scholarship together, recognising that this would not always be easy, and that tensions would exist that I would need to navigate carefully.

After my daughter was born with Down syndrome in 2005, I spent many years volunteering and working to support other families, including co-founding a Down syndrome support group, chairing a local parent carer forum and delivering training and workshops. When I started my doctoral research, I was already fully embroiled in the world of special educational needs and disability (SEND) and I hoped that my experiences and knowledge of the SEND system would be helpful. It did mean, however, that at times it became difficult to know where the doctoral research started or finished, as my multiple roles and experiences could not be neatly separated out.

Before the conversations started with parents who had kindly agreed to take part in the research, I arranged to have an initial telephone call to introduce myself, discuss my research interests and to agree how we might engage together. Instead of the traditional consent form, I developed a 'shared agreement' document setting out my commitment to the parents alongside their consent to participate. Once they signed and returned this form, I co-signed and returned it to signify how this was a partnership rather than a relationship where I, as researcher, would be extracting and using their stories as data to analyse. This helped set the tone for the research relationship ahead. I was also able to use the entanglement of motherhood and scholarship to provide additional support and care for the parents engaged in the research. I shared with them a personalised document with national and local support organisations listed if they needed additional support. For one parent, my husband and I prepared a list of questions we wished we had asked when visiting schools, following a request for support for visiting potential secondary schools. For another, I used my personal knowledge of the SEND system to make introductions to support organisations and to draft templated letters.

I knew that life as a parent of a disabled child could throw unexpected curveballs and it was important that the mothers' lives took priority over their engagement in the research. Shortly before each research meeting or call, I would check that the time and day was still OK, allowing them the opportunity to postpone without feeling that they might be letting me down. Sometimes meetings were rearranged due to family illness, or because a mother wanted to go on a school trip with her son, and sometimes because I needed to move the time and date of the meeting because of issues arising in *my* personal life – for instance, needing to prepare for my daughter's education tribunal hearing. We had a shared understanding that our home lives must come first.

The mothers valued being able to speak to someone who they felt understood what they were going through, describing the conversations we had as therapeutic and helpful: as one parent described 'to actually be able to sit and talk to you and to have, you know, having a few hours of your time and you know how it works. And you know, you can empathise and you understand; it's been really useful for me.' Similar to what Van Osch describes above, the 'safe spaces' that were born out of an orientation to care in the field not only implied an ethical stance, but also added richness to my engagements with these mothers.

***

Our positionality as mothers that shared, or had an affinity with, some characteristics of our participants provided us with a unique opportunity to engage dialogical, conversational approaches in the field. This enabled us to develop meaningful relationships and address problematic power relations during fieldwork. Motherhood *can* be a valuable, intersubjective experience for fieldwork that enriches our positionalities, the building of rapport and the process of knowledge production.

Entanglements and embodiment in/outside the field

Personal experiences of motherhood and power imbalances in fieldwork

Elsemieke van Osch

Being pregnant during my fieldwork meant that I could relate somewhat to what it must have been like for some mothers to live an entire pregnancy, including postpartum period, in a large-scale reception centre with limited privacy and sanitary facilities, noise and smells that become unbearable with heightened senses during pregnancy. The bodily changes and discomforts I went through made me aware of what it must have felt like for them. Of course, I cannot even imagine the extent of the many difficulties that come with this.

Sharing the experience of my pregnancy with my participants enabled me to have conversations that would otherwise be out of reach. My changing body would often trigger memories of participants, both mothers and fathers. They would reflect on their pregnancies and the good and bad moments they had lived through. Céline, a Congolese single mother, vividly told me the story about the moment her contractions started in the reception centre, including about the frightened looks of the male receptionist who had to drive her to the hospital. She herself was not frightened, because 'it was her fifth', she explained. Two mothers expressed how anxious they were giving birth with medical staff that they could not communicate with. Yara, a Syrian mother who spoke English, explained how she had accompanied another mother to the hospital for the delivery. She felt quite anxious because she herself had only given birth through C-sections. My changing body led to increased rapport and the telling of stories that might not otherwise have been shared with me.

While this reflexivity into my own changing social reality provided embodied knowledge on the epistemological complexity and messiness of social realities (mine as well as theirs), at times it also elicited the fierce power imbalances. In many moments, my struggles or worries as a mother were nothing compared to the daily reality my participants were facing. At times I felt bad for expressing these struggles so bluntly because they describe the privileged position that I was in, having the safety and comfort of my own home, and the stable, nurturing environment for my children that many other parents dreamed of in that difficult period.

My pregnancy and the birth of my third son in the second year of my fieldwork turned out to be an emblematic example of power imbalance in the field. When I announced my pregnancy to the staff of the reception centre, this led to me being 'excluded' from visiting the asylum centres because of the perceived risks this would pose to my unborn child, a protective measure of Belgian labour law. This was not a random or unexpected decision, it was a general measure that

I was well familiar with, having worked as a social worker before. Unfortunately, there was no room to negotiate an exception as an independent researcher; the staff in the reception centre did not want to take responsibility in case anything happened. Because some of my participants also were pregnant or gave birth during their stay in the same reception centre, I understood these bureaucratic, protective measures as contradictory, reflecting the privileges of my position as a white, European woman. Taking this friction as an analytical starting point, these embodied experiences enabled me to understand how the border of the nation-state can manifest itself aggressively in the intimate sphere.

Dealing with personal challenges during research

Sharon Smith

> This morning I planned to write some more of my thesis. I know what I want to write about, have the necessary resources saved. I started the day well, even writing a couple of hundred words before taking my daughter to horse therapy this morning. But then I had to respond to emails about her forthcoming tribunal hearing. I now can't think of anything else, and that familiar tightness across my stomach has returned. I revisit the document I was working on just a few moments ago and it could be in a foreign language. My feet and legs are restless, I feel shaky, tears welling in the corners of my eyes blurring the words I am typing. I wish it was not like this …

During the period of the research, I had to challenge the local authority about my daughter's educational provision via a tribunal process, a situation which had a considerable impact on my ability to focus or find time for my research. It resulted in a rollercoaster of frustration, self-blame, despair at not being able to resolve the situation amicably, anger and disappointment, as well as guilt for not having enough time for my research.

I completely underestimated the emotional and physical impact this process would have on me while also undertaking fieldwork. I found that when waiting for an email response or a document to be sent by a specific deadline, I simply lost my ability to focus and was almost paralysed with worry. I felt that I was failing at being a good wife, mother, friend *and* PhD researcher. Even reading a short journal article was too much. I could not face meeting with parents in the study, as I did not want to come across as that angry mother, bitter at how the system was treating me. I did not want my experiences to have a negative effect on them. Meetings had to be postponed and emails were not responded to as quickly as usual.

It was through this experience that I started to recognise the importance of embodied knowledge and feelings, as both my mind and my body were being negatively affected by the intense stress I was going through. Several parents engaged in the research were also going through the tribunal process, meaning that I had a greater understanding of what they might be going through. More importantly, it was this deeply personal experience that led me to realise the importance of 'embodied knowledge' (Strom, 2021), through a heightened awareness of my body. The way that the tribunal affected me led me to affect theory in a way which, I believe, has more resonance now that I am not only engaging with it on an intellectual level but with my body as 'an ontological site of becoming' (Braidotti, 2022, p. 113). The personal struggles that I went through led me to explore new theoretical avenues, recognising the embodied, relational and affective lives of the parents I was working with. My experiences also made me feel even more passionate about ensuring the findings of the research are disseminated widely, so that others could gain a better appreciation of the challenges faced by mothers of disabled children.

***

How can our embodied mothering experiences bring us closer to our fieldsites? In this section we have reflected on unanticipated entanglements and synergies between our private experiences and our participants' lives. While these entanglements at times might have been emotionally challenging for us as researchers, they also gave us unique, embodied knowledge about some of the challenges faced by our participants, which enhanced our research enquiry. This heightened awareness of the embodied realities and embedded subjectivities of ourselves and our participants also provided opportunities for developing care and recognition towards our participants – and ourselves – inside and outside the field.

Messy trajectories and institutional challenges

Ethnographers have a long historical tradition of going to 'the field' accompanied by family members. Views on the presence of family members in fieldsites are often gendered: for men there appears to be no problem, but when female ethnographers take their partner and/or children with them abroad, they are allegedly distracted, biased or not taken seriously. These gendered assumptions about the supposed pitfalls of conflating the productive with the reproductive extend into the academic realm as well, where women – especially mothers – can be seen to be at a distinct disadvantage in an environment where care can sometimes be seen to be 'on the periphery' and 'children are all but absent' (Evans and Grant, 2008, p. xviii).

Motherhood and care work is often invisible in universities. In our experience, our identities as carers are erased to make room for the (false) illusion that this is merely confined to the private domain. One example is how pregnancy during a PhD can be frowned upon. From personal experience and that of colleagues, this is associated with either a lack of ambition or an abuse of scholarship funding (gaining an extra year to complete the PhD), as if growing a new human is something 'relaxed'. This can lead to a working environment in which one does not always feel safe to talk about the feelings and worries one is facing at home. In the case of motherhood specifically, while we recognise that 'too much of the mummy thing' can risk one's 'credibility as a competent, capable and serious academic' (Bueskens and Toffoletti, 2018, p. 15), with the result that we avoid talking about the issues we are facing, we suggest that opening more spaces for these conversations could transform the office/academy into a safe space to offload, to discuss challenges faced both in the field and at home, and the intersections between them. Doing so could break down gendered assumptions that place care work and mothering outside the academic realm and reduce these parts of our identities to the private sphere.

Undertaking ethnographic research requires dedicated time and space. Having care responsibilities alongside fieldwork means that sustained periods of uninterrupted time with few external stimulants are non-existent. In order to find the time to work we must create 'hybrid' working spaces, reading articles and attending online seminars while standing in the kitchen cooking a meal. While this can lead to feelings of not managing to achieve well in either part of life, or feeling constantly torn between the two, it can also be an opportunity to think differently about what it means to undertake ethnographic research. The coevalness of academic research and family responsibilities can lead to benefits from this 'in-between' space where unformed ideas can gestate. It is in these spaces where fascinating connections are made that can push thinking further (see also Van der Tuin and Pekal, 2023, p. 48). We often found ourselves simultaneously watching a research seminar on our phones while undertaking household tasks, reading a journal article in the park while our children played or responding to an email from the side of a swimming pool. Indeed, it was frequently in these moments, outside what might be considered formal scholarship, that we found ourselves asking more questions, making connections, pushing our thinking further in a way that might not have otherwise emerged.

BOX 5.2

New care spaces 'in the field'

Elsemieke van Osch

Meeting participants with your children can also be a way to share, be vulnerable and open up to your participants. I met families at a playground, had them over for lunch and was invited over to their new homes, which they were eager to have filled with guests. I took this decision for both personal reasons and reasons related to my vision on ethnography, but it proved very valuable. It has completely transformed my experience of fieldwork.

Fieldwork and academia provide a certain flexibility and autonomy to decide your working hours. This can enable new temporal-spatial boundaries between work–care realities, reshaping them to make your fieldwork work around care responsibilities; picking up children from school when leaving the fieldsite (as some of our participants would have the same rhythm); and then writing field notes in the evening after putting children to bed or recording them while walking back from school the next morning. In our research, the experiences of 'shared time' (e.g., daily routines around schooling hours, starting of school holidays) we had with participants was a subtle nudge to a more horizontal background to our relationship: it positioned us in relationships towards our participants as mothers inhabiting a shared social reality. Yet, while, on the one hand, fieldwork and childcare can work well together, enabling one to structure the week flexibly as needed, together with participants, considering key events in the academic context as well, on the other hand we must be cautious that because of gendered perceptions within the university we, as mothers and carers, do not fall in the trap of constantly doing *more* in order to prove we are successfully juggling home and research (see also Jenkins, 2020).

BOX 5.3

An orientation to care in the supervisor-student/researcher relationship

Sharon Smith

I was concerned about being seen to be struggling or 'falling behind', but through the relationships I had built with my supervisors I was able to trust them with my worries and they were able to offer suggestions for self-care – for instance, they suggested taking some time off after COVID-19 home-schooling to recover before returning to my enquiry.

We are acutely aware that our academic trajectories diverge from the conventional and anticipated route. However, the entanglement of our home lives and fieldwork has led us to generate insights that might otherwise not have been possible. Due to additional responsibilities, it became necessary for us to not only accept that there would be disruption and delays, but also to embrace these more 'organic rhythms' (Ulmer, 2017, p. 203). Indeed, we agree with Summers and Clarke who suggest that ideas, 'like pregnancy', cannot always be hurried (2015, p. 245) and more time and care might be required to support their incubation. Taking longer to complete a research enquiry is therefore not to be seen as a negative. Rather than attempting to explain away 'delays', we seek to demonstrate the benefits of orienting our research practices towards care. We simply need to ensure that our research outputs reflect the time taken to care for ourselves and for our participants' needs throughout the process, and what this looks like in practice.

Conclusion

In this chapter we have discussed the intersections between care work and engaged, ethnographic fieldwork as a counter to the assumption that the two are incommensurable. By providing readers with snapshots into our ethnographic practices, we shared personal, intellectual and emotional challenges of being in the field while caring for dependent others. Dissecting both the opportunities and challenges of our positionality as mothers, we strive to carve out a space for reflexivity that goes beyond the field, and instead involves a comprehensive discussion of how our own changing social realities might resonate in the relationships we forge. Reflexivity into our own changing social reality and, with it, our re-positioning in the field, provides embodied knowledge – related to our own embodied experiences in the field – on the epistemic complexity and messiness of social reality (ours, as well as our participants'). Moreover, it has the potential to reveal how power imbalances can intimately manifest themselves in our social relationships, laying bare structural mechanisms of in/exclusion.

By bringing motherhood into research it became possible for us both to develop more care-full approaches to undertaking research. This enabled us to access knowledge/s that otherwise would have remained out of reach, as well as to reciprocate by providing support, and creating safe spaces for sharing and being vulnerable. Through making visible the challenges of motherhood, and acknowledging our full selves in the field including the labour we put into our daily lives, we were able to create a new space and way of interacting that enabled new forms of knowledge and care to be produced in the field. Reflecting on what contemporary ethnographic practices ought to look like and what commitments we should strive for as engaged researchers, considering the complexity and fluidity of our own social reality and our care responsibilities, as well as the ways in which these enable us or make us vulnerable in the field, enables a more inclusive, decolonial approach to research that is less about 'the Other' as our object of analysis – which often reduces them to their most vulnerable characteristic (e.g. 'refugee' or 'at risk'). Instead, in our shared vulnerability as well as in acknowledging each other's social relations, the focus turns to the relational knowledge/s and insights we co-create in our encounters.

Recommendations

1 **Develop an ethics of care.** This means manoeuvring the tides of social webs of interdependent relationships, being attentive to changing needs and worries and being responsive to these, when possible allowing you to develop more care-full approaches to ethnographic research.
2 **Embrace being 'differently productive' and build uncertainty into your planning.** Build flexible spaces in your schedule, which can be last-minute filled to meet both the demands of our unpredictable caring roles and static academic timescales. Consider using a 'narrative CV' (Royal Society, 2023) to demonstrate how your caring responsibilities have influenced your work as well as being able to account for gaps in the chronological timeline of your CV.
3 **Identify ways to look after yourself.** Being flexible and responsive to care needs also functions in relation to self-care; you may need to take a reading day at home when your baby has not slept all night, when your child has been sick or when a challenging situation requires you to emotionally recharge. Normalise and remove guilt from these needs.
4 **Establish boundaries and trust within your supervisory relationships.** It is important to keep supervisors up-to-date with both research progress and developments at home. It is sometimes difficult to not become despondent when you feel you have not enough work to show in a supervision meeting, or when you (again) have to explain your personal situation when discussing why the project is not progressing in a neat linear

trajectory. This is where developing trust and transparency in supervisory relationships is paramount for finding support and reassurance and for care-fully pushing you to keep giving the best of yourself. We are grateful to our supervisors for their support in this approach.

5 **Be willing to be vulnerable**. As we described above, being vulnerable in the research relationship helped build rapport and created a safe space where participants felt comfortable to share their doubts and emotions. It also removed tensions in the researcher–participant relationship when we spoke up about our own struggles, and it led to conversations we might otherwise not have had.

Further reading

Braukmann, F., Haug, M., Metzmacher, K. and Stolz, R. (Eds.) 2020. *Being a Parent in the Field: Implications and Challenges of Accompanied Fieldwork*. Bielefield: Transcript.
In this edited volume parents (both mothers and fathers), ranging from early career scholars to professors, discuss relevant aspects related to their positionality in the field, as well as knowledge production in relation to their parenting roles.

Farrelly, T., Stewart-Withers, R. and Dombroski, K. 2014. 'Being there': Mothering and absence/presence in the field. *Sites: A Journal of Social Anthropology and Cultural Studies*, 11(2), 25–56.
Contrary to the other readings, this journal article reflects on the absence of children during fieldwork. The authors describe how their children's absence is made present to them in their fieldwork encounters, and how this influences their relationships, observations and experiences in the field.

Mattingly, C. (2005). Toward a vulnerable ethics of research practice. *Health*, 9(4), 453–71.
Through reflections on fieldwork experiences, the author reflects on relational ethics, calling for vulnerability in the relationship between researcher-participants.

Tan, P. 2020. Unseen roles of women during COVID-19: How the echo of an 'Mummy, I love you' from a six-year-old during a Zoom meeting redefined mothering. *Journal of the Motherhood Initiative*, 11(2), 211–17. Available at jarm.journals.yorku.ca/index.php/jarm/article/view/40615 (accessed 26 September 2023).
This photo essay describes how the author experienced shifting spaces and temporalities of being a researcher, mother and educator for her child during the COVID pandemic.

References

Barnacle, R. 2018. Research education and care: The care-full PhD. In Bengsten, S.S.E. and Barnett, R. (Eds.), *The Thinking University: A Philosophical Examination of Thought and Higher Education*. Cham: Springer. pp. 77–86.

Braidotti, R. 2022. *Posthuman Feminism*. Cambridge: Polity Press.

Bueskens, P. and Toffoletti, K. 2018. Mothers, scholars and feminists: Inside and outside the Australian academic system. In Black, A.L. and Garvis, S. (Eds.), *Lived Experiences of Women in Academia: Metaphors, Manifestos and Memoir*. Abingdon: Routledge. pp. 13–22.

Childers, S.M. 2015. More mother than others: Disorientations, mother-scholars, and objects in becoming. In Young, A.M. (Ed.), *Teacher, Scholar, Mother: Re-envisioning Motherhood in the Academy*. Lanham, MD: Lexington. pp. 111–26.

Evans, E. and Grant, C. 2008. *Mama, PhD: Women Write about Motherhood and Academic Life*. New Brunswick, NJ: Rutgers University Press.

Jenkins, K. 2020. Academic motherhood and fieldwork: Juggling time, emotions, and competing demands. *Transactions of the Institute of British Geographers*, 45(3), 693–704.

Kittay, E.F. 2020. *Love's Labor: Essays on Women, Equality and Dependency*. 2nd ed. Abingdon: Routledge.

Noddings, N. 1986. *Caring: A Relational Approach to Ethics and Moral Education*. Berkeley/Los Angeles/London: University of California Press.

Palmer, D., Washington, S., Silberstein, S., Saxena, P. and Bose, S. 2022. Socializing doctoral students the feminist way. *International Journal of Qualitative Studies in Education*. Available at doi: 10.1080/09518398.2022.2061737 (accessed 16 January 2023).

Rogers, C. 2015. Who gives a damn about intellectually disabled people and their families? Careless spaces personified in the case of LB. *Disability and Society*, 30(9), 1439–43.

Royal Society 2023. *Résumé for Researchers*. Available at royalsociety.org/topics-policy/projects/research-culture/tools-for-support/resume-for-researchers/ (accessed 12 March 2023).

Strom, K. 2021. Learning from a 'lost year': An autotheoretical journey through anxiety and panic. *Capacious: Journal for Emerging Affect Inquiry*, 2(3), 2–24.

Summers, F. and Clarke, A. 2015. In-betweenness: Being mother, academic and artist. *Journal of Family Studies*, 21(3), 235–47.

Ulmer, J. 2017. Writing slow ontology. *Qualitative Inquiry*, 23(3), 201–11.

Van der Tuin, I. and Pekal, A. 2023. On generative and generational interlinkages and intersections: Interdisciplinarity in humanities, culture, and art. *Qualitative Inquiry*, 29(1), 45–54.

6

FIELDWORK AS A CODED-AS-BLACK WOMAN

Sandra Fernandez

Summary

This chapter guides students in exploring issues surrounding how they may be perceived in their fieldsites because of values placed upon skin colour alongside expected gender roles. The author details her own experiences doing research in Egypt, demonstrating how skin colour and gender can be both the source of varying degrees of discrimination and advantageous in navigating certain contexts. Students should be able to prepare themselves for potential differences in treatment, regardless of how they self-identify. The author offers a starting point for students in making choices that impact gathering data, maintaining their safety and halting unwanted behaviour.

Table of contents

Introduction..79
Perceptions of race and gender at the fieldsite...80
Adjusting your fieldsite...81
Being seen as harmless..83

On reaching an impasse 84
Think more than your counterparts 84
Self defence 86
Using your privilege 87
Conclusion 88
Recommendations 89
Further Reading 90
References 90

Introduction

Sex and race are no more natural than gender (Kobayashi, 1994, p. 76) but they are some of the many categories used in our social world to determine who does what and the limits of interpersonal interaction. We often forget that people experience privilege and oppression intersectionally, i.e through the lens of skin colour, gender, religion, and more, simultaneously (see Crenshaw, 1989). Maya Berry et al. (2017, p. 544) agree that academic and research spaces still see the white male experience as the default and that this is one of its weaknesses:

This hypermasculine social context highlighted a shortcoming of activist research: attentiveness to the ways that multiple inequalities (e.g. race, class, gender, sexuality) affect research participants has not been accompanied by a serious discussion of how these participants can reproduce those power relations with racially marked women researchers.

Furthermore, and especially in the UK context, internalised ideas about what it means to be a researcher and what it means to be coded on the basis of skin colour reinforce keeping silent about negative experiences in the field. Throughout higher education, whiteness is still centred as the norm, with work being done to incorporate the lived experiences of non-white British nationals and internationals still lacking. As women researchers of colour it becomes an assumption and a given that we open ourselves even more to dangerous situations during data collection, as reflected by Berry et al. (2017, p. 552) who say that through listening, the notion of women as passive is reinforced, while the intimacy that comes from this act makes us vulnerable.

As an anthropologist and woman with a mixed background who is coded by others as Black, I have continuously had to negotiate my multiple positionalities in relation to the field. I was born to a mixed African father and a mixed North American mother in Europe, and I have lived in the UK for over twenty years. My Masters research was conducted between 2008 and 2010 at the American University in Cairo, with people with one Egyptian parent and one non-Egyptian parent, people I could easily relate to because we were constantly being asked the same questions: Where are you really/originally from? Which place do you prefer? Where would you rather live?; questions that demand a direct association with one geographical location rather than many. My work focused on understanding how people made comfortable spaces for themselves in Cairo, which at the time was a place unwelcoming of difference. For my PhD I worked with anti-sexual harassment groups between 2014 and 2015, hoping to understand how they created safe spaces. It was only in my PhD, however, that I began directly addressing the role skin colour played in my work, and in the following sections I detail the different ways I adjusted and renegotiated my presence in Cairo to conduct my fieldwork.

Because there is also a history of slavery in the Arab context, I relate to what one author in Berry et al. (2017) writes about Black flesh as 'rapeable'. The authors each give accounts of being sexually assaulted, having their safety threatened, or being expected to sleep with gatekeepers in order to gain access to their fieldsite. Certain postcolonial contexts can override a Black woman's claim to rights, and her body becomes flesh to be eaten. The author takes the idea of eating flesh from Dana-Ain Davis who describes fieldwork as 'flesh-eating' and goes on to elaborate:

> 'Because our research depends on intimacies…I wonder if as Black feminist practitioners we engage in ways that makes entry points for external forces/ideas/virus/people easier to enter us…Cultural capital can be understood as flesh and therefore we are always in danger.' (p. 546)

In short, the fact of racism can override any social mobility or status acquired, and people react directly to the position they think you should occupy according to skin colour. To be clear, racism and sexism exist to varying degrees all over the world, a burden I am sure many of you already contend with in your daily lives.

It is with these ideas in mind that I present the following suggestions on preparing to conduct fieldwork as a woman of colour. I will also include a suggested reading list at the very end. These suggestions are by no means applicable to all situations, but serve as a starting point towards solidifying your own judgement as a burgeoning researcher.

Perceptions of race and gender at the fieldsite

EXAMPLE 6.1

An Egyptian friend had offered to take me to Khan El Khalili, a souq which was also a popular tourist spot for buying a range of souvenirs and gifts. My friend was directing me to the clothing section of this souq, leading me past the winding covered alleyways towards wider, uncovered streets lined with makeshift metal stalls dressed in rows of jeans, novelty t-shirts, polos, abayas, and other fare. As we walked down the street, every other step I was faced by different men who would say 'brown sugar' in a low voice as I passed. After about the sixth utterance, I turned to my friend and expressed my discomfort. She told me I was misunderstanding their intention.

'This is a compliment', she said.

The above took place within the first months of coming to Cairo, and I use it to demonstrate the slipperiness of how harassment, gender roles, and racial bias are perceived and defined. This was not the first time I had been harassed since arriving in Cairo, nor was it the first time harassment had referred to my skin colour. This exchange is also an elaboration on how sexual harassment was normalised and rationalised away in early 2000s Cairo. During the years leading to the revolution, people began to force the issue of sexual harassment into public debate, but in 2006 when I arrived, sexual harassment was either blamed on the harassed, justified in ways similar to what my friend had said, or its existence was flat out denied. This did not change the fact that it was endemic, and how it was enacted according to skin colour and stereotypes.

Blonde women, non-white women, and women who coded as Eastern European received more harassment than others. Walking the streets of Cairo men would shout the names of different African countries at me, and when talking to people in passing, they would refuse to accept the idea that there were Black people outside of the African continent. Women coded as African were often associated with prostitution, and Nubian Egyptians also found themselves discriminated against alongside the large population of mostly Sudanese refugees who resided in Egypt.

The other side of this coin is pursuit of whiteness. Skin lightening was commonly practised in Egypt, so much so that it was difficult to find skincare products without lightening agents. All of this occurs alongside the entrenched view that women are conditionally granted access to public space by men, with sexual harassment being rationalised as a method of punishing women for 'improper' conduct (Abdel Hamid and Zaki, 2014). In my experience, all women entering the public sphere were harassed, regardless of appearance and clothing.

This account is to demonstrate the multiple layers behind the use of racialised forms of harassment; and while some of this information was readily available, some of it I had to learn through experience. Background reading and thorough online research is crucial in understanding how people might react to your presence and appearance, as is connecting with other scholars of similar positionalities who have conducted research at similar fieldsites. For further ideas and suggestions on how to go about this, please refer to Spector and Sutton's chapter in this book.

Adjusting to your fieldsite

EXAMPLE 6.2

The metro stopped at a crowded station, and the crowds moving in and out of the women's car against each other and then against the crowds moving along the platform caused a slight halt. Dressed in summer whites, one of the police officers made his way to the women's car, and upon entering it, began bellowing at a young boy who was standing by the doorway. As he yelled, a woman in abaya and hijab jumped up and ran to the boy, explaining to the officer that she was his aunt and he was accompanying her. This was not enough; the officer declared the boy too old to be on the women's car (there was a maximum age for boys being chaperoned by their female relatives) and both were ejected. Having done this, the officer turned towards me, and began bellowing at me to get off the car. Having been in this situation too many times to count in the year since I had returned to Cairo, I raised one of the headphones that covered my ears and said 'ana mish ragul' (I am not a man). The officer's eyes widened, and, in English, he said 'OH! Sorry sorry!' and left the car.

This situation occurred while I was working in anti-sexual harassment. I had decided to do away with the added stress of hair management by close cropping it (the politics of hairdressing in Cairo is too complicated to go in to here). This decision brought with it a whole new set of racialised gender issues; on the streets of Cairo the sexual harassment I received dropped significantly, but when I was harassed it was more along the lines of ascertaining which gender role I should be fulfilling. Old men would stop in the street and exclaim '*Eh da?!*', literally 'What is it/this?!'.

It was more problematic on the metro, which had separate cars for women that I rode because harassment is common on the regular cars. I began to enter the women's car expecting a woman to approach me and tell me I was on the wrong car, or to have to explain to the metro police that I was not a man. These experiences taught me that for women, gender was mainly embedded in clothing and hair, as the fact that I wore jewellery did not enable people to recognise that I was not a man. This was an issue not necessarily reserved for women of my skin colour, as an Egyptian friend and another European friend had similar experiences on the women's car of the metro.

This story raises a question of whether or not researchers should try to 'conform' to a given fieldsite. For me, my skin colour already meant in many places, I would stand out no matter what, and my experiences in Cairo before the revolution had shown me that changing my attire did not lessen the amount of harassment I received, nor did it make day-to-day exchanges easier. I did not seek to actively force my notions on to others, but I had decided that if people were going to form their opinions around a fixation with my skin colour and presumed gender role, so long as my choices were not offensive, the differences would not affect my fieldwork in a negative way (which they ultimately did not).

BOX 6.1

How you choose to adapt yourself to your fieldsite is entirely up to you, and while it is important that you consider how your appearance and positionality affect data collection, you should never put any aspect of your health and wellbeing at risk. Experiences of sexism and racism, even in the form of microaggressions, can build up, making it difficult to work under any circumstances. *It is important to make sure you have thought about what makes you feel threatened and ensured you have adequate support from supervisors, the university and the necessary institutions. Universities have obligations towards your health and safety, and it is imperative that they uphold their responsibilities.* You should not be expected to sacrifice your wellbeing for your research, nor should you be expected to support the structures that perpetuate racism and sexism.

While I was doing fieldwork, a number of people had asked why I had not chosen to wear the *hijab*, suggesting that wearing the *hijab* would help to mitigate my Otherness in the Egyptian context. I explained to them that wearing the *hijab* would symbolise for me, a condoning of the harassment that I was enduring. When I told an Egyptian friend these stories, she added that I could not wear the *hijab* anyway because it would also symbolise to others that I was Muslim, which I am not. If you do choose to change yourself to blend in better, be sure you know how you are trying to blend in and if it will achieve the goal you seek. You should also be aware that it is often the burden of women to make these types of changes in the first place. Women are historically seen as the bearers of culture, which is reflected in the tendency in many places for women to wear 'traditional' clothing while men present themselves as more 'modern'. Berry et al. take the notion of women's bodies as battlefields for defining social boundaries and apply it to academia: white male researchers are argued as using the bodies of women researchers to define the standard, as 'key battlefields for truth in our discipline' (2017, p. 554).

Being seen as harmless

When I did fieldwork in the mid-/late 2000s, it was mostly interview based, and the people I talked to never questioned my position as a researcher. In post-2011 Cairo however, there was a resurgence of the fear of foreigners as destabilisers of the country. Journalists in particular were being targeted, and my plan to carry my DSLR camera was abandoned, save for during specific events. It appeared that a person of colour carrying a DSLR was fine, as I found out when my bag was searched at a metro stop. At the time, all persons entering the metro were being searched, but when I explained my research to the officer, I was allowed to pass. My white female flatmate, on the other hand, would have been considered more suspicious, being more readily suspected to be a journalist. I had been asked by both Egyptians and other researchers if I was Sudanese, which led me to believe that part of the reason I was able to do things my white counterparts might not have been able to was because I was mistaken for Sudanese, and as such, not necessarily seen as a threat. This reinforces my earlier recollection of being in Cairo where people refused to believe I could be non-African. The downside of this is also embedded in the ways people had reacted to me: my research was not considered serious because it was me who was conducting it. Conversely, you may be perceived as part of the group as a result of skin colour or gender. You would then become party to a form of embodied learning that others may not have access to by mere fact of who they are. In such cases be wary of the kinds of assumptions that both you and your interlocutors may be making. As Kobayashi says (1994), what are the questions you are not asking? What are the questions your interlocutors are not asking? What are the things that may not have occurred to either of you?

It is fairly common in academia for doctors and professors of colour to be treated with less respect than their white peers, and in a similar vein you may find yourself in spaces where people find it hard to believe you are a researcher, or do not treat you with respect commensurate with white researchers. In such cases, you have the choice to reinforce your authority if doing so does not adversely affect your data collection. Younger Egyptian female researchers have told stories of having to gain authority through the practices they deployed for data collection: formalised interviews, surveys and note taking. Providing this structure serves as a constant reminder of your position as a researcher to others, and the ritual of data collection in many cases can seem more like traditional ideas of what research looks like to non-researchers. Being taken less seriously/seen as harmless can have both benefits and drawbacks, and you should consider when and under which circumstances you may need to navigate or challenge these assumptions.

At the same time, I cannot stress enough the importance of keeping yourself safe. Berry et al. (2017) provide very jarring accounts of how being taken less seriously can overlap with being seen as more sexually available, indeed rapeable, to people in a given fieldsite. In all of these cases, the threats to and violations of these women's safety were seen as justifiable through the idea that being a person of colour or being seen as part of the community on some level gave men in power rights over these researchers' bodies.

On reaching an impasse

After landing in Tunis, I was queuing for passport control while two elderly ladies poked my back, telling me to move forward. When I was called to the counter, I handed over my passport and, after looking through it, the officer called over his superior. Confused, he began to ask the supervisor (in Arabic) how it was possible I was Belgian. The supervisor said he did not see what the problem was and that if I had the passport I must be Belgian. The officer persisted: but how is she Belgian? The supervisor said if I have a passport and identification card, then I must be Belgian, at which point I asked in Arabic if they wanted to see my identification card. They both ignored me, and this back and forth continued for a little longer, until I asked for a second time if they wanted to see my identity card. This time, the supervisor said he would, and I presented my identity card for them to examine. The supervisor then said to his subordinate 'See? She has the passport and the identity card. She is Belgian. There is no problem.' As this was happening I could hear a woman with a distinct London accent answering questions about where she lived and what her occupation was. The officer stamped my passport and handed back my documents, and as I turned to leave I noted that the woman who was still stuck at the other passport control counter was darker than I was.

After my first arrival in Cairo, I was regularly asked by passport control if I had a second passport or if I was Sudanese. I later discovered that asking the former question was a way of suggesting one had 'non-Western' origins. Skin colour marks people as having specific histories, backgrounds and occupying specific classes in the minds of those who do not bear that skin colour. In doing research, there are going to be times where you will be faced with people who are just not open to the idea that having a certain skin colour does not lock you to a certain 'non-Western' geographical location, or the ensuing arguments put you, your relationships or your research at risk. It may also just be that sometimes the situation is like that I experienced in passport control: the exchange is too brief. In whatever you do in the field, you need to find a place within yourself where you can come to terms with various outcomes and reactions to your presence, including the possibility that you cannot change people's views on the role you 'should' occupy as a racialised and gendered being. Life as you currently live it will have already equipped you for this to some extent, but be prepared to extend this to your research and fieldwork.

Think more than your counterparts

I had called a taxi to take me from my flat in Maadi to visit a friend on the island of Manial. After entering the cab, I messaged my friend to let him know I was on my way and the driver began to ask the usual questions: where I was from, what I was doing in Cairo, if I was married. At this point in time it was common for women to lie and say they were married, which I did in hopes of avoiding further questioning. I was still messaging my friend when the driver asked a question I had never heard before: are you pregnant? I gave an ambiguous answer, and messaged my friend what had happened. His response? To call me and tell me not to hang up the phone. I proceeded to detail everything that happened in real time as the driver took me in a different direction to where I was supposed to be headed, to an area called Moqattam, and parked his car at the base of a set of flats. He then told me to wait while he exited the car and entered the block of flats. I contemplated running, but was unsure where to run to as there were no other buildings in sight. By this point my friend had informed another one of our friends, and they were also debating what to do. After about ten minutes a completely different man approached the taxi, got in and explained he would be taking me to Manial. Without further conversation, this man took me to my original destination and I did not have to pay extra for the detour. After making sure that I was indeed alright, my friend who had been on the phone the entirety of the taxi journey explained that in addition to the fact that asking if a woman is pregnant is a method of ascertaining if they had had sex, Moqattam had a reputation for being a part of town where many women are raped; his main concern was that that would have been my fate had he not been on the phone.

***

I had walked the length of the Mohandiseen shooting club which separated my flat from that of my friend and, after dinner and a long catch-up, began the walk back to my flat. The area around the shooting club sometimes had many loiterers, either in groups or in parked cars, as there were a few stands that sold fruit, colas and burgers, so there were many people about. I was focused on my phone, still messaging that same friend, but had begun to suspect I was being followed. I tensed as two youths picked up their pace, one of them reaching for my phone as they went past. Instead of carrying on, after a number of metres they turned around and came back in my direction, the same youth this time trying to tip my phone out of my hand as they passed. I picked up my pace and began to wonder if I should circle around to avoid them finding out where I lived, or if I should confront them, but knew that their willingness to engage in such an overt manner and the fact that there were two of them would be problematic. In a mix of fear and frustration, I entered a store I shopped from regularly, and explained to the owner that I was being followed by youths I did not know; after offering me a seat, he sent his son out to have a look. After about ten minutes the son returned, saying that everything seemed normal, and offered to walk me the few metres to my flat.

***

In such situations, you have to either have a plan, or be able to improvise quickly and, if possible, see things coming in a way many others do not have to (but many of us do). We can speculate that it was lucky that I was in constant contact with friends while in the taxi, but what they could do in that situation was limited. It may be worth having someone who knows that if they haven't heard from you in a certain amount of time they should call a relevant organisation, authority and the university, but keep in mind they all vary in their capacity to handle such situations (see 1752group.com). Doing fieldwork will most likely resemble your current daily life, but more intense, more unrelenting and with even fewer options for refuge (if you have options for refuge in non-fieldwork life in the first place). This is similar to advice given to pre-fieldwork students about planning for their research in general: always have alternatives and multiple back-up plans for doing research, even for potentially life-threatening cases like these. We must interrogate ourselves as part of the process of producing ethnography, but also as part of the process of planning for our own wellbeing given how people are socialised to react to racial and gendered cues. This is not to place the onus entirely on women of colour, but to equip us to draw others to a point where they begin to participate in exchanges which do not leave us doing the majority of the work, or having to alter and minimise ourselves to prevent trespasses on our minds and bodies. We can aim to reach a point where we no longer have to do the extra work to keep ourselves safe, but for now these strategies can assist with personal safety and field research.

I have been comparatively lucky in my experiences in Egypt; I know many women who were sexually assaulted while living there, and it is because of this that I issue this piece of advice. As is hinted by the taxi story, saying that you are married does not always prevent harassment, and single/unaccompanied women are always seen as either a threat or fair game. As Berry et al. (2017) note, help is not on the way and, while you may be lucky enough to have a strong support network to get you through whatever may happen, you need to prepare as if you are on your own. Furthermore, I agree with their postulation that doing research as a non-white woman can amount to simultaneously advocating for your own rights while respecting and possibly advocating for the rights of the people you work with. The act of doing research requires data-collecting methods, such as participant observation, that can make research participants reproduce specific social dynamics they see as normal but rob researchers of their humanity in the process.

As academics, we are told we hold a certain privilege that mitigates any violent experiences we may have. This argument claims that by speaking up we separate ourselves from the communities we work with, but in my case, when working in anti-sexual harassment, we were a group of people already speaking up against gendered violence; while I had the privilege of being able to leave that does not mean that I stopped experiencing racialised gendered violence. This argument seems predicated upon the idea that (racialised gendered) violence occurs 'over there' when in fact it happens everywhere.

Self defence

My friend and I had decided to go for dinner, and were making our way back to our flat in downtown Cairo. As we began to cross a large, open square, we noted a man walking within centimetres of my friend; she turned sharply to face him. Startled only slightly, the man said 'Sorry, but your breasts are so beautiful.' My friend grabbed this man by the arm and began punching him in the chest. The man panicked and tried to wrestle free from my friend's grip. Because of the spike in sexual harassment, I had been carrying a medium-sized stick for self-defence. My friend, aware of this, handed her much smaller bag to me and demanded the stick, which she used to continue beating this man. The man then broke free and began to run across the square; my friend took off right behind him. I waited patiently for her to return, which she did after about ten minutes.

In this story, my friend was in a position where she was confident enough to know she could handle whatever situation unfolded. If you are in a situation where you are not as confident, I would not advise doing what she did. It is important to defend yourself, but be aware of the legal frameworks in place and the potential aftermath. What happens if the person retaliates? Will the police take the matter seriously? If they do, is the information you give them protected? What are your psycho-social resources? At the same time, I would advise that you plan multiple strategies for handling situations in advance, much like the thought process I described when the youths were following me. This is not to place the burden on the targets of harassment, but to deal with situations where it has yet to be acknowledged that the burden to end the gender inequalities that support harassment is on everyone. Returning to Berry et al., one of the authors was told that blackness was seen as a 'flesh that attracts sexual violence to itself' (Berry et al., 2017, p. 545) and it was her responsibility to compensate 'for having a Black female body'. You should be prepared to defend yourself not only when your safety is threatened, but when your positionality is challenged. Living in Cairo was in many ways a course in survival for me. To walk the streets and go about my day-to-day life, I had to be hypervigilant, watch for possible signs of harassment on the horizon and take extra steps to safeguard myself. I experimented with masculinising my gait, taking wider strides and making my body take up more space. I walked in the streets instead of the pavement to keep from being cornered by groups of men and took different routes to get to the same destination. I even switched to wearing large headphones over my ears to both block out catcalls and signal to men I wasn't listening.

Using your privilege

This can mean many things, but often refers to nationality and class markers. In both cases of my research, one of my privileges was being a student at the American University in Cairo, whose prestige carried a lot of weight in Egyptian society. My capacity to pay for a foreign education in a sphere where most people could not and did not pay for education heightened my foreignness; while I was protected in some respects, I was not spared milder forms of racist behaviour and sexual harassment. The presumed protection of being connected to the American University in Cairo changed with the death of Giulio Regeni, who had been conducting PhD research in Cairo when his body was found by the side of the road, showing signs of torture, in January 2016. An event like this can remind you of how quickly situations can change, and that having multiple plans and safeguards in place is paramount. There is no straightforward answer for such a seriously dangerous situation, so make sure you have thought this through – if possible with advice from your supervisor and ethics committee. It was in this climate that Rassa Ghaffari (2019) was conducting her fieldwork in Iran, making affiliation with a local university more problematic, and she ultimately chose not to. In Erica Townsend-Bell's (2009) case, what protected her while doing research in Uruguay as an African American woman was the fact that her class markers and nationality coded her as not likely to be Uruguayan. She noted that her clothing and hair set her aside from Afro-Uruguayans, identifying her as middle class. This placed limits on her interaction with Afro-Uruguayans but increased her access to other Uruguayans, and granted her proximity to 'whiteness'. This did not always work out, and sometimes she found that some men mistook her for a prostitute, a stereotype of Black women also common in that part of the world. For me, the question of nationality, as hinted in previous stories, made me seem more of an anomaly. Many Egyptians did not believe I could be Belgian because of the belief that there were no Black Europeans.

In short, take stock of the privileges that you have as part of your positionality and try to figure out how these may help you navigate being in your fieldsite. What aspects of your identity make it easier for you to embed yourself safely in a given locale? What are the elements that may seem disadvantageous in one place that could be advantageous in another?

Conclusion

Communicating the difference in what your skin colour means to you and what it means to your interlocutors require long-term, individualised and context-dependent reflection. More than other advice given, there is no pre-set structure or road map. Anything we do must be done with the research community in mind, but also with the above advice regarding your safety front and centre. Think about your context, your role in the space you occupy, but beware the idea of fieldwork as suffering or a rite of passage, and think back to the boundaries you have set for yourself. Fieldwork will be an extension – and possibly an intensification – of the life you already know, so try and brace yourself for this. This is not to say that the fieldwork experience will be terrible and negative. As angry, stressed and scared as being in Egypt made me at times, I also have a wonderful love for Cairo and made some of my closest friends there. Cairo helped to solidify who I am, and helped to identify what really matters to me, but also brought me face to face with unshakeable forms of racism and sexism, previously only experienced in subtle forms. To be clear: racism and sexism are global problems which is why it is important for us to discuss and think through how to address these issues.

There is a point that can be applied to a number of stories I have already told, and is most likely something you already have experience with, but it is important to reiterate in light of the different ways discrimination, racism and sexism manifest themselves. With the rise of populism, whiteness is once again reinforced as the baseline criteria for belonging in many societies (Essed et al., 2018, p. v), and the deployment of racism in the way terrorists and criminals are profiled has signalled a return to older forms of dehumanisation found in the colonial legacy. Essed et al. write:

> Dehumanisation can be absolute, as in the animalisation of Blackness; it can also be relative as in equating being Black with a lesser cultural, social or psychological degree of being human, thereby normalising (imagined) characteristics of Whiteness as the epitome of humanity.
>
> (2018, p. vii)

As a species, we are still a long way from disconnecting the meanings we place on skin colour and being male or female from the realities of the people we encounter and our bodily practices. This means finding a way to keep going despite this current reality, to be able to look after yourself, do the necessary work and pick your battles.

Recommendations

1 **Research the local histories with regards to gender and race roles in your expected fieldsite**. Make sure you know as much as you can about the locale you are about to enter, and how people are likely to react to your positionalities.
2 **Do not expect to change yourself completely to accommodate your fieldsite or fieldwork**. Try to gain a sense before entering the field of the levels to which you may have to adjust, but also the levels to which you are willing to adjust. The boundaries you draw for yourself must be supported by your supervisors, your institution and any support networks you may have.
3 **Being taken less seriously can both help and/or hinder research**. You need to contemplate the impact your positionality has on data collection and if you wish to take advantage of these potentialities. Data collection should not be at the expense of women's safety and sanity, but no project is risk-free, so there will be choices for you to make.
4 **Prepare for the fact that some people will act threateningly towards you because of perceived gender/skin colour roles, and that defending yourself will be complicated**. There is no 'follow these instructions and all will be fine'. If you can, establish links with the local community in ways that foster potential support. Be aware of the legal system alongside social beliefs that may work with you or against you in a situation of danger. Consider this work by North South Feminist Dialogue: 1752group.files.wordpress.com/2021/09/8583a-nsfd-handbook-final-23july-2.pdf
5 **Take stock of the privileges you have as possible safeguards**. Consider how certain qualities take on a different meaning when the context is changed, and how you can benefit from this in the field. Make plans that include worst-case dangerous scenarios.

The suggestions given here are by no means complete, nor should they be, but I offer these reflections based upon my own experiences in hopes of providing a foundation for future and current researchers to build upon. I do not endorse a neo-colonial position of dictating to different cultural contexts how to engage with people from all walks of life, but I offer suggestions on how to begin to dismantle the engrained idea that women and women of colour must suffer in order for research to progress.

Further reading

Berry, M.J., Arguelles, C.C., Cordis, S., Ihmoud, S. and Estrada, E.V. 2017. Toward a fugitive anthropology: Gender, race, and violence in the field. *Cultural Anthropology*, 32(4), 537–65.
The authors give the reader accounts of just how problematic things are when doing social science research as a non-white, sometimes coded as insider, females, and while it may be a very triggering read, I consider it essential.

Duhe, B.J. 2019. *Dear White Anthropology Grad Students: A 'How To' Guide for Successfully Interacting with Students of Colour in Graduate School*. Self-published on Amazon.
This author directly addresses issues US postgraduate students of colour have with their white peers, with supplementary advice to professors/lecturers and many examples relevant to non-US contexts.

Essed, P., Farquharson, K., Pillay, K. and White, E.J. 2018. *Relating Worlds of Racism: Dehumanisation, Belonging, and the Normativity of European Whiteness*. London: Palgrave Macmillan.
This book offers a series of chapters engaging with blackness and whiteness in different contexts, and will provide the reader with a broader understanding of the varying embodiments of blackness and whiteness alongside the range of racist behaviours.

Ghaffari, R. 2019. Doing gender research as a 'gendered subject': Challenges and sparks of being a dual-citizen woman researcher in Iran. *Anthropology of the Middle East*, 14(2), 130–42.
This author provides an anthropological take on negotiating insider/outsider identities with attention given to questions people with mixed identities have faced vis-à-vis insider/outsider and the power, status and mobility a Western passport can provide.

Nash, M., Nielsen, H.E.F., Shaw, J., King, M., Lea, M.-A. and Bax, N. 2019. 'Antarctica just has this hero factor …': Gendered barriers to Australian Antarctic research and remote fieldwork. *PLOS One*, 14(1), e0209983.
The authors discuss how certain parts of the world are rendered harder to access for women using the idea that exploration is a 'men only' endeavour, really highlighting how spaces and research in general still defaults to the male experience and perspective – for example, when dealing with urinating and menstruation.

Pierre, J. 2013. *The Predicament of Blackness*. Chicago: University of Chicago Press.
This book focuses on the interactions between African Americans/the African diaspora and Ghanaians and gives nuanced and detailed accounts that demonstrate the differences in how blackness is perceived and embodied, including its connection to whiteness through colonial history, purchasing power and skin lightening.

References

Baron, B. 2005. *Egypt as a Woman: Nationalism, Gender, Politics*, Berkeley: University of California Press.
Berry, M.J., Arguelles, C.C., Cordis, S., Ihmoud, S. and Estrada, E.V. 2017. Toward a fugitive anthropology: Gender, race, and violence in the field. *Cultural Anthropology*, 32(4), 537–65.

Crenshaw, K. 1989. Demarginalizing the intersection of race and sex: A Black feminist critique of antidiscrimination doctrine, feminist theory and antiracist politics. *University of Chicago Legal Forum*, 1(8), 139–67.

Essed, P., Farquharson, K., Pillay, K. and White, E.J. 2018. *Relating Worlds of Racism: Dehumanisation, Belonging, and the Normativity of European Whiteness*. London: Palgrave Macmillan.

Ghaffari, R. 2019. Doing gender research as a 'gendered subject': Challenges and sparks of being a dual-citizen woman researcher in Iran. *Anthropology of the Middle East*, 14(2), 130–42.

Hughes, A. 2016. Exploring normative whiteness: Ensuring inclusive pedagogic practice in undergraduate fieldwork teaching and learning. *Journal of Geography in Higher Education*, 40(3), 460–77.

Kobayashi, A. 1994. Coloring the field: Gender, 'race', and the politics of fieldwork. *Professional Geographer*, 46(1), 73–80.

Townsend-Bell, E. 2009. Being true and being you: Race, gender, class, and the fieldwork experience. *PS: Political Science and Politics*, 42(2), 311–14.

7

SEX, SEXUALITY AND THE ETHNOGRAPHER IN THE FIELD

Shannon Philip

Summary

This chapter looks at the important role of sexuality within different stages of ethnographic research. The chapter looks in detail at the sexuality of participants, the sexuality of the researcher, the wider sexual politics playing out in any fieldsite and the consequences these have in understanding sexuality in and through ethnographic research. Through exploring the importance and consequences of 'sexuality' in carrying out ethnographic field research, the chapter highlights the analytical value of being aware of sexuality and the sexual politics within ethnographic fieldsites; it also explores what it means to be an ethnographer with a sexuality doing research in particular context with participants who have a sexuality of their own. From a research methods point of the view, the chapter highlights some of the dangers in not unpacking and accounting for sexual politics of the fieldsite, as well as suggesting some useful strategies and methods to approach safe and effective ethnographic fieldwork with sexual politics in mind.

Table of contents

Introduction 93
'Seeing' sexuality: before, during and after fieldwork 93
Sexuality and ethnography 94
Sexuality of participants 96
Sexuality of researcher 97
Sexual politics of the field 99
Recommendations 101
Further reading 101
References 102

Introduction

The chapter starts with an ethnographic vignette of 'smart boys and sexy girls' wherein sexuality of the research participants, the researcher and the fieldsite are presented together where sexuality and its application in the field can be 'seen'. This section on 'Seeing' sexuality will also allow us to build an analytical understanding of sexuality before, during and after fieldwork. The next section unpacks the links between sexuality and ethnography as highlighted in the vignette and the following section specifically addresses the sexuality of the research participants. Then the next section looks at the sexuality of the researcher doing the fieldwork and research. Following that the final section looks at the sexual dimensions of the field more broadly and then offers a summary and some practical recommendations for students carrying out ethnographic research.

'Seeing' sexuality: before, during and after fieldwork

EXAMPLE 7.1

One evening after work two of my male informants, Raj and Aditya, took me to a shopping mall in Delhi to hang out and do some window shopping on a boys' evening out'. Both Raj and Aditya made an effort to dress up in smart shirts and tight trousers and gelled their hair in a stylish quiff for our outing. We met outside the mall at a bus stop and greeted each other with hugs and warm smiles and then the three of us walked to the mall. En route the two young men asked me to take several photos of them in various poses with the mall in the background. Raj explained to me that these photos were for his social media accounts.

After security checks at the entrance of the mall, we entered it and walked towards the central courtyard. As we were walking Aditya and I were looking at the shops with their big display windows and talking about the clothes on sale. Suddenly, Raj pushed between Aditya and me and moved his arms over our backs and put them across our shoulders. Then, without saying anything, holding both me and Aditya close by our shoulders, Raj slowed our walk. He then turned Aditya and me sideways, our three bodies closely touching each other, turned away from the shop and towards the courtyard. As Raj guided our bodies to turn, I noticed a group of three young women walking towards us.

The young women were also stylishly dressed in jeans and T-shirts and were smiling and enjoying time with each other. The girls we were about to pass us and I could feel Raj's arm tense on my shoulder. Then Raj and Aditya became silent and they stared at the group of young women without saying anything to me. I did not understand what was going on; I looked at both of them in confusion. Raj quickly nudged me with his elbow and suggested that I too should look at the group of young women about to pass. At that point, I followed his instructions and joined them in looking at the group of young women approaching us.

As the women came closer to us, I noticed that two of them looked directly at Raj and myself and smiled. Raj in turn smiled too and said 'Hullo' to them. Raj's greetings made the women giggle even more and they smiled warmly as they passed. Raj then used his arms to push Aditya and myself even further so that we were now behind the young women, looking at them smiling and walking away. At that point Aditya quickly turned to Raj and me and said 'What sexy babes (maal)'. The young women did not turn back to look again and carried on their window shopping. Raj and Aditya, thrilled with the exchange with these young women, turned away too and carried on with our walk through the mall.

This vignette has several themes around sex, sexuality and the sexual politics that need careful unpacking for any ethnographer interested in critically thinking about sex and sexuality. The vignette also involves dimensions and assumptions about sex and sexuality that need to be thought about pre-fieldwork and during the fieldwork, as well as after leaving the field. For example, before going on fieldwork, it is important to understand the dating habits and courtship patterns of groups one is studying so that 'unusual' or 'new' forms of courting practices seen above are not seen simply as forms of 'violence' or 'male aggression', but rather are thoroughly contextualised. Likewise while in the field such practices should not be looked down on or morally judged or discouraged by researchers; instead, there should be space given to fully understand the 'sexual and social field' in which the ethnographer is operating. Finally, when away from the field it is also important to reflect on field notes about where social interactions are taking place to bring out hidden sexual and gendered dynamics that shape those contexts.

Sexuality and ethnography

Sexuality has important consequences for the ethnographer, not just in the process of doing ethnography, but also through the analytical points brought out through understanding the role of sexuality in a given fieldsite. In the vignette we see that there is no explicit sex or sexual acts within the narrative; however, I want to demonstrate in this chapter the profound role of sexualities with regard to the researcher, the participants and the fieldsite more broadly.

There is now a considerable literature on the role of gendered positionality of the researcher within fieldwork (see McDowell, 2011, for example). However, little has been written about the role of sexuality within fieldwork, particularly within ethnographic fieldwork which often requires a highly involved and immersive effort from researchers in gathering data. Yet, as various scholars point out, sexuality in all societies and across histories pervades every aspect of social existence and often plays a crucial role in shaping social relations and social orders (Srivastava, 2007). The myriad roles of 'sexuality' may be to foreground a particular moral order, or to express desire, or to discipline and control (Foucault, 1990) or, indeed, to celebrate and enjoy physical acts of sex with other people (Philip, 2017). However, at the same time sexuality cannot be reduced to a simplistic notion of a fixed 'sexual expression', but has to be understood as a changing and politically charged field that has social significance. Hence 'sexuality' as a theme has profound significance for ethnographers who are going into various fields, even if their focus is not on gender or sexuality. Understanding and acknowledging the power of sexualities and their operations within fieldsites will allow researchers to identify their structuring role in order to unpack them carefully and critically before going into the field, as well as while carrying out fieldwork and when analysing data from a field trip.

In the vignette with Raj and Aditya, based in an urban context of New Delhi in India, the site of the mall where the vignette is set is charged with sexual politics. We saw in the vignette, for example, a brief exchange between the young men and women who do not know each other but nonetheless engage in flirtatious interaction with each other. Throughout my fieldwork in Delhi, such practices of initiative conversations and communications with members of the opposite sex were commonplace among young men and women who often lived and moved around in same sex settings. Hence, the mall or other spaces where men and women could freely meet were exciting spaces of encounter and desire, as several urban ethnographers of young people have pointed out (Trivedi, 2014).

In such cases, as an ethnographer working closely with young people, it is important to be open to the possibility of various forms of sexual encounter, which we may or may not be used to or agree with. For example, in the vignette I personally, as the ethnographer, found it difficult, impolite and often outright hostile to stare at women as a way of trying to initiate conversation with them. My own prejudices, regarding such behaviour as sexist and violating, meant that I often judged those of my male informants who carried out such practices. However, as I discovered in the field, the sexual politics and the sexual practices of the site meant that young people coded various acts very differently to the way I understood them. As various ethnographers working in India have pointed out, such approaches from young men cannot simply be read as violence because they are often reciprocated and received positively as a way of wooing and attracting a mate at bus stops, malls etc. (Osella and Osella, 2006). Indeed in the vignette and throughout my time in the field, I found that most young women also engaged with men and expressed their sexual, romantic and personal desires through such forms of contact. Hence, as a researcher, understanding how sexuality was thought of and practised among my informants was an important part of the fieldwork experience for me.

In my ethnographic experience and in conversation with colleagues doing ethnography I have found that sexuality is often a dimension that is not talked about or critically articulated. Unless researchers are explicitly studying themes of gender or sexuality, these dimensions operate largely through a heteronormative framework. I have often heard my female colleagues say how assumptions are made about their desire to marry and bear children. Likewise for LGBTQ+ researchers, assumptions around their heterosexual or 'normal' way of life are often made with problematic consequences for researcher–participant relationships.

As a queer-feminist young man, researching largely 'heterosexual' men in the context of India, my own sexuality and the sexuality of my participants were important aspects of my research experience, as well as important analytical themes in my ethnography. In India, while carrying out the bulk of my early research, homosexuality was illegal; hence, it would have been easy to reduce homosexuality to the margins and view it as difficult to research. However, as I discovered through my research experience as a gay man, the very essence of heterosexuality in Indian society was defined by and through the marginalisation of homosexuality. Thus it did not matter if homosexuality was legal or not because the social order tried to keep reproducing a heteronormative framework through a highly complex politics of sexuality. Within such a context, the sexuality of the researcher, the sexuality of informants and the wider sexual politics take on a huge significance in how individuals, as well as the researcher, belong within their fieldsite, and how it is understood and legible within their sites and the data they gather.

To explore how ethnographers may critically engage and be aware of sexuality within their fieldsite, in this chapter I propose a few simple steps and guidelines that can help ethnographers think about the sexuality of their informants, their own sexual positions and the broader sexual politics of the field. I will unpack the vignette by trying to explore the sexual dimensions of the fieldsite in how they relate, first, to the participants and informants that we seek to study; second, to our sexualities as researchers; and, finally, within the broader politics of the field.

Sexuality of participants

Among the young men I was working with, heterosexuality was the norm and assumed to be a given. The normative power of heterosexuality was so strong among my informants that they never had to tell me they were 'straight' or ask me if I was 'straight'; it was always simply assumed that we had a shared and identical sexuality. With heteropatriarchy as the norm in most conventional social worlds, most ethnographers operate and carry out research in heteronormative contexts. Heteronormativity is the process of normalising heterosexuality to the extent that 'gay' or 'lesbian' identities are marked and smaller subcategories within the social order. Within heteronormative contexts the assumption is that most people are heterosexual and that they lead lives in which heterosexual marriage, reproduction and penetrative penal–vaginal sex are the norm. Of course, the social forms this heteronormativity takes will be different in Cairo to Brussels or Jamaica – they depend on the society being studied – but the foundational attempt at making society normatively heterosexual remains powerful.

In this context, participants too operate from a heteronormative position where they view the world as heterosexual without realising the political and social consequences of this. For them, having a girlfriend or boyfriend of the opposite sex, talking about and sharing desire about the opposite sex, perceptions of their own bodies and the bodies of others, heterosexual marriage and the desire to reproduce children and domestic values of their families are normalised and taken for granted. As an ethnographer, being aware of the ways and forms heteronormativity shapes the lives of our informants is crucial as their understanding of sexuality underpins and is foundational to how they view the social world. Even ethnographers not studying sexuality will benefit by being aware of the way in which heteronormativity operates and structures lives of the people they work with.

For example, while out 'roaming' my male informants would often pull me or each other by the shoulders or by our T-shirts and, without saying or explaining anything, physically turn their bodies to look at a woman passing by, as in the vignette. No discussion was needed as to whom or what the object to be consumed and watched usually was. The embodied masculinities discourse, working collectively through our bodies, only allowed space for a heteronormative way of 'looking' and being for young men – as a collective and publicly shared construct. A situation like this requires the ethnographer, regardless of whether they share the same sexual desires or not, to follow the social lives of their informants and adhere to their heteronormative way of looking at the world and of acting in order to remain a participant-observer within their fieldsite.

Within heteronormative societies, there are also important communities that are not heteronormative and could include various gay or lesbian families or spaces, as well as social worlds of transgendered persons or intersex persons. In most heteropatriarchal societies, such social worlds are given a marginalised position even in the most 'economically developed' societies; in the worst-case scenario they are totally rejected or criminalised. Hence, depending on the context, when conducting research with informants who are heavily stigmatised in their communities due to their sexuality or sexual practices, the researcher should be prepared to face stigma by association. It is possible that people in the community who might not know the researcher's objective may start attributing to them the same 'reproachable' behaviours of their research participants. For example, a female ethnographer working with female sex workers in a social context where there is hostility to sex work might experience negative social reactions through association. This can be difficult for the researcher to deal with emotionally, but when conducting research with marginalised populations it is to some extent unavoidable. To mitigate this, it is important to clarify one's role and objective in the community as widely as possible, while at the same time not alienating the marginalised young people one is seeking to reach and understand. Being stigmatised by research association with a particular group can have a detrimental impact on the wellbeing of a researcher, and the institutions and organisations commissioning the research should provide support for researchers who may find themselves in such situations. This brings us on to looking at the ethnographer's sexuality too.

Sexuality of researcher

This vignette has several important themes around the sexuality of the ethnographer which need unpacking too. While out roaming around in Delhi doing fieldwork with young men, I often found myself being pulled by the shoulders or by my T-shirt, without warning, and being made to physically turn my body to look at a woman passing by. As this demonstrates, among the young men I was spending time with there was an assumption that their heterosexuality was shared with me and their normalised heterosexual way of 'looking' and being a young man was similar to my own.

Likewise, the experiences of queer ethnographers also have various dimensions within their fieldsites. In the case of the vignette above, my sexuality was something I could not personally discuss with my informants. Most of my informants, who only enjoyed sexual contact with women, were embedded deeply within heteronormative cultures which depended on homophobia to define itself. The source of what I could say and what I could not say became an interesting point of analysis within my work and thinking around how sexuality structures ethnographers' experiences while carrying out ethnography.

I was constantly afraid of the way I was standing, my voice, the way my hands were moving or what the expression on my face was and how my eyes were scanning the scene; at all points I was afraid of being 'caught'. It was only in the intimacy of being with one informant at a time that I really ever felt completely at ease with my informants. The group homosocial dynamic, in particular, I felt required me to be careful and alert. At the same time, young men confessed to me their close bonds with other men but these were always through the language of 'bhai' and 'yaar'. However, in a 'gay park' I did meet informants who enjoyed having sex with men; with them I could be more open about my homosexuality which meant that I was closer to them in a way I could not be with the other informants.

I perceive my own masculinity to be subordinate within the dominant ways of being a man in India because my sexuality is hidden, illegal and deemed as being subversive. I understand the benefits of making my sexuality public because it will allow me to build open and honest relationships with my informants which are crucial for ethnographic research. However, there may also be a strong negative backlash as a result of being an openly gay ethnographer in the field, as experienced by other queer researchers (Krishnan, 2014).

For female ethnographers a similar complex and gendered dynamic operates in negotiating their sexualities in the field. Several female ethnographers explain the unwanted advances made on them by male participants or other men in the field on the assumption that they are not just heterosexual but also 'free' and hence approachable (see McDowell, 2011, for a discussion). These unwanted advances can have profoundly negative effects on the wellbeing of the researcher and jeopardises their relationship to the field, their safety and their personal sense of dignity. Several female colleagues have explained to me how they would 'pretend to be married' in heterosexual marriages to deter men or unwanted advances from people in the field. However, for lesbian or trans persons doing ethnography this is further complicated by the heteronormative social ordering which marginalises their sexuality and sense of self.

Having grown up in India and attended an all-boys' school I have trained myself to be reflexive and aware of my embodied masculine performance; I have become adept at 'passing as straight' when required. Likewise, women and trans persons too have to think about strategies that they would be comfortable in applying and using when faced with unwanted attention or the practicalities of gaining access without having to divulge personal details that they are not comfortable sharing. For women who are anti patriarchal marriage, or trans persons who seek not to assimilate, or non-conforming ethnographers more broadly negotiating a highly heteropatriarchal field it is not an easy experience and can have safety risks attached. However, what is also important to remember is that these points of friction between the researcher and their fieldsite are also generative experiences which have strong analytical value. In my case, for example, given the experiences outlined in the vignette, I found that my sexuality not only allowed me to be critical and aware of the forces that shape 'appropriate' male behaviour, but also helped develop a sensitive and empathetic approach to understanding young men's realities and the functioning of heteropatriarchy in and through men's bodies and their social worlds. An alternative situation that I also envisage is that my informants will feel more open to discuss 'hidden' issues around sex and gendered relations due to my perceived 'sexual deviance'. Given that I hope to form meaningful bonds with my informants, I expect that I may be able to negotiate when and how I make my positionality explicit.

Finally, creating any ethnographic knowledge requires empathy and understanding (Mills and Morton, 2013). This is particularly true when trying to study people in the context of gendered and sexual relationships that surround their social worlds. This task will often require questioning several things that are taken for granted and also being patient around discussions that I might politically and personally disagree with. Nonetheless, it is the task of the ethnographer, particularly when studying groups like heterosexual men who are presumed to be powerful and privileged, to not demonise them but rather create empathic knowledge about the expectations, pressures and vulnerabilities they might be experiencing. Likewise it is also the duty of the ethnographer to fully account for the vulnerability and challenges faced by sexual minorities within a heteropatriarchal context, as well as being aware of the researcher's own positionality of privilege or vulnerability with regards to their sexuality. These points bring us to explore the broader sexual politics of the field itself.

Sexual politics of the field

As we see in the vignette, Raj and Aditya's sexuality and their relationship with their own bodies and the bodies of other men are different to how they react to women and their bodies. In the vignette, for example, we see the male informants sexualising the bodies of young women and calling them 'maal' or sexual goods. Yet at the same time the bodies of other men are seen as non-sexual and can be touched or held without any sexual connotations for them. In this setting, as a homosexual ethnographer, I may view their touching of my body as a sexual act; however, for them it is an act that is not necessarily sexual and is often performed from a position of a heterosexual brotherhood. But the sexual politics of any field operate in many different directions and through different bodies, so cannot be classed as fixed or made static as queer theorists have long argued (Puar, 2018). Hence it is important to keep in mind the messy and often complex flows of sexual politics and desire within any given ethnographic field and how they might operate in intersecting and contradictory ways.

In ethnographies where older women have studied younger men, for example, the older female ethnographer is not classed as a sexually active woman and hence approached very differently through ideas of maternal bonding (McDowell, 2011). However, a younger female ethnographer working with older men may not similarly be approached through a paternal bond and could be more easily sexualised by participants. Hence the sexual politics of any field, much like an intersectional approach to gender, also requires the ethnographer to understand the multidirectional flow of sexual desires and values in any given context. In and through understanding some of these sexual politics, an ethnographer can come to a much richer and more nuanced understanding of the field itself.

As feminist human geographer Doreen Massey (1994) explains, the very fact that someone feels 'out of place' or they are deemed as being 'out of place' by others in a social context hints to how such a 'place' is socially constructed and who is within it and who is outside. Applying this idea to sexuality, we can think about which sexualities are welcomed in which spaces and which sexualities are made to feel 'out of place' or unwelcome. Often, in a heterosexual context where heterosexuality is normalised or is normative, other sexualities are 'minorities' and are often marginalised. In such contexts the sexual dynamics of the field shape how sexualities are performed, policed and practised. However, at the same time these practices of social spaces and their sexual politics are not fixed and are constantly being negotiated in any fieldsite for any researcher.

Likewise, a colleague who works on female sexualities in her fieldsite of a girls' college hostel found that young women would often want to engage in sexual encounters with other women, but would have to 'distance' themselves from being branded a lesbian and hence would joke about such sex and try to assert their heterosexuality while clandestinely engaging in sex with women (Krishnan, 2014). In such cases, for me, the role of the ethnographer is not to establish a truth or a true sexual identity for their participants; the analytical value lies in understanding why and how sexual politics in a particular field operate and what this might tell us about the fieldsite itself.

For LGBTQ+ ethnographers going into various contexts, a similar playing with the sexual politics within their field becomes a strategy for safety and for maintaining a liminal position and identity without compromising their sexual orientation or identity. For example, for lesbian female researchers faced with the question of 'marriage' in their field playing with sexual politics might mean suggesting that the researcher is 'not married yet'; this would allow for a possibility which can be imagined in various ways by the participants but also allows the researcher to not lie or provide false information. In my experience the idea of 'not married yet' was a useful way in which, as a young queer male researcher, I could critically unpack the assumptions and values placed on young men like myself, but also allow space for their moral and social imaginaries to operate in a unspecified future, while also maintaining my own sexual politics. As a strategy I felt comfortable and safe in negotiating the sometimes violent heteronormative society of India by actively engaging and playing with the broader sexual dynamics of the field.

Conclusion

In this chapter I have demonstrated how the politics of sexuality have a profound impact for ethnographers in the field, as well as the ethnographies they produce. I have argued that the sexuality of the participants, the researcher and the broader sexual politics of the field have important consequences for ethnographers doing ground-level research in any social context. Sexuality, as I have demonstrated, draws in the researcher, the lives of participants and the broader social setting of a fieldsite in very complex yet profound ways. Not being aware or sensitive to these dynamics can render the ethnographer vulnerable in the field but could also have a strong negative impact on the analysis and data that is gathered. The chapter has tried to demonstrate that being aware of the important role of sexuality in the field can allow the ethnographer to carry out safe and sensitive research, as well as form better and more honest relationships with participants.

Recommendations

1 **Do not take a judgemental or moral approach towards sexual and gendered lives of participants** – approach them analytically and critically to understand their logics.
2 **Remember that all participants, old and young (including the researcher) are sexual beings who create and shape their sexual and social fields.**
3 **Be aware of 'sexuality' and its various manifestations rather than assuming heterosexuality as the norm** – look at the cracks and processes of heterosexuality
4 **Do not assume 'homosexuality' looks the same everywhere; be aware of the different forms bodies and sexualities can take** – for example, gay marriage or 'straight' married men engaging in sex with other men.
5 **Study the dating, courting and sexual politics of the group of people and context you are going to be observing, regardless of the subject of your enquiry.** Having or not having sex or performing sexual acts does not equate to sexuality – all human bodies are sexual, social beings.

Further reading

Abu-Lughod, L. 2016. *Veiled Sentiments: Honor and Poetry in a Bedouin Society.* Berkeley: University of California Press.
Ethnography which shows tensions of being a woman researcher and accessing the field and its sexual and gendered politics.

McDowell, L. 1999. Gender, Identity and Place: Understanding Feminist Geographies. Cambridge: Polity.
A UK-based ethnographer who highlights the role of bodies, identities, spaces, time and gender all interplaying.

Menon, N. 2012. *Seeing Like a Feminist.* New Delhi: Zubaan, with Penguin.
An easy-to-read feminist guide to see sexuality, gender and bodies in various contexts and social settings.

References

Foucault, M. 1990. *The History of Sexuality*. Harmondsworth: Penguin.
Krishnan, S. 2014. *Dispatches from a 'Rogue' Ethnographer: Exploring Homophobia and Queer Visibility in the Field*. Available at www.anthro.ox.ac.uk/sites/default/files/anthro/documents/media/jaso7_1_2015_64_79.pdf (accessed 2 October 2023).
Massey, D. 1994. *Space, Place and Gender*. London: Polity.
McDowell, L. 2011. *Redundant Masculinities? Employment Change and White Working Class Youth*. Chichester: John Wiley.
Mills, D. and Morton, M. 2013. *Ethnography in Education*. David Mills, Missy Morton: London: Sage.
Osella, C. and Osella, F. 2006. *Men and Masculinities in South India*. London: Anthem.
Philip, S. 2017. Caught in-between: Social developments and young men in urban India. *Journal of Gender Studies*, 27(3).
Puar, J.K. 2018. *Terrorist Assemblages: Homonationalism in Queer Times*. Durham, NC: Duke University Press.
Srivastava, S. 2007. *Passionate Modernity: Sexuality, Class and Consumption in India*. New Delhi: Routledge.
Trivedi, I. 2014. *India in Love*. Delhi: Aleph.

PART 3

WORKING WITH INTERLOCUTORS

8

BETRAYING LOYALTY: MANAGING DIS/TRUST AS ETHICAL FEMINIST PRAXIS

Hareem Khan

Summary

Drawing from ethnographic explorations of fieldwork, homework and feminist and critical praxis, this chapter explores how relationships enacting trust as well as distrust are configured through women's demonstrations of establishing boundaries and confronting power. This chapter incorporates 22 months of ethnographic fieldwork in the ethnic beauty industry in Southern California to highlight the ways trust and distrust are mediated by the raced, gendered, classed and religious identities of those involved in ethnographic contexts and the ways academic institutions can do more to prepare researchers for managing these experiences with a feminist compassion grounded in ethics.

Table of contents

Introduction 105
Blurring boundaries: Navigating familiarity and betrayal during fieldwork 106
Familiarity, friendship and trust 108
Suspicion, betrayal and distrust 109
Understanding power in relationships 110
Methodological insights: Reconfiguring relationships in and out of the field 110
Observing relationships in the field 111
Interview challenges and reconciling conflicting narratives 112
Conclusion 114
Recommendations 115
Further reading 116
References 116

Introduction

What does it mean when relationships shift, as in, when they flow from one state of being to another or occupy multiple states simultaneously? How do ethnographers, who have the privilege of 'entering' and 'leaving' the field, remember and consequently write about the fluid trajectories of these relationships in ways that challenge their perception of how friendships are formed, sustained, ruptured or rendered impossible during research? Ethnographic methodology is not immune to reflexive critique from within and outside the social sciences when it comes to such relationships. However, I am moved by the continued influence of relationships on our own development as ethical and feminist ethnographers in the context of research inherently laden with its own power differentials.

My research is situated in the South Asian beauty and wellness industries in Southern California. I have been employed and carried out research in beauty salons and supply stores that cater largely to South Asian diasporas in the United States. These are predominantly diasporic women's spaces that in many ways I grew out of and my career trajectory compelled me to grow back *into*. I became more curious about the ways women who participate in this ethnic industry negotiate their racialised subjectivities as the service sector continues to expand to reach a more multiracial and multiethnic clientele. These curiosities eventually shaped the directions of my fieldwork methodologies. They raised questions around what it means to conduct research grounded in a feminist and ethical praxis in a context I was familiar with through my shared identities with many of my research participants.

Questions concerning the possibilities and limitations of feminist ethnography have existed since the inception of feminist ethnographic pursuits that resulted from a crisis in anthropology as well as in feminism (Abu-Lughod, 1990; Haraway, 1988; Stacey, 1988). This has received close attention as the 'third world woman' became a subject (and object) of ethnographic writing and in the context of writing *about* ethnographic writing. Historically, Western feminism has homogenised third world women's – and I would add diasporic women's – experiences, extracting them from their material, historical and cultural contexts and, thereby, creating the singular 'third world woman' (Mohanty, 1984). As a result, not only are third world women often transformed into one singular subject during the course of fieldwork, but they are, at times, represented as all equally oppressed, subjugated and victimised. These ideas have emerged throughout ethnographic writing and have compelled many ethnographers to speak out about the way we do our methods and who we do them for. Ultimately, it also becomes a question of how we write. Carole McGranahan explains, 'When we read an ethnography, we expect to meet people, not just categories of them' (2020, p. 6). This often becomes a challenge when doing ethnography because one is expected to dismantle these homogenising categories, but at the same time one must acknowledge their existence. As some of you can relate, it is the stories emerging from ethnographies that can be moving, transformative and provocative. However, I would like to focus on the relationships that allow for such stories to be told and raise questions about the blurry boundaries that often structure these relationships.

Ethnography calls into question the fragility of relationships in the field, their ever-present potential to rupture and the ways academic institutions prepare (or, rather, don't prepare) us for these experiences. The subtext of 'fragility' here is *trust,* and I am curious about how trust and loyalty (and, consequently, betrayal and distrust) are inextricable from how relationships are built, understood and, ultimately, written about in the social sciences. Drawing from ethnographic explorations of fieldwork, homework and feminist and critical praxis, this chapter addresses how friendships built around trust and distrust are actually configured through women's demonstrations of establishing boundaries. Specifically, in this chapter, I incorporate 22 months of ethnographic fieldwork to illustrate how migrant women from South Asia manage and navigate these mechanisms of betrayal and loyalty, drawing this analysis from earlier works of feminist ethnography.

I end with some thoughts on the production of reflexivity in our writing that often only allows our processing to commence once we have 'returned' from the field. How does this distance morph our understandings of betrayal during research and what limitations does this distance pose for new as well as seasoned ethnographers? Additionally, I offer some thoughts on what institutional support can look like when it is integrated with the day-to-day of fieldwork. The insights gathered here are to support you as you consider the ways you navigate your own relationships with the people you meet during fieldwork.

Blurring boundaries: Navigating familiarity and betrayal during fieldwork

The boundaries structuring relationships in the field are often very fluid. They change form throughout daily interactions, as well as due to shifts in the political, social and economic contexts in which research is being done. To illustrate this, I'll draw from my own experience visiting ethnic beauty supply stores, salons and training institutes where services, including threading hair removal and henna, were taught.[1] Most of the women I met and interviewed were South Asian migrants, predominantly from Nepal, Pakistan and India. Among this group, I was usually read as a South Asian woman myself (and eventually Muslim once people learned my name or when they noticed that I observed Muslim holidays and religious traditions). This visibility in the form of familiarity served as a catalyst *and* a liability in the course of building relationships in the field. While sometimes these relationships were built on intimacy through our shared identities as South Asian women, these identities also limited my agency as a qualified researcher by positioning me as a fictive daughter, resulting in my sense of obligation around following particular social and behavioural codes. My desire to be liked by everyone and be taken seriously as a researcher, at times, made me oblivious to the racial, gendered and classed dynamics that structured these relationships.

By openly identifying as a first-generation South Asian American Muslim woman of Indian and Pakistani descent, I was situated both within and apart from the industry where I worked and carried out research. Scholarship on critical ethnography points to the importance of being cognisant of these positions as they relate to the research site and our research participants (Behar, 1997; Bhavnani et al., 2014; Haraway, 1988; Marcus, 1995; Rosaldo, 1993). My positionality constituted dilemmas in the field where the comforts and frustrations of home were projected onto my fieldsites, forcing me to come to terms with my position as simultaneously 'researcher' and 'daughter'. Depending on the context, I was read as belonging to or outside the boundaries of 'community' established by the individuals I met during research.[2] These blurring and re-forming boundaries of 'home' and the 'field' shaped my opportunities to do ethnography in profound ways (Bhatia, 2007; Gupta and Ferguson, 1997; Visweswaran, 1994). At the same time I was an ethnographer, I was also a friend, legal advisor, mediator, daughter, researcher met with suspicion and researcher met with warmth, at some points embodying many of these positions simultaneously.

Figuring out how to work through blurring and re-forming boundaries is a central tenet of ethnographic fieldwork. For me, this duality between 'ethnographer' and 'daughter' shaped my access to fieldsites and research participants significantly. In her important piece 'Situating locations' (1996), Jayati Lal ponders the division of 'Self' and 'Other' that un/fortunately is part and parcel of ethnographic research and argues that as researchers we 'occupy multiple and fluid locations' (p. 186). In my case, several business owners as well as workers in the industry positioned me as 'daughter' or 'friend', yet with some distrust due to my classed position as an academic. This did not altogether extinguish the possibility of other forms of relationships emerging, a realisation I came to much later. Additionally, there were certain assumptions I made concerning access due to my shared identity as South Asian, Muslim and a woman that were challenged by the women in the beauty sector. While opening up some doors, these identities also worked to inhibit my navigation of the beauty and wellness industries because they pointed to the ways I was separate and distinct from beauty industry workers. In the following two sections, I highlight the ways both trust and distrust emerged during my fieldwork.

Familiarity, friendship and trust

Beauty salon labour is deeply physical and emotional. It requires one to stand for at least eight hours a day and engage actively with customers, which can be non-stop during busy shifts. The latter form of beauty labour is 'emotional labour', a term coined by sociologist Arlie Hochschild in her 1983 book *The Managed Heart*. It refers to the management of feelings that has become part and parcel of many of the occupations making up the service industry. In the context of my employment at various salons, I found that the most arduous aspects of the work included managing a customer's dissatisfaction with their service, handling disputes between workers and performing enthusiasm in helping customers in order to sell cosmetics. It was a challenge for me to perform sincerity in a relationship that I had largely come to see through my pre-fieldwork research and personal experiences as transactional. However, over time, I started to question that presumption and built meaningful relationships with regular customers as well as the other employees and business owners in the salon. Friendships were made possible and strengthened with continued contact over the duration of my fieldwork even while the forces of capitalism buttressed these interactions.

Hochschild made it clear that emotional labour constituted relationships within the context of work. As I continued to carry out this type of labour in the salons, outside the salon space relationships resulted that in some ways transcended the realm of labour. For example, I carried out a significant portion of my fieldwork and interviews during the month of Ramadan in 2015 and 2016.[3] As an observing Muslim, I was fasting during the hours I was also doing ethnographic work. I was formally and informally employed across three salons in Southern California and the days I had to fulfil my front desk duties while fasting were definitely the most taxing. At first, on the one hand, I remembered thinking how Ramadan could negatively interfere with my access to fieldsites and informal spaces where my research participants had more candid conversations. For example, I often felt like I was missing out on invitations to lunches, dinners and social events during the evening, which was when I had to be home to break fast with my family or attend a prayer or event at the mosque. On the other hand, my Muslim identity also had the impact of facilitating conversations between other Muslim business owners and workers who confided in me about the ways their visibly religious identities marked them as peripheral members of a heterogeneous South Asian community. I worked at one salon that was owned by a Pakistani Muslim woman named Tasneem and we developed a deeper bond during Ramadan while we both fasted and talked about Muslim identity as it played out in the beauty industry. These insights were instrumental in pushing me to think about race, identity and power in ways that my original research questions had not and that my pre-fieldwork coursework did not prepare me for.

Throughout my fieldwork, I was fortunate to have generally positive relationships with most of the employees and business owners I met. Sometimes we would get together for a quick grocery story run or pick up some coffee or just idle near our cars in the parking lot chatting. These moments made me forget that I was even doing fieldwork at times, which was *not* fieldwork done right; it was actually fieldwork done naively. This is not to say that friendship is impossible while doing ethnography but, rather, it is a reminder to question how we perceive friendship in the midst of other conflicting emotions that also occur during fieldwork, including betrayal, distrust and suspicion. More succinctly, what forms of power reveal themselves within friendships in the field, especially when things start to go awry? This question will be explored next.

Suspicion, betrayal and distrust

Tasneem, mentioned earlier, co-owned two beauty salons with her husband, which offered a range of services from threading hair removal to bridal make-up. I used to visit one of her salons during slower afternoon hours and would sit with her and the other workers while they shared their experiences, often lamenting about the increasing competition and heavy deflation of beauty service prices. This economic climate made it difficult to stay afloat in the market despite the increasing popularity of services associated with ethnic Otherness. Tasneem eventually invited me to 'intern' at one of her salons, an unpaid job managing the front desk and keeping a written record of services completed. During the first couple of months at one salon, I became close to two of the beauty technicians who were hired by Tasneem. Most of the time, it would be me and the two technicians onsite while Tasneem and her husband managed their other salon, 20 minutes away. We swapped stories, ate and shared snacks and, as we became closer, these two technicians started to share their experiences of working for Tasneem, which, at times, challenged the generous and sacrificial image she laid out for me as their employer.

Eventually, I became suspicious to Tasneem as I started to build a friendly rapport with her employees, potentially threatening the social order of the salon. She was evidently uncomfortable with the relationships I was forming at her site, so she moved me, without explanation, to the other salon where she spent most of her time, implying that I could maintain this position only under surveillance. After reacting to this situation with immense frustration and disappointment, I tried to configure these emotions into an understanding of how my dual position as 'researcher' and 'daughter' was bound with power and privilege that could be read as betrayal in a highly precarious and competitive market. These are not new reflections; navigating betrayal has been a part of carrying out fieldwork since its inception. Judith Stacey questioned whether betrayal was inherent to fieldwork methods, leading me to rethink not so much how to avoid betrayal, but render it inescapable and something to manage ethically and responsibly (1988). She writes, 'I find myself wondering whether the appearance of greater respect for and equality with research subjects in the ethnographic approach masks a deeper, more dangerous form of exploitation' (p. 22). She works through an experience of betrayal in her own fieldwork in Silicon Valley to understand that the role of the researcher is always that of someone who can *leave* the field, which is not the same privilege afforded to women who cannot leave.

While I did try to push back on Tasneem's decision, I ended up adjusting to my new role at this other salon where I was permanently relocated. I also did not want to put the first two technicians I met in a compromising position, so I stopped visiting the original site, lost touch with the other workers and was unable to interview them or meet with them outside their work hours. As I have shown, one relationship can change form throughout multiple interactions. My relationship with Tasneem started off with a familiarity and trust around our shared identities as Muslim women. That, however, shifted over time due to the closeness I formed with her employees, disrupting the class hierarchies of the salon. I bring these moments up to both address the fact that relationships can change during fieldwork and also to comment on the ways these relationships exhibit the nature of power in the field.

Understanding power in relationships

The tensions around trust and distrust were simultaneously mediated by the raced, gendered, classed and religious identities of all of us involved in ethnographic research. I was aware of the role of positionality in doing ethnographic work ethically; however, I still bought into the idea that my intentions being honest, inclusive and transparent was enough without acknowledging that it was the right of the research participants to analyse my position based on their own experiences and identities. Kamala Visweswaran (1994) argues that the ruptures in fieldwork relationships that enact feelings of betrayal are often based on the ethnographer's assumption that a 'universal sisterhood' exists between researchers and their participants. This framing immediately calls into question the patronising orientation ethnographers can have when it comes to collecting, listening to and writing about knowledge production. It also reveals how 'the process of knowing is itself determined by the relationship of knower to known' (p. 48). While *betrayal* best expressed the emotional dimensions of Visweswaran's relationship to the participants at her fieldsite, I am curious about what a deep critique of and confrontation with *trust and loyalty* can imply for the transformative potential of critical ethnography and feminist epistemology.

Some of my earlier emotions around feeling betrayed or feeling like I was untrustworthy eventually subsided, transforming into something more generative. I started to pay attention to the financial precarity of small business owners, which stirred a general climate of suspicion and competition in this niche market, further compounded by any researcher's presence. This precarity exposed the relationship as more nuanced, one that eliminated the need to point fingers. Tasneem and I still keep in touch, texting each other on birthdays or religious holidays. My relationship with her taught me that friendship is inherently entangled with axes of power, trust and distrust that leaves it susceptible to rupture. It took me time to accept that our friendship was not any less real because of this fragility and her suspicions. This dis/trust can and should be used as an analytic to situate power in the field as well as in knowledge production 'after' the field.

Methodological insights: Reconfiguring relationships in and out of the field

The expectation that ethnographers are going to be forming relationships with those they meet in the field is often centred in preparation for fieldwork. Another important layer to this is the fact that ethnographers will also be spending a significant amount of time *observing* relationships in the field with the added responsibility to record and write about these observations ethically. This raised serious methodological concerns for me during my research. While in the first section of this chapter, I explored the blurring boundaries of trust and distrust between researcher and research participants, this section takes as its central point the 'observation' and 'interview' and what an ethnographer may have to confront when they observe those blurring boundaries take and lose form between others in real time.

I will return to the beauty salon to illustrate the ways loyalty is the currency through which relationships are structured between workers and their clients and workers and their employers. I show how the observations I made between other participants in the beauty industry were not separate from the ways I was also entangled in these networks. I then reflect on the nature of conducting interviews in a context where one might receive conflicting narratives around loyalty and betrayal. In the preceding section of this chapter, betrayal was discussed more as a feeling, whereas here it emerges through a confrontation with the researcher's own loyalties. Whose story gets precedent when it comes to time to record them? Whose story ultimately gets included in the dissertation? How can the tensions surrounding loyalty and betrayal transcend the fieldsite and be exhibited through our writing? These questions will not be resolved in this section, but I will discuss how they revealed themselves through my fieldsite and interactions.

Observing relationships in the field

I focus on a threading salon that I visited regularly. Threading is a deeply intimate skill and catalyses feelings of loyalty between employee and client. The premise and promise of loyalty are created from the first encounter between these two individuals and depend on whether the client is satisfied by the service provided. Many other factors go into the rating of satisfaction, including the ability to perform the service well, provide customer service and appropriately exert the necessary emotional labour. These efforts communicate to clients that workers have experience and that they are willing to adhere to the client's needs.

One of the technicians I met at a threading salon in Southern California, Deepa, had been an employee at this location for almost two decades and was viewed by her employer as the most loyal employee the salon had ever hired. Deepa was a devoted grandmother and cosmetologist whose popularity became obvious within my first hour of observing her. People arrived in large groups of family and friends to get their eyebrows threaded solely by her. When I worked at the front desk, I would notice how many clients would come in requesting to be seated with Deepa, even though there were two other technicians on site who had no wait times. People ended up waiting over an hour for Deepa to work her skill onto their faces. Many times, when clients were not able to wait an hour or longer, they would ask Deepa about her next available shift and proceed to make a formal appointment with her.

'Loyalty' is a noun that is thrown around very loosely in the beauty business world. It is a subjective quality, invoking certain connotations of honesty, devotion and sacrifice as part and parcel of its conceptualisation. In the context of the South Asian beauty industry, loyalty is *earned* through client satisfaction. If clients are loyal to the artist, they are also loyal to the company and its brand, raking in more regular clients for the business. Employees in the industry define this loyalty as necessary for their livelihoods, as the more clients that request them, the more likely they are to tip due to the nature of the personal relationship. Conversely, these relationships could easily rupture if a technician fails to meet the expectations of the client.

I often recorded these patterns as they played out in daily interactions. I noticed how often a popular technician was getting requested by new and regular customers and I observed the ways they strengthened those relationships through banter, sharing of personal information and humour. I also observed the ruptures stemming out of customer disputes or employee frustrations. As a front desk receptionist at three salons, I was often drawn out of my role as observer into one as mediator. As a result, loyalty and betrayal were not just experiences I was observing but ones I was actively preserving, soothing, or managing. As much as we might be prepared for roles of participant and observer, I was not prepared for how to navigate these roles simultaneously. For example, tensions could occur between an employee who misunderstood a client request (due to English not being their native language), resulting in a hostile and racist reaction from a customer. Stepping in to manage this relationship while not severing ties with the customer raised ethical considerations for me. Specifically, if I am committed to anti-racism, shouldn't I have told that customer to leave and never come back? But what if the employee does not want to lose this client? How do my personal politics shape these interactions and how do I process them in my field notes later?

Reflecting on the ways I was entangled in these networks I was committed to recording and observing accurately helped me work through these recurring dilemmas. The trust and distrust with Tasneem and other business owners were connected to the ways employees and clients built relationships and the ways they relied on my role as a receptionist to manage these blurring boundaries that could easily slip into feelings of betrayal. Going back to Jayati Lal's provocation that we occupy fluid positions in the field, I show how this manifested through my role as participant observer and interviewer, the latter of which will be explored next.

Interview challenges and reconciling conflicting narratives

Semi-structured interviews were often where I processed the dynamics I observed in the salon. During these lengthy conversations, research participants would delve into the meanings of loyalty and betrayal, adding more nuance to the experiences I was otherwise just witnessing or managing. I learned that loyalty is couched as a potentially positive attribute of client/employee relationships; however, serious concerns are posed for businesses when one of their employees develops an extraordinarily committed and loyal client base. It morphs from an advantage for a business to a threat of its demise. Employees and business owners like Tasneem often used the English word 'loyal' to describe their employees' relationships to management and the business, which was also often interchanged with the language of 'appreciation'. Tasneem would often say, 'They don't appreciate', as a way to position 'they', in this case, her workers, as unappreciative of the opportunities Tasneem has been able to provide, with disloyalty being a marker of this under-appreciation.

This raised many methodological challenges for me during the course of fieldwork. I often collected conflicting narratives from workers and employers that made it difficult to situate these experiences into my larger writing project. For example, Tasneem described her relationship to her employees in the following way:

> I take them [employees] to the apprenticeship programme till they get the licence. They didn't even know how to talk sometimes, some people, but I helped them to get on their feet to, you know, to stand. Some people appreciate it, some people not. Some people cheat you, but you know, what can you do? That's my goal: to help some people. In future, also, I want to do that for my coming new generation. When I retire, at least I can teach.

Tasneem's insistence on giving back to her community through training is what gives the rhetoric of empowerment its form. She lamented that sometimes workers take advantage of this generosity by proving to be disloyal. Sometimes women left her salon to open up their own threading businesses within close distance of Tasneem's, taking their clients with them. Employees also commented on the heightened surveillance they experienced through the salon security cameras and the ways the employers tracked their relationships with customers, increasing the incentive to leave for opportunities with more autonomy. The importance of ethnography is that it can allow room for these conflicting narratives to reveal something bigger about the structural conditions under which people work. However, this reward doesn't always alleviate the challenges of writing about betrayal and conflict in a way that honours each individual experience.

These moments from the field help to think through the fluidity of ethnographic methodologies. In writing my dissertation, I grounded my observations of trust and distrust through my own experience as a formal and informal employee, acknowledging the ways I also inhabited these networks and the ways my own recordings of these events constituted what Donna Haraway refers to as 'partial perspectives' (1988). As feminist ethnographers who are committed to studying power and its differential impacts on the lives of migrant women of colour, betrayal is not simply a methodological hurdle to relationship-building, but also an analytic that can generate new possibilities for ethical praxis and ethnographic writing. In the next, and last, section, I reflect on the ways institutions can support ethnographers during fieldwork – specifically in the realm of managing the blurry boundaries of relationships as well as writing about them. While ethnographers are extensively trained theoretically in positionality, reflexivity and, in some cases, feminist ethnography, I will add some specific recommendations to the list that can support us in centring a feminist ethical practice in our daily research as well as our daily writing endeavours.

Conclusion

The central aim of this chapter was around navigating, observing, managing and recording the blurring boundaries of relationships as they exist in the field. Much of the material covered here is drawn from my own experiences as an ethnographer doing immersive qualitative research in what I have identified as the ethnic beauty industry. I began with an acknowledgement of the dual ways in which I was often perceived by my research participants. For example, due to my shared identity as a South Asian woman, who was often younger than the individuals I was meeting in the field, I was read as fictive daughter. While this worked to facilitate some relationships in the field, it also served as a liability when it conflicted with my being perceived as researcher/ethnographer. I draw from my experience with a small business owner, Tasneem, to reflect on these questions. This relationship brought out some of the tensions that form between loyalty and betrayal that coexist and have the possibility to nurture and generate new forms of thinking about relationships. Ultimately, for the ethnographer, this becomes an important moment to address the role of power in structuring our fieldwork and how to ethically approach these concerns as they play out in real time.

In the second section of this chapter, I looked specifically at two staple ethnographic methodologies: the observation and the interview. Participant observation is often incorporated into our pre-fieldwork training; however, I was not prepared for moments where these roles happen simultaneously. I reflected on what sorts of challenges are posed when one is not only observing relationships, but, in some cases, also managing them in ways that may or may not align with our own ethical position. In the case of interviews, I raise the question of what happens when we record and collect conflicting narratives from our interviewees. For example, in the case of my work, I was interviewing business owners who had a different reading of loyalty at their salons compared to their employees, who often read this loyalty through another lens. This is not a problem with an easy fix, however; I use this space to think through how I am also entangled in these networks of relationships even while I am observing and recording them.

The final section brings forth five recommendations that can better support ethnographers as they navigate the blurry boundaries of relationships in the field. Some of these require a shift in theoretical orientation and others require us to seek out institutional support and spaces where we can process these moments as they occur rather than after the fieldwork has already been conducted. Had I had access to these kinds of supportive spaces, I believe I would have managed some of my relationships with employees and business owners differently. One of the rewards of doing ethnography is that a lot of our research necessitates a comfort with fluidity and spontaneity. However, in this chapter I try to combine these rewards with the urgent questions of ethics and praxis that also emerge. Fluidity should not just be a romanticising characteristic of ethnography, but should be woven into how we think about the stakes of our work and the meaning of our work to our research participants. For me, these questions highlight the processes of racialisation that sustain the beauty industry, illustrating the ways migrant women and other women of colour working in this industry negotiate their relationships and what generative challenges these negotiations pose for ethical practice grounded in critical and feminist ethnography.

Recommendations

1 **Be critical of bureaucratic ethics.** We are trained to fill out Institutional Review Board applications, design detailed consent forms, often protecting the institution itself rather than research participants. This framing of fieldwork cannot account for the fluidity of relationships and the ways they change. Think about ethnographic ethics in ways that transcend the institutional language of ethical conduct. What does ethical practice mean to your research participants rather than to the academic institution?
2 **Participate in and organise workshops that disrupt the stages of fieldwork.** Workshops focused on relationships would allow us to reflect on the trajectory of relationships in the present as opposed to retroactively processing their development once we have 'returned'. Themes could include relationship-building and the sustaining and rupturing of those relationships; confronting power; and encountering our raced, classed and gendered selves within these matrices. Ideally, the readings, themes and discussions would function fluidly to reflect the changing needs and concerns of the participants and remain loosely structured as a means of support.
3 **Keep a positionality journal.** Fieldwork can tend to get categorised into 'types' of fieldwork, including participant observation, surveys, semi-structured interviews and so on. Much of what we actually experience in the field may not fit into any of these categories. Keep a separate writing space solely for recording and observing these emotions and their impacts on shifting understandings of positionality.
4 **Do homework beyond anthropology.** Consider what 'homework' looks like in various fields and identify the types of support structures or spaces that might be helpful during research. Additionally, the navigation of our raced, gendered and classed selves must be centred in our training, drawing from feminist ethnography, Black and Indigenous anthropology, and critical ethnography.
5 **Write for all.** Catering for an audience that is not solely academic and comprised of a spectrum of individuals interested in these topics (including our own research participants) will strengthen your project and allow you to continue building a critical eye towards academic institutions. If you are unable to find critical digital sites where you can get your work peer-reviewed, I encourage ethnographers to curate a public-facing written or visual blog (perhaps using Instagram) where the themes that are important in your research can surface through various modalities. This critical eye can be used to bolster our current programmes and departments and better train and support students.

Notes

1 Threading is a hair removal technique that involves the friction of intertwined cotton threads across the face, which pulls out fine hair from the roots. Henna refers to a skill that uses a plant-based paste to draw intricate designs and patterns on the body and hands. Both skills are often marketed in the US as originating from South Asia.

2 For more explorations of the insider/outsider dynamic in the realm of ethnographic fieldwork, see Shukla, 2003, and Young, 2004.
3 Ramadan is a holy month for observing Muslims during which it is believed that parts of the Q'uran were first revealed to Prophet Muhammad. During this month, Muslims fast, pray, give charity, build community and reflect to commemorate the spiritual significance of this month.

Further reading

Bolles, L. 2013. Telling the story straight: Black feminist intellectual thought in anthropology. *Transforming Anthropology*, 21(1), 57–71.
This important article traces the contributions of Black feminist thought within cultural anthropology and provides crucial theoretical and methodological insights that all ethnographers who are committed to feminist and anti-racist work should consider.

Lal, J. 1996. Situating locations: The politics of self, identity, and 'other' in living and writing the text. In Wolf, D.L. (Ed.), *Feminist Dilemmas in Fieldwork*. Boulder, CO: Westview Press, 185–214.
Jayati Lal compels us to think about positionality in the field and to intentionally locate our 'self' in relation to the 'other' and it is important reading in the field of feminist ethnography.

McGranahan, C. (Ed.) 2020. *Writing Anthropology: Essays on Craft and Commitment*. Durham, NC: Duke University Press.
This edited volume offers many short essays reflecting on the nature of ethnographic writing across moments, disciplines, writing styles and theoretical orientations. It pushes the boundaries of conventional ethnography by raising important questions around identity, systemic violence, urgency, race, experimental writing and much more.

Visweswaran, K. 1994. *Fictions of Feminist Ethnography*. Minneapolis: University of Minnesota Press.
This text is transformative in thinking about the possibilities (and impossibilities) of carrying out feminist ethnography ethically. It raises questions about the role of power in relationships formed between a woman ethnographer and her research participants through an understanding of race, class, gender, sexuality and status.

References

Abu-Lughod, L. 1990. Can there be a feminist ethnography? *Women and Performance: A Journal of Feminist Theory*, 5(1), 7–27.
Behar, R. 1997. *The Vulnerable Observer: Anthropology that Breaks Your Heart*. New York: Beacon.
Bhatia, S. 2007. *American Karma: Race, Culture, and Identity in the Indian Diaspora*. New York: New York University Press.
Bhavnani, K.-K., Chua, P. and Collins, D. 2014. Critical approaches to qualitative research. In *The Oxford Handbook on Qualitative Methods*. Oxford: Oxford University Press, 165–178.

Bolles, L. 2013. Telling the story straight: Black feminist intellectual thought in anthropology. *Transforming Anthropology*, 21(1), 57–71.

Gupta, A. and Ferguson, J. 1997. *Culture, Power, Place: Explorations in Critical Anthropology*. Durham, NC: Duke University Press.

Haraway, D. 1988. Situated knowledges: The science question in feminism and the privilege of partial perspective. *Feminist Studies*, 14(3), 575–99.

Hochschild, A. 1983. *The Managed Heart: Commercialization of Human Feeling*. Berkeley: University of California Press.

Lal, J. 1996. Situating locations: The politics of self, identity, and 'other' in living and writing the text. In Wolf, D.L. (Ed.), *Feminist Dilemmas in Fieldwork*. Boulder, CO: Westview Press, 185–214.

Marcus, G.E. 1995. Ethnography in/of the world system: The emergence of multi-sited ethnography. *Annual Review of Anthropology*, 24, 95–117.

McGranahan, C. (Ed.) 2020. *Writing Anthropology: Essays on Craft and Commitment*. Durham, NC: Duke University Press.

Mohanty, C. T. 1984. Under Western Eyes: Feminist Scholarship and Colonial Discourses. *Boundary 2*, 12/13, 333–58. doi:10.2307/302821

Rosaldo, R. 1993. *Culture and Truth: The Remaking of Social Analysis*. Boston, MA: Beacon.

Shukla, S.R. 2003. *India Abroad: Diasporic Cultures of Postwar America and England*. Princeton, NJ: Princeton University Press.

Stacey, J. 1988. Can there be a feminist ethnography? *Women's Studies International Forum*, 11(1), 21–7.

Visweswaran, K. 1994. *Fictions of Feminist Ethnography*. Minneapolis: University of Minnesota Press.

Young, A. 2004. Experiences in ethnographic interviewing about race: The inside and outside of it. In Bulmer, M., and Solomos, J. (Eds.), *Researching Race and Racism*. Routledge, 199–214.

9

SOCIAL MEDIA AS METHOD

Branwen Spector and Theodora Sutton

Summary

Ethnographic research is increasingly entangled with the internet and social media, used both by the researcher as a method and by one's interlocutors. Yet literature on this subject rarely reflects the practical and affective experiences of the researcher, and offers limited guidance on conducting quality research while prioritising the safety and mental health of the researcher.

This chapter discusses the co-authors' experiences working with online communities both on- and offline. While acknowledging that this fast-changing field can often result in data and method becoming quickly outdated, this chapter provides suggestions and strategies for using the internet before, during and after fieldwork. Importantly, it includes advice on managing online and offline relationships with interlocutors, negotiating access, consent and boundary creation – all relatively new subjects in this field and necessary for both interlocutor and researcher's interests and safety.

Table of contents

Introduction	119
Pre-field research	121
While you're in the field	124
Intimacy and boundaries	127

Post-field research 129
Conclusion 130
Recommendations 131
Further reading 132
References 133

Introduction

Ethnographic research requires engaging with participants to gain a deep understanding of their culture. These days, this includes the online social landscape, be it through social media, Google Maps, or even email inboxes. These virtual spaces form layers of social environments that are inextricably linked to the physical world, without which we are left with an incomplete picture of the field.

Social media provide valuable resources and networks for researchers conducting their work on- and offline, but they also inspire new methodological questions and raise complex ethical and methodological concerns, particularly around protecting oneself and one's research participants. In our experience as digital ethnographers, the university's emphasis often fell on protecting interlocutors while we and our peers frequently felt vulnerable in this new digitally mediated landscape. How do digital methods reimagine the power dynamics between anthropologist and participant? How do we surf this new wave of challenges, retain our sanity and deliver our research?

In this chapter, we will answer the questions we struggled with while conducting our own research online. On the one hand, digital technology allowed both Spector and Sutton to conduct research across geophysical distance and dangers and risks in their fieldsite, helping them to mediate their exposure to physical and psychological harm. On the other, conducting research online also opens up new issues and risks, including overexposure, difficulties managing boundaries and managing ethical implications. This chapter will unpack what it currently means to use social media as a research method, and provide an inclusive framework for starting your own ethnography online.

Going digital

Spector conducted research among both Palestinian refugees and Israeli settlers in the Occupied Palestinian West Bank, using Facebook, WhatsApp and experimenting with online dating platforms such as Tinder to explore the means by which these platforms are integrated into everyday security and mobility practices, as well as finding them useful as tools for conducting research in hostile fieldwork environments.

Her research never intended to focus explicitly on social media, but during her time in the field she noticed how people integrated social media into their daily lives to navigate the violence of life under occupation. Different social media platforms were used to conjure material relations and understandings of material space from the immaterial platforms to find ways to move safely around the physical space of a region with strict but fluctuating controls on mobility. As such, she was a researcher simultaneously studying the use of social media, using it as part of her methodology and relying on it for her own safety.

Sutton studied a community in the San Francisco Bay area who annually attended a New Age, 'digital detox' retreat. Her fieldwork ostensibly focused on non-users, yet online life became a large dimension of her ethnography once detoxers returned home and congregated on a 'secret' Facebook group. Gaining access to this group, and adding her participants on Facebook, Instagram, Snapchat and Twitter with her own personal accounts, helped her to understand detoxers' focus on spiritual self-improvement and desire to get ahead in life. Yet at the same time there were methodological drawbacks; and using personal profiles to connect with participants only served to exacerbate the confusion regarding the nature of Sutton's relationship with them.

Using our own experience as early career researchers, we respond to gaps and tensions in the literature on digital ethnographic methodologies around consent, safety, privacy and access for both research participants and researchers. We describe our own challenges, with a particular focus on the novel method of using one's own social media as a research tool. We also note the highly localised nature of social media and discuss the opportunities that digital platforms offer in revealing localised cultural layers, gaining access and aiding in managing the emotional difficulties of fieldwork.

On- and offline

As anthropologists now living in a digital world, there will almost always be a digital dimension to our fieldsite. We view this as an opportunity to learn even more about our interlocutors and to watch human nature play out in new and revealing ways. There has historically been a tendency to view offline and online as two separate worlds, with the actual world as more authentic and the online as a pale imitation. However, digital anthropologists emphasise that the online realm is not separate or elsewhere, nor is it less authentic or 'real'. Instead, it is mapped onto our actual-world experiences; as we have seen in recent years, politics, art, lifecycle events, economic activity, sex, all take place *both* on- and offline.

Taking this approach allowed Spector to understand how 'places' were manifested online through social media by their residential communities; how refugee camps used Facebook pages to connect with diasporic refugee communities by reporting on the goings on of the camps online; how gated communities also used Facebook pages as message boards and boundary markers for residences; and how surveillance at state and community level played into these relations. This allowed her to develop an understanding of the role of social media in navigating space and representing communities at both local and global levels while being mindful of her relation to social media users as an outsider.

Although Sutton's interlocutors attended a digital detox, technology was still part of their everyday lives once they returned home, where they added the people they had met in the woods on Facebook, Instagram and Snapchat. The San Francisco Bay area is home to many tech giants; the area was perceived by her informants as the cutting edge of technological invention. It was this very digital ubiquity which her interlocutors had grown tired of, and they wanted to seek out what was, in their vocabulary, the opposite: off-grid camping in a forest. Yet the internet was a necessary part of their ordinary lives. After the offline retreat, social networks became an extension of Sutton's fieldwork, without which she would not have been able to see sides of her participants that were vital for her findings. In the woods, she saw people without make-up, playing games and crying in group therapy exercises, but online, she saw the ways they extolled the virtues of therapeutic techniques and garnered hundreds of likes for polished photographs of themselves. Through situating their use and non-use within the context of their lives, she learned more about her interlocutors' personalities and views, as well as how they imagined the role of technology in society.

Pre-field research

Asking the right questions

The age-old saying goes that 'on the internet, nobody knows you're a dog'. If communicating only online, there is no real way to validate or determine the authenticity of one's research participants; they could feasibly lie about who they are or how they look. Context is vital to understand who is talking and why. When using both on- and offline methods, it can be easier to put online behaviour in context and understand what role the online behaviour plays in their lives more generally.

Take time to reflect on your approach, and why the specific platforms you plan to use are the most appropriate for your topic of study. If your participants already use a specific digital tool, it may likely be the best one for you to research them with; if participants would be more comfortable talking to you from their own home, a video call may encourage them to answer at greater length and in more detail. Your priority should be to put your participants at ease and to understand their perspective. Online communication with participants, particularly those that are anonymous, could be more honest and responses might be more reflective. Remote research can increase opportunities to participate, especially for people with physical disabilities (Bowker and Tuffin, 2004) or those with caring duties (Chapter 5, this volume).

Technological choices not only shape your access and richness, but also the kind of arguments you can make with the data you gather. Data gathered online can be qualitatively different, and this will affect the types of research questions you can ask at the start of your project. It is important to consider the kinds of questions that you are asking and whether they are suited to online research, since the types of knowledge that you will glean (James and Busher, 2009).[1]

However, conducting online-only research can result in gaps in your knowledge. On the one hand, you might not know how that online life interplays with how they move through the world, and how the way they act online differs from how they act in other settings.

Class, economic standing, religion, family – all might be obscured online. On the other hand, you might feel that sense of belonging from an online forum, or know what makes your interlocutors laugh, and perhaps laugh along with them. You might be able to map social clusters and groups, and see who is closest to whom. You may even know intimate information such as when people wake up or go to sleep, and find that you are able to learn their innermost aspirations and values.

Making inroads

Social media can and should be used to locate information and contacts before travelling to the field, if you are indeed doing so. Location tags can help you get your bearings both geographically and culturally, while blogs, news articles and videos filmed in the area are all good starting points.

Some towns and cities have privately or municipally operated Instagram feeds. These can serve as primary tools for locating interlocutors or for following local news dynamics, and can be a key part of pilot research or preparation for an ethnography. Spector used Facebook 'place' pages as ways to search for people to meet before she formally entered her fieldsite, building a list of faces she would go on to recognise in person. The Facebook page for the Israeli settlement where Spector conducted her work functioned as a community message board for exchanges, services rendered and adverts for public events. Spector used this page to locate several active community members (archivists, activists and language teachers) who went on to serve as important gatekeepers in her fieldwork.

Establishing contacts in the field before arriving can help with practical issues such as housing and visas, and these individuals may be able to help as contacts for emergencies and safety issues. Local women's groups online can be useful for newcomers to a region and pose a safe space for (women-identifying) researchers to ask questions and make contacts. When reaching out, be sure to outline your project and explain why they in particular might be the right person for you to be in touch with.

Sutton researched AirBnB housing close to train stations in Oakland, aiming to use public transport, but found it difficult to understand the scale of the American style 'grid' of roads on Google Maps. Even after using street view to 'walk' from her AirBnB to Ashby BART station, she was shocked at how inhospitable the streets were to someone moving on foot. Sutton lived with her 'host' who went on to lend her camping equipment and be listed as her emergency contact, as well as offering guidance while she navigated the San Francisco Bay area as a newcomer. She also used sites like Meetup as a way to learn about common meeting places and hobbies, building a picture of a city even before leaving her accommodation.

While some interlocutors may be contactable prior to meeting them, others may need to be met face to face first. In Sutton's fieldwork she found that meeting informants at their retreat or at reunions – even briefly – was welcomed by her participants as an appropriate moment to then connect with them online. After attending the retreat, she was granted entry to their 'secret' Facebook group, as well as private message threads where more exclusive events were organised.

Having added her interlocutors on Facebook, she was also able to see which events they attended, providing vital information on their interests and behaviour outside the community.

Using your own social media

When you initially contact interlocutors, they may themselves research you to assess your credentials. This step may make the difference between them accepting or declining an invitation to participate in your research, so think through how you present yourself as a researcher online. In Sutton's research, the degree of formality was key to connecting with her interlocutors; she found it was important to be approachable rather than emphasise her academic affiliation. Rather than relying on a university profile, she used her social media profiles to soften and humanise the image of a researcher.

Sutton's use of her own social media profiles was particularly appropriate for embedding herself in the community: a gesture of mutual trust between researcher and interlocutor. However, this can result in making yourself vulnerable to your interlocutors and it becoming harder to maintain professional distance. Sutton's Facebook profile detailed more than ten years' worth of her personal information, including photos, statuses and conversations. Such an exchange of information may, in fact, be appropriate when we consider ethnographic research as an exchange, rather than extraction, of cultural information; or that fostering authentic relationships is more ethical, rather than less (Oakley, 1981).

Using her own social media led Sutton to be tagged in pictures, statuses and comments by her interlocutors, through which she learned more about how social media played a part in their gatherings and relationships. In doing so, however, they inadvertently de-anonymised themselves by placing their full name alongside hers, in a clash between formal procedures and the reality of online ethnography.

In Spector's research, her modesty and political affiliations were the most important aspect of her online presence. Photographs of herself, what she wore and where they were taken, with whom she was photographed, who she had friended and what she chose to like on Facebook were all interrogated by people she met. In a politically fraught fieldsite, a misstep in any one of these areas could lead to a setback in her research. In the conservative Muslim setting of her research, she had already updated and edited her public profiles to respect local codes of morality for Facebook, removing pictures of alcohol or dress not in accordance with local customs, yet this was not thorough enough for the more curious of her research participants. Regardless of where you are conducting your research, it is important to not take any element of your digital body language for granted.

Knowing the fraught nature of the relationship between the two groups she was conducting research with, Spector opted to operate two parallel Facebook accounts: one her original, personal account, with which she had befriended Palestinians and a second, newer account to use among Israeli settlers, to allow her to manage relations with each group separately. She asked friends from outside the field to befriend the more recently established second account, to make the second, new account look 'real'.

Self-presentation online has become a crucial aspect of research in today's world. As you engage with a new group of people and attempt to understand what matters to them, it is important to strike a balance between your own safety and privacy and the desire to connect. Achieving this balance can be challenging, and it is normal to make some missteps along the way.

BOX 9.1

You may similarly want to create a separate profile and hide photos depicting yourself conducting activities considered immoral to those among your interlocutors. It is worth keeping in mind, however, that social media is a way in which we as outsiders are referenced and understood by outsiders; if your online presence does not reflect the information you tell people, or makes it appear as if you are hiding something, this may impact the relationships you are trying to build. If in doubt, check the Facebook pages of people in your fieldsite to see what they do and do not divulge online.

While you're in the field

Digital armchair anthropologists

Using social media allows us to, as Shireen Walton notes, 'return to the proverbial and physical "armchair"' (2017, p. 166) – the place where anthropology began – but this time, she can do so while simultaneously participating and immersing herself in the field. Due to violence and embassy closures in Iran, Walton (2017) conducted much of her fieldwork on Iranian photobloggers from England.

Mirroring this approach, Spector used social media as a technological workaround. Struggling with strict physical barriers, limited public transport and unsafe road conditions, as well as a health condition that impacted her ability to travel, Spector used Tinder as a way to conduct fieldwork in hostile conditions, safely and remotely chatting with geographically proximate but socially inaccessible participants for her research, building networks of contacts from her home less than 10 kilometres from her fieldsite.

Spector also used Facebook and WhatsApp to conduct this kind of semi-remote fieldwork when necessary. On the days when she wasn't able to access her fieldsite, she used the local town's Facebook page to contact locals – for example, posting questions on the page asking if there was a town archivist or historian who she might speak to. Other users of the page got back to her with recommendations, and through this snowball method she was able to set up meetings for the following days while chatting through messages.

In addition to overcoming such 'involuntary immobility' (Elliot et al., 2017), digital armchair anthropology can make research more financially accessible for those in expensive fieldsites or with limited research funding. The opportunity to eliminate travel costs may change *who* is able to do ethnography. For those with disabilities, dependants, or other circumstances which restrict their travel, online ethnography can welcome more would-be anthropologists to the discipline. Finally, with fewer flights to and from fieldsites, the research will have a smaller carbon footprint.

Putting the 'participant' in participant observation

How exactly should we participate when we do ethnography online? It can be tempting to not participate at all; online worlds can lend themselves well to 'lurking' (Hine, 2008), which can be an extremely effective way to gather data. This method, however, raises important ethical issues; we know that posting online tends to be for specific imagined audiences and that users often do not anticipate the full 'public-ness' of their online lives (Nissenbaum, 2010). There are, however, various methods for signalling your presence as a researcher. Conducting research on Tinder, Spector made her presence as a researcher obvious by posting the relevant information about her intentions in her profile bio and reiterated this message when she chatted with her matches. While some people interpreted this as a 'cover' for romantic intentions, Spector was mindful not to mislead people given the nature of the app, and cut contact with people who didn't confirm their informed consent to take part in her work.

If possible, ask community gatekeepers for advice, or for them to introduce you to an online group – this will help to legitimise your presence, foster trust and gain informed consent. Posting an introductory paragraph on the social media spaces you use may also help your interlocutors choose whether they allow you to watch their sociality online. When studying the digital detoxers' Facebook group, Sutton asked the retreat organisers if she could introduce herself in this space with a post, but they opted against it, concerned that it would alter people's behaviour and skew her findings. As a result, many community members may never have known she was there. It was through her long engagement with the community and attendance at events, however, that she hoped that her presence was common knowledge.

Participation in the Facebook group remained a difficult tension for Sutton; posts from detoxers often spoke of their transformative experience at the camp and love for the community, with comments underneath agreeing and sharing touching stories. Others asked for advice on how to feel 'awesome' again, or how to stop a boyfriend from checking his phone all the time. Sutton felt unable to participate in offering life advice or sharing her experiences, which were so heavily coloured by the values of the group; she did, however, 'like' posts and use the group to ask for lifts, housing and to sign up to events.

While working with Palestinian refugees, Spector was mindful of the wider surveillance environment of the research setting under occupation. Although the Palestinian refugee Facebook pages were public, posting was restricted to page administrators to protect user anonymity as it was commonly understood that these pages were surveilled by the occupying Israeli military. Spector, acting on the advice of local friends, retained a silent and 'lurking' presence on the digital space of these pages, and only discussed them with friends in an offline capacity, as her presence in the setting as an outsider could easily be confused with Israeli surveillance.

Both co-authors needed to use the internet to participate fully in their fieldsites. Participation feels very different from spectating: it is an emotional risk that leaves you vulnerable. Whenever possible, avoid 'lurking' and ask yourself how you can engage with your participants. When participation risks rejection – and the dissolving of your project – this may, unfortunately, be an even more important question to ask yourself. Are you the right person to be conducting this research? Do your participants want to be studied? Remember that all hurdles in the research process are part of your data; and that failing to gain the access you hoped for can, in itself, be a highly revealing and useful finding.

Safety and online research

The primary considerations in conducting an ethnography should be the physical and mental safety of yourself and your participants.[2] Conducting research online can open up hundreds if not thousands of potential research contacts and opportunities, but researchers must keep their safety in mind when arranging to meet in person. Arrange to meet new contacts in public and be mindful of setting clear expectations about the meeting – sending your participant an information sheet ahead of time, asking whether they would be OK with the interview being recorded and establishing how long it will last. As researchers, our interest can be misconstrued as romantic, friendship, therapeutic, or otherwise different from how we see ourselves. In traditional ethnographic methods, a wedding ring has often been worn by women researchers who hoped to discourage unwanted attention or misunderstandings of male informants. The digital equivalent might be foregrounding a significant other in social media profiles; Sutton strategically made her profile picture feature her boyfriend, since her participants were often single, in a similar life stage to her and seeking to build relationships by attending the camp.

Social media platforms such as Facebook and Twitter are often co-opted by state security agencies to share data in exchange for grounds to operate in those countries. In many regions of the world it is widely accepted that social media platforms are not secure means of communication. As a result, researchers should be wary of both the information they divulge and solicit, and those they befriend online.

BOX 9.2

Find out about how people in your fieldsite conceive of social media networks in relation to surveillance. Be wary of trying to initiate conversations about sensitive subjects, such as personal lives, habits, or political activity online. Be aware that attempting to initiate these conversations on online platforms may position you in the eyes of your interlocutors as linked to surveillance organisations. Researchers must be aware that, as outsiders, requesting or raising sensitive subjects or data over Facebook, or even the act of befriending people can be mistaken as colluding in surveillance activities and/or put people in danger.

Intimacy and boundaries

Ambient presence

In 'My profile: The ethics of virtual ethnography' Driscoll and Gregg (2010) point out that connecting with informants online can feasibly involve a higher degree of intimacy than 'any other kind of ethnography', taking into account the 'ambient technologies regularly used to signal when people get up and go to bed, what they cook, what TV they are watching or how they are getting along with their partners and their colleagues' (p. 19). For anthropologists, this can prove to be an immensely useful increase of access, since we seek the taken-for-granted aspects of culture and sociality.

During Sutton's fieldwork she was made privy to detoxers' Instagram stories, Snapchat posts and Facebook activity, which often displayed private or mundane aspects of their lives that she would not have been able to see otherwise. What she saw her participants post was crucial to her understanding of them; while in an interview they might say one thing about social media, they might later contradict themselves in how they behaved.

This kind of 'ambient presence' can help to foster a sense of intimacy with our participants – we are more available to our participants, and might find ourselves chatting with them while relaxing or in bed. Mundane, frequent and everyday conversation conducted via social media and smartphones can often lead to a sense of intimacy between parties. Often this kind of chit chat facilitation can pave the way to friendship or the status of a confidant with the participants in question.

However, being constantly accessible by your interlocutors can also be a great drawback to ethnography in a digital era. Spector found that befriending men often led to them feeling that they had a direct line of communication to her at all hours, and was often messaged by men sending flirtatious messages late in the night, something considered inappropriate by local social standards. Spector countered this by establishing working hours for her Facebook; she would not reply to messages after a certain time, or at all if they were inappropriate.

After collapsing into bed after a long day and watching *The Great British Bake Off* on Netflix, scrolling on her feeds to see what her friends were up to in England, Sutton could receive several messages from participants about interviews and gatherings over the coming days, or questions about her project. Because she used the same platforms that her participants did, both work and leisure were coexisting in the same online 'space'. Although the pressures of conducting ethnography can stress researchers to never decline an invitation and pursue all feasible leads, this is not a realistic or healthy way of working. Sometimes it's important to be unavailable; to mute conversations, go on aeroplane mode, or take a day to enjoy your fieldsite as a tourist.

Acquaintances, friends, lovers

While acting as researchers, we are also human beings; we need friends, down time and support, and we need these even more so if living in a foreign country. But Spector felt conflicted about the friendships she established through using Tinder as a way to meet local Israeli settlers. On the one hand, she was grateful for and interested in the data on their lives they shared with her, and the intimacy of the platform simulated a close relationship. On the other, she found their politics hugely divergent from her own, and wasn't comfortable sharing her own views on settlement with them. With some participants, she also didn't always feel confident that meeting in person was mutually understood as a research and non-romantic encounter. Spector worked hard to prioritise informed consent of potential interlocutors she met on Tinder, and struggled with her own sense of professionalism. 'Whatever my intention is in a new conversation with a Tinder match or Tinder interlocutor,' she explains, 'I have always informed them that I'm a researcher of Israelis.' Being honest, however, has not removed a sense of confusion and guilt. 'Despite maintaining honest relations with my Tinder matches, I feel a twinge of guilt when using data I've gleaned from conversations or people I've met from Tinder, as if this is somehow not legitimate anthropological knowledge.'

Just as Spector's participants suspected her academic research as a 'cover' for romantic intentions, Sutton's hoped that her research was a 'ruse' for her to find her own community. At the digital detox retreat, Sutton's informants placed a high value on creating deep, spiritual connections with each other. Sutton had attended countless mutual help exercises in the woods that facilitated sharing with strangers, where women wept and where she hugged them tightly as tears fell on her shoulders; where her interviewees had told her about their childhoods, their depression, anxiety, divorces, loneliness and grief.

Watching their vulnerability, Sutton sometimes felt guilty that she was there to study detoxers rather than connect with them on the level they wanted. At other times, she yearned for friendship to help mitigate such emotionally exhausting fieldwork. In addition, the use of Sutton's own social media facilitated a sense of closeness that Sutton feared was unprofessional. Was she first and foremost their friend or a researcher?

Ethnography will always include relationship dilemmas like this, but connecting with informants on social media can muddy the waters of the already complicated researcher–participant relationship. The bonds implicit in relationships formed on online platforms can be interpreted differently in different cultures, and by different individuals. While Instagram might, to you, be just a list of people you have met at one point, to another person it might be a community of best friends. The important thing is to consider your relationship from your participants' point of view, and to be open and honest with them about your motives as a researcher. Anticipating those differing interpretations of what bond you are making when you connect online might help in identifying misunderstandings or help you position yourself more clearly.

This begins to illustrate why online ethnography might require more caution around the creation of personal boundaries. Online access might exacerbate the sense that you have little control or boundary between yourself and your participants, yet, as researchers, we need boundaries in place to protect our own emotional stability. This is all the more important when there is the possibility for vicarious trauma. When attending a vicarious trauma workshop after fieldwork, Sutton felt 'ridiculous' for having studied privileged, relatively wealthy people in San Francisco, while others in attendance had studied refugees and other highly vulnerable groups. Nevertheless, emotional transference can happen in any setting; indeed, the personal boundaries Sutton tried to enforce for herself during fieldwork were at the mercy of a therapeutic retreat specifically designed to break them down.

Ask yourself: what is different about my role in this place as a researcher versus if I were here as myself? While it can be wonderful to connect deeply with participants, be mindful of your vulnerability and the different roles you need to play. We recommend you create clear boundaries between professional and personal life, as well as rituals to transition between them, both on- and offline.

Technology as escape

The use of digital technology in ethnographic fieldwork can create new problems, but it can also fix older ones. In the midst of stressful or difficult actual-world fieldwork experiences, the laptop or smartphone itself can represent an escape – a bubble of comfort. Whatever is happening in our fieldsite, as long as we have access to the internet, we can sink into an online world of familiarity, friendship and entertainment.

Tremblay writes about fieldwork: 'bring movies. Watch them. Bring trashy (or good) novels. Read them. Malinowski did it, ain't no shame in it' (2014). We emphasise that you are allowed to be comforted by your social media and by the connections that social media foster – if Tumblr, your favourite Youtube channel, or reading tabloid gossip from home helps, be sure to use it as important mental time out.

Offloading is an important element of fieldwork,[3] but in fieldsites in a different time zone from home, calling friends and relatives is sometimes not possible. While Sutton received online counselling from her university, these sessions with a new counsellor were shorter in length and could only help her so much. After difficult interviews Sutton would record herself on her iPhone voice memos as a way of offloading her emotional experience, while simultaneously documenting an important interview reflection. In this way, her devices were a comfort and emotional aid, even if a person wasn't listening to her problems, her phone – and her future self – was.

Post-field research

Managing relationships after fieldwork

Lines of communication can be immensely useful in the writing up stages of the PhD; if willing, these contacts can serve as helpful aides in writing up, fact checkers, or even remote photographers. Joining Facebook groups or knowing relevant corners of social media through which to follow reactions to local or regional news events, changes and so on can allow you to continue your fieldwork from afar.

However, Spector found the constant exposure to the violence and political unrest of her fieldsite through Facebook difficult to manage upon her return. Since she did not want to sever connections with the Facebook friends she had made, she reduced her use of Facebook, moving communication and friendships with friends and family to other platforms to allow her to mediate her exposure to content relating to her fieldsite.

It can also be challenging to move on to the next stage of the research project. Sutton found that while it was helpful to have research data in among posts from friends and family when gathering data, it began to feel confusing and inappropriate during the later stages of analysis and writing up. It was all too easy to see a new theme arise and want to rewrite a chapter to include this new and exciting data. Drawing a line under the time you spent gathering information can be helpful to avoid repeatedly extending the scope of what you will write about.

Continued connection, facilitated by the internet, complicates the relationship we have with participants after the research has ended. Sutton continued to struggle with the online connections she had made and was anxious about the expectation for continued friendships; a couple of people she met suggested meeting in England. She eventually moved her informants onto a new Facebook profile to take them out of her personal social media space as well as to better obscure their names and identities. However, she still felt guilty and conflicted. The edges of this 'list' that she moved to a new profile were blurry, and some informants who she was good friends with are still also connected to her personal Facebook, Instagram, or Twitter profiles.

BOX 9.3

It can be guilt-provoking to feel that you have intensely connected with your participants while you needed to gather data, then stopped contact with them when you left. Find ways to keep in contact with them at a rate that you feel comfortable with, perhaps weekly or monthly, or by providing key updates at your own pace. Consider how you can manage those relationships realistically and with compassion towards yourself.

Conclusion

In this chapter, we have provided an overview for how to go about an ethnography of social media, from the choices you make at the start of a study, to the ones you make as you finish your research project. We have also explored how age-old anthropological problems are being reimagined in the digital world. Using personal social media profiles for ethnographic research can exacerbate the complex researcher–participant relationship, causing guilt and imposter syndrome for early career researchers trying to navigate the fieldwork process. Digital tools can aid in the emotional experience of conducting fieldwork, providing support and respite.

We emphasise that safety and emotional wellbeing are paramount in using social media in your research project, but equally hope that early career researchers can feel emboldened, both in using novel digital methods in their research and in including their own complex entanglements with online platforms and participants in their writing up, just as we have begun to do here. We encourage researchers to embrace the nuanced issues we have raised in order to do justice to the rich set of environments our digital ethnography can take place in. We hope that by sharing our experiences and the lessons we've learned, we can inspire others to open up about the problems they encounter during their research. It may be challenging to be honest about the frictions of fieldwork, but doing so can help future generations of researchers feel reassured that fieldwork is always a messy and complicated affair.

Recommendations

1 **Use social media to establish contacts in your fieldsite before you arrive.** Strategically use social media to build connections before your fieldwork begins, establishing a foundation of trust and access. Seek guidance from gatekeepers and local groups to legitimise your presence and foster a sense of community.
2 **Review the content of your social media accounts before adding research participants.**
3 **Craft an online presence that aligns with your participants' expectations.** Consider using your social media profiles as tools to establish rapport, but be cautious about what information you make available to your participants.
4 **Be aware of how people relate to and use social media in relation to local surveillance practices.**
5 **Maintain awareness of the digital security landscape in your fieldsite and consider potential risks associated with state surveillance.** Be aware that this may limit your participants' ability to speak freely with you and ensure that you are as transparent as possible with them to protect their safety.
6 **Set boundaries around how and how often you will communicate with research participants online.** Consider setting aside dedicated 'offline' time to avoid being constantly accessible to your participants and ways to transition into clocking off from your research project.
7 **Don't be too hard on yourself.**
8 **Recognise that conducting ethnography, especially in the digital age, is a multifaceted and complex endeavour.** Embrace the challenges and frictions that come with it and don't hesitate to discuss these complexities openly in your research.

Notes

1 These points are informed by Rebecca Eynon who teaches this approach in her Digital Interviewing class at the Oxford Internet Institute.
2 Chapter 11 (this volume) engages more with emotional safety during fieldwork.
3 See Chapter 11 for more on this.

Further reading

Backe, E.L. 2015. Playing along: Fieldwork, emotional labor and self-care. *The Geek Anthropologist*, 24 July. Available at thegeekanthropologist.com/2015/07/24/playing-along-fieldwork-emotional-labor-and-self-care/ (accessed 3 October 2023).

This piece explores the emotional and practical realities of fieldwork and the fear of 'failure' in the field; by talking about frictions and failures we can prevent new cohorts of anthropologists from assuming they are alone in their struggles.

Blanes, R.L. 2006. The atheist anthropologist: Believers and non-believers in anthropological fieldwork. *Social Anthropology*, 14(02), 223. doi:10.1017/S0964028206002552

This article explores the challenges of conducting research among those with radically different beliefs in a religious context.

Evans, A. 2017. Tinder as a methodological tool#EmergingDigitalPractices. Available at allegralaboratory.net/tinder-as-a-methodological-tool/ (accessed 3 October 2023).

This article explores the use of the dating app Tinder as a tool for meeting new research participants and making cultural observations in fieldwork.

Eynon, R., Fry, J. and Schroeder, R. 2017. The ethics of online research. In Fielding, N., Lee, R. and Blank, G. (Eds.), *The Sage Handbook of Online Research Methods*. London: Sage. pp. 19–37. doi: 10.4135/9781473957992.n2

This chapter discusses the ethical issues that tend to arise in internet research, and how these may differ from traditional forms of research.

Hargittai, E. (Ed.) 2009. *Research Confidential: Solutions to Problems Most Social Scientists Pretend They Never Have*. Ann Arbor: University of Michigan Press.

The predecessor to *Digital Research Confidential* (see below), this book explores the methodological issues that rarely make it into the final write-up of research projects.

Hargittai, E. and Sandvig, C. (Eds.) 2015. *Digital Research Confidential: The Secrets of Studying Behavior Online*. Cambridge, MA: MIT Press.

This book embraces the reality of digital research, with all the problems that may arise during a research project, and shares the behind-the-scenes stories of researchers who needed to improvise and adapt in the face of difficulty.

Oakley, A. 1981. Interviewing women: A contradiction in terms. In Roberts, H. (Ed.), *Doing Feminist Research*. London: Routledge and Kegan Paul p.221–242.

In this chapter, Oakley finds that traditional interviewing methods are absurd and unethical since they tend to only view interview subjects as a way to obtain data; in contrast, feminist interviewing would allow for the reality of a two-way relationship that brings more integrity to the research process.

Spector, B. 2021. Uneven ground: Infrastructures and mobility among refugees and settlers in the Occupied West Bank. Doctoral thesis. London School of Economics.

This thesis details the chapter author's experience using digital ethnographic techniques: see Chapter 2 for a full breakdown.

Sutton, T. 2020. Digital re-enchantment: Tribal belonging, New Age science and the search for happiness in a digital detoxing community. Doctoral thesis. Oxford University.

This thesis explores frictions between a highly online millennial and a group of New Age, digital detoxers, as Sutton joins them for a technology-free retreat in the forests of Northern California.

References

Bowker, N. and Tuffin, K. 2004. Using the online medium for discursive research about people with disabilities. *Social Science Computer Review*, 22(2), 228–41. doi: 10.1177/0894439303262561

Driscoll, C. and Gregg, M. 2010. My profile: The ethics of virtual ethnography. *Emotion, Space and Society*, 3, 15–20. doi:10.1016/j.emospa.2010.01.012

Elliot, A., Norum, E.R. and Salazar, N.B. (Eds.) 2017. *Methodologies of Mobility: Ethnography and Experiment*. Oxford: Berghahn.

Hine, C. 2008. *Virtual Ethnography: Modes, Varieties, Affordances*. London: Sage. doi:10.4135/9780857020055

James, N., & Busher, H. 2009. Online interviewing. SAGE Publications Ltd, https://doi.org/10.4135/9780857024503

Nissenbaum, H. 2010. *Privacy in Context: Technology, Policy, and the Integrity of Social Life*. Stanford, CA: Stanford University Press.

Oakley, A. 1981. Interviewing women: A contradiction in terms. In Roberts, H. (Ed.), *Doing Feminist Research*. London: Routledge and Kegan Paul.

Tremblay, J. 2014. *10 Tips for Surviving Anthropological Fieldwork*. Available at allegralaboratory.net/10-tips-for-surviving-fieldwork-blogging/

Walton, S. 2017. 'Being there where?' Designing digital-visual methods for moving with/in Iran. In Elliot, A., Norum, E.R. and Salazar, N.B. (Eds.), *Methodologies of Mobility: Ethnography and Experiment*. Oxford: Berghahn.

10

DOING FIELDWORK IN AND ON CONTEXTS OF VIOLENCE AND INSTABILITY

Caitlin Procter

Summary

This chapter reflects on the challenges of doing ethnography either in contexts of violence or on subjects related to violence. It is grounded in a broad understanding of the scope for violence and fieldwork to interact. It moves away from the assumption that 'violent fieldwork' only happens in specifically 'violent places', and invites readers to consider if and how their topic or fieldsite might engage with questions of violence. I consider how violent topics or violent spaces can interact with core issues surrounding access to research participants, consent and the building of reciprocal trust. I then discuss the entanglements of privilege when confronting violence during fieldwork, before turning to the importance of working with compassion, both for yourself and your research participants.

Table of contents

Introduction 135
Who should be thinking about violence and fieldwork? 136
Building trust surrounded by violence 138
Confronting your privilege 141
Compassion for yourself and your interlocutors 143
Conclusion 145
Recommendations 145
Further reading 146
References 147

Introduction

For a long time, there has been an assumption that discussions of violence and safety in fieldwork are reserved for researchers working in 'violent places far away'. The reality is that violence – in its myriad forms – can interact with fieldwork whether conducted in a conflict setting or a place that is generally considered to be safe. It is often the case that the setting of fieldwork can be ostensibly safe, but the subject under study is a violent one. Concepts of violence are also, to some extent, relative, depending on what an individual researcher is accustomed to. For instance, the ways I experienced violence during fieldwork are different from the experiences of people intimately related to the context in which I worked; I have no family history of violence in that setting, nor have I grown up with the inherited stories of violence from other generations in my family. These are all aspects of the intersection of violence and fieldwork which are often not considered.

I start this chapter by challenging the hierarchies of 'danger' that often permeate discussions surrounding ethnography on subjects and contexts of violence. When violence can mean so many different things to different people in different contexts, it is unhelpful to try and provide blanket advice on how to navigate it. Instead, I engage with three core issues that arise throughout the fieldwork process in relation to fieldwork in violent places and on violent subjects. The first is the way that violence makes it difficult to build trust among interlocutors. The technicalities of access and consent are well-worn topics in discussions surrounding fieldwork preparedness, and it has now been established in ethics guidance that written consent – particularly in heightened security contexts – is often inappropriate (for example, ASA, 2021). However, the way that violent contexts or subjects can interact with the ability to actually do ethnography – that is, developing trusting relationships with interlocutors with whom you can have repeated conversations over a prolonged period of time, as opposed to one-off interview encounters – has generally been less discussed. The second core issue is that, as a researcher, at some point you 'leave' your research participants – even if you live among them. This is part of the job: to remove yourself; have some analytical distance; and take this work to a wider audience. This entails a lot of privilege, and when you have seen the worst of humanity, and know your interlocutors are continuing to live it, is extremely hard to do. Confronting that privilege is a necessary challenge to face while working in, or on, violent contexts. Finally, to do this work, it is important to maintain compassion for yourself and for those you work with. If compassionate practice relates to the acknowledgement and understanding of the myriad experiences and responsibilities we share as ethnographers, here it means being able to talk about the experiences and responsibilities that doing fieldwork in and on violence entails. This means being able to talk to your interlocutors not only to gather data, but about the research process and its effect on them; as well as being able to acknowledge the impact of what you have seen and heard on yourself.

This chapter draws on my experiences of fieldwork in refugee communities in Palestine (East Jerusalem, the West Bank and Gaza) during my doctoral and postdoctoral research. My research focuses on children and youth, and the ways that they navigate the many structures of violence that comprise their everyday lives. As such, my fieldwork primarily involved listening to people's accounts of violence. More times than I would like to remember, it also involved witnessing their experiences of extreme forms of violence and discrimination. Prior to my doctoral fieldwork, having previously worked in Palestine in the humanitarian sector, I understood the immediate violence and brutality of military occupation; the daily discrimination and humiliation my research participants would be subjected to; the devastating conditions in which many of them were forced to live; and the structural nature of this violence. I was not prepared for the impact that 'observing' and hearing stories of violent experiences on a daily basis for 18 months would have on me, nor was I prepared for navigating my privilege in relation to that. The ways that the personal circumstances which enabled me to leave the context I worked in still make me question how I write about it. Typically, when students and early career researchers are encouraged to think about the ways violence might interact with their fieldwork, the emphasis is on how to stay physically safe, how to keep research participants safe and make sure the research in question 'does no harm'. Thinking through the long aftermath of what researchers might carry with them as a result of this work is often neglected.

Who should be thinking about violence and fieldwork?

In the past decade there has been a welcome increase in literature reflecting on the many entanglements of violence and fieldwork, and particularly on how to do safer research in contexts of instability. In political science and conflict studies in particular, there has been a wealth of publications related to ethnographic methods in contexts of violence (Cronin-Furnham and Lake 2018; Millar 2019; Rivas and Browne 2019; Grimm et al. 2020; Weiss et al. 2023). From this critical body of work, it is evident that attention to the multifaceted ways that violence can interact with fieldwork is deserving of greater attention both from institutions and individual researchers.

There remains, however, a tendency in academic departments to emphasise fieldwork safety as relevant only to those researchers working in settings of war, conflict or clearly defined violent spaces. The focus is often on students travelling to violent places to undertake research, with little or no consideration of the implications for students from places of violence conducting research in their own communities; for students working on violent subjects in places generally characterised as safe; or the kinds of unexpected violence that can occur in any setting. This sets up troubling hierarchies of what violence is and is not, as well as ignoring the more mundane aspects of violent environments and the challenges therein.

My research took place both on a violent subject and in a violent place – yet in many ways, the most extreme violence that I personally encountered was one that I did not anticipate: that is, the many repeated conversations I had with interlocutors about violence they had experienced. Hearing their accounts of violence; the impunity with which the perpetrators got away with it; coming to understand the devastating knock-on effects this had on people's daily lives, hopes and dreams; and feeling that research was a very power less way to make any difference to these situations was paralysing. Because *this* experience of violence could happen in almost any context, it is critical to think broadly about how violence might intersect with your fieldwork. For instance, your research may not be directly related to a violent subject, but may involve hearing (repeated) stories about violence. It may involve interacting with individuals who have perpetrated violence or abuse, either personally or through the structures that they represent. It may also involve interviewing or engaging with individuals who have the power to change this situation, but who are not prepared to ameliorate it. Or these same individuals may express their indifference to a situation you find abhorrent.

Alternatively, your research may include the direct observation of physical attacks, instances of abuse, degradation, or other kinds of maltreatment (as described in Chapter 2). You may not experience or witness any such forms of maltreatment directly, but work for a prolonged period in an environment of visible threats of violence. Your work may also involve spending time in and understanding the unsafe living conditions of participants, who may not have access to food, water, heating, electricity or other essentials. Circumstances related to your own living conditions during fieldwork might also involve violence; the only option of accommodation available to you may feel insecure, or you may be made to feel unwelcome by members of the community where you are living, or by your research participants themselves.

Your work may involve none of the above, but you may still be subjected to unexpected instances of violence during your fieldwork, such as theft, robbery or an assault of some kind which may or may not be connected to aspects of your identity (as discussed in Chapter 6). If you are undertaking this work alone, without the support of colleagues, a partner or family members close by, you might experience feelings of loneliness or isolation; and if you are undertaking fieldwork with family members in tow, you may be overwhelmed with responsibility for their safety and wellbeing (as discussed in Chapter 5).

I pose these scenarios to articulate that it is not only because you directly experience violence, or work in a context known for its violence of violence, or on a specifically violent topic that you might experience it in some form. There are psychological consequences for anyone working in or on violence, and even more so for those who are not prepared (see Chapter 11). In broadening the scope of who should be thinking about violent encounters during fieldwork, it is also important to raise the question of who should be doing fieldwork in contexts of, or on topics related to violence. To return to Chapter 1 of this book, it is good ethical and professional practice to seriously consider if this kind of ethnography is right for you, and whether you have the capabilities to do it safely. Driven by anger about a particular issue, passion for social justice, or sometimes a level of arrogance, junior researchers are often captivated by the study of violent contexts or subjects without thoroughly thinking through what this kind of work will entail. As this chapter suggests, being untrained or unprepared for your own work ultimately risks creating more dangerous situations for your research participants and those you interact with during fieldwork, as well as for yourself.

Building trust surrounded by violence

EXAMPLE 10.1

Early in my fieldwork, I was invited to attend an NGO-led workshop for young women in a community centre in a refugee camp about risks associated with early marriage – the marriage of individuals before reaching the age of 18. The head of the community centre had offered to help connect me with young people living in the camp to interview, and thought that those attending the workshop could be a good place to start. She suggested I stay at the back of the room, and initially introduced me as a volunteer. Her concern was that, as generally there were few non-Palestinians taking part in such events at the centre, people might assume I was either a journalist or an aid worker, and would not feel safe to express their views freely in either scenario. The workshop itself was a fascinating insight into how European donor-funded projects oriented around a Western construction of childhood (as applicable to anyone under the age of 18) fundamentally jarred with the strategies of young people in the community to keep themselves safe. Marriage – particularly to someone not living in the camp – was seen by many teenage girls as a critical way of protecting themselves. I sat at the back of the room listening, wishing I had first explained my research and sought the consent of all these young women to record their ideas. After the workshop, I started to introduce myself to some of the participants and to try and explain my research. A few hung back to talk with me, and we swapped numbers, chatted and made plans to meet in the following days. Many others smiled politely and quickly excused themselves. One young woman invited me home for lunch. She lived in a part of the camp I hadn't visited previously. I tried to make light conversation as we walked, asking about what she thought of the workshop, her family and her interests. She abruptly cut me off, saying 'Can you walk a bit faster?' Eyes on the road ahead, she walked quickly and with purpose, holding my hand to lead me through the streets to her family home. We passed what looked like it might be a small school. I stopped to ask her what it was but she continued walking – 'I don't know, OK? Come on let's go.' I wasn't sure if she was worried about the safety of the streets where we were; if she was worried about being seen outside with me; if she was regretting her decision to invite me home; or if this was her usual way of walking and interacting with the space. As I came to know her over time, I realised it was all of the above.

This vignette offers three different insights into the ways that violent spaces can complicate the process of gaining trust from interlocutors and, subsequently, access to them and their consent to partake in research over a prolonged period. The first is the ways that violent spaces jar with the typical image we have of 'doing ethnography'. To do effective participant observation, you will be constantly 'working': observing, note-taking, thinking, planning, being flexible, being friendly and open, rejecting lines of enquiry and considering new ones. As this vignette demonstrates, the idea of an always open and friendly ethnographer contrasts somewhat with the experience of daily life in violent spaces, or with people who routinely experience forms of violence. For instance, 'hanging out' is often impossible beyond the home or a confined space when there is violence in the streets. Similarly, people who routinely experience violence or abuse may be uncomfortable spending long, undefined stretches of time with you, or subjects of conversation may be abruptly closed because someone else comes into the room, or the conversation has become too difficult. When people live in or have profound personal experiences of violence, they may feel discouraged from speaking with strangers or individuals not known to be trustworthy.

The second issue relates to the need to gain the trust of multiple 'gatekeepers' in order to spend time with the people you really want to talk to. The woman in the vignette above did not turn out to be particularly interested in my research, but introduced me to many of her family members and friends who were. Before 'gaining access' to her and her networks, I had to gain access to the community centre. Establishing and demonstrating solidarity and support within the community turned out to be a critical first step. I volunteered at this centre for months of my fieldwork, supporting the teaching of different activities as well as writing funding applications in English. Building a sense of reciprocal trust among research participants can take a long time in any context, but often requires a greater depth of engagement when addressing sensitive topics or working in challenging settings. This includes finding ways to navigate community practices that may not align with the requirements placed on you as a researcher by your institution, ethics committee or insurance providers (see Textbox 10.1 below). All of this is inevitably much easier to do in contexts where your personal politics align somewhat with your research topic. Demonstrating solidarity as a way of building trust when doing research with actors with whom you do not agree can be a much greater challenge. Yet, as McNeil-Willson (2020) has argued, demonstrating openness and willingness to learn is often one of the strongest hands you can play in fieldwork. He argues for the importance of approaching clandestine groups with transparency, suggesting that the vulnerability that honesty involves on the part of the researcher is often both recognised and rewarded by research participants. In contrast, covert research risks damaging the researcher–researched notion of trust, and subsequently of ethics, and potentially limits the possibility for future researchers to undertake studies with the same groups.

EXAMPLE 10.2

Gaining consent from young adults under the age of 18

When young people grow up in violent settings, this can often result in those young people adopting adult-like roles from a younger age, in order to protect themselves or their families. For example, young people might get married as teenagers; they might leave their family home to find work; they might adopt positions of authority in gangs or armed groups; or they might adopt the caregiver role for older members of their family. In these instances, it would be both offensive and meaningless to require the consent of their parents or caregivers simply because they are under the age of 18. Age-based definitions are often a hard line in ethics approval processes. In my own research, I have navigated this through the process of establishing a 'trusted other' with research participants under the age of 18 for whom it does not make sense to consult their parents. Hanin was 17 years old and mother to a young baby. Hanin's husband had recently been detained. She lived in the apartment they shared, in the same building as her husband's brother and his family. When I told Hanin about my research she was eager to meet and to talk further. Since she had not lived with her parents for two years, asking for her parents' consent to take part in the research would not have been appropriate. Instead, we agreed upon her sister as a 'trusted other'. The agreement was made between Hanin, her sister and myself, that Hanin would tell her sister about any concerns she might have related to things she shared with me, and that I could similarly speak to her sister if I had any concerns about information shared by Hanin.

A third way that violence interacts with trust is closely linked to ongoing consent and knowing how to manage the data you are not permitted to use in your research. In the anonymised vignette above, the ways that young people presented ideas around what they considered to be protective of their futures became fundamental to the way I discussed these issues going forward. While what I heard in the workshop informed my thinking, I did not directly use anything shared at the workshop in my analysis. Of course, this can be the case in any context, but in communities where violence of different kinds is prevalent, the potential for ongoing research over a prolonged period can be seriously limited. It is highly likely that your work will be interrupted at different stages. During my fieldwork, political circumstances changed at short notice, directly impacting the extent to which interlocutors were able or willing to meet with me, making a long period of fieldwork in this community necessary. In the days and weeks following any violent attack on or within the refugee camp, interlocutors were slower to respond to messages suggesting we meet, or vague about their plans. My fieldwork was characterised by multiple military invasions in this community, during which people did not want to leave the house unnecessarily. I would often meet up with interlocutors after work for a quick coffee or to accompany them on the journey home. Many were uneasy about what may or may not happen next, and it was a difficult time to try and have in-depth conversations.

I persevered with these short meetings in order to maintain contact with research participants. Several months passed like this, until it was possible to resume longer meetings in the camp again with ease. During these 'non-research' meetings we had many conversations that had nothing at all to do with the topic of my research. On numerous occasions, interlocutors would clarify that a conversation we were having was not for research purposes: *this isn't for the research, right? I'm just telling you this as a friend!* Inevitably, everything I heard and understood from these young people contributed to my understanding of their social worlds and the way I analysed the data that had been collected with their consent. However, whenever I was directly asked not to include things, I did not count the information shared as data for analysis. When working in or on contexts of violence, it should be anticipated that participants will share information that they then subsequently withdraw, or you deem that it would be unsafe for participants to have this information made public. One part of this is knowing the legal requirements in the context in which you work – for instance, if you are obliged to disclose your data to relevant authorities. The other is in working out how you can move forward in your analysis with this knowledge, but not specifically drawing on this data. In my experience, I continued to make notes about everything, but marked with an asterix the pages of fieldnotes that contained information that participants had asked not to be used in the research. Inevitably, whatever I learned from interlocutors contributed to a broader picture of their lives, but this method meant that when it came to data analysis, I could clearly remember which data could be used, and which could not.

Violence as context or subject can make the process of gaining the trust of research participants a challenge. The issues discussed here are by no means exhaustive but serve to demonstrate why it is important to think broadly about the ways violence might force you to adapt your approach to gaining access, gaining consent and, ultimately, maintaining trust.

Confronting your privilege

Asking people to let you into their lives to ask questions and try to understand their circumstances opens us up to profound learning and deep human connections, but is intrinsically an act of vulnerability and humility for all parties. The kinds of friendships that grew out of my own experiences of violence alongside research participants made it difficult to think of these individuals through the methodological terminology of 'research participant' or 'interlocutor'. At the same time, issues of our difference become even more stark as we experienced violence together, and circumstances which I could leave and others could not.

As Abdelnour and Abu Moghli (2021) have argued, researchers who engage in political reflexivity can be much better equipped to critically understand, and hold to account, the actors and structures that perpetrate violence. It can, however, bring a flip side, in which we identify so strongly with our respondents that we put aside any issues that might be troubling for us: 'It's not that bad for me,' 'I can always leave the situation', 'I have the emotional and financial resources to address this while my participants do not', etc. (Markovitz 2019; Procter, Spector and Freed, 2024). Confronting privilege in fieldwork is critical for the production of ethical and reflexive ethnography. It is also very important to recognise that spending months engaged in the violent experiences of others takes its toll on you. In the context of my doctoral fieldwork, I knew that I was exhausted, but kept pushing myself to do more every day, telling myself that if I was a 'real ethnographer', I wouldn't find it so difficult. I brushed aside my own discomfort at hearing repeated stories of violent attacks, pain, loss and destruction because this was part of the job.

Vicarious trauma

───── **BOX 10.1** ─────

Vicarious trauma was first described by trauma psychotherapists Lisa McCann and Laurie Pearlman in 1990. It is a trauma response induced by hearing about traumatic experiences of others, generally in a professional capacity, and results 'from the fact that we open ourselves to deep knowing about the experiences of others'.

───────────────────

Vicarious trauma has a cumulative effect, developing over time with long-term contact and engagement with people who are struggling. Typically, it can lead to overstepping boundaries that you might have previously set for yourself, and overextending your work beyond that which you can do. Having high expectations of yourself and your work can – if not taken seriously – leave you feeling overwhelmed and hopeless.

One way to manoeuvre around your own reflexive questions of privilege and your 'right' to feel challenged when confronted with stories of violence or situations of instability is to reflect on your own methodological training. *How much real-life experience do you have in interviewing or otherwise engaging with individuals who have lived through deeply horrifying experiences?* I had significant experience in doing so as part of an organisation, but not as a researcher, working alone without a team to oversee my work. *Have you received any training in interviewing?* My own academic training was rigorously theoretical and involved no practical elements of interviewing or listening skills. If this kind of training is not readily available at your institution, propose it to your department and, if necessary, seek out training avenues beyond the university. For example, a good starting point might be the Samaritans Listening Skills course. *What will you say and do in response to difficult conversations?* It was in this regard that I often felt entirely inadequate. I had prepared documents with suggestions of organisations or individuals that research participants might be able to contact for different avenues of support, but this is where ethnography really differs from other kinds of interviewing. While it might be appropriate to leave a research participant that you meet only once for one prepared interview with a list of follow-up contacts, when you see that person regularly and come to engage with them on different levels, doing so can be inappropriate. In fact, the most helpful thing to come from my pre-prepared sheet of contacts for research participants was to go through it with them and hear about how unhelpful many of these organisations had been to them, and the complexities of accessing support. *Do you feel equipped to stop, or exit from an uncomfortable or otherwise inappropriate reaction or interaction?* Doing research in or on violence can quickly blur personal boundaries, especially in circumstances in which you have experienced similar kinds of violence as your interlocutors. This uncomfortable position can sometimes lead us to cross lines that we had previously resolved not to, or to break institutional ethics and risk assessments. This could mean oversharing of personal information and ways to stay in contact (see Chapter 9 on managing online relationships with interlocutors) or being drawn into friendships or relationships that make you feel uncomfortable.

Compassion for yourself and your interlocutors

Whether you are a survivor researching violence that you have yourself experienced; someone who lives in a context of violence doing research in your own community; or someone who has lived in safety and without harm, trying to understand the experiences of others, working in or on topics of violence is often accompanied by a sense of exhaustion from being on high alert all the time. Before embarking on this road, it is important to think about what you can endure. It is also important to think through alternative routes for research ahead of time, so that if the work becomes overwhelming you can limit the sensation of paralysis and can shift gear towards another research question instead. Fatigue and exhaustion can impact our ability to make good, safe and ethical decisions, and our willingness to be constantly engaged with our interlocutors.

Above all, you are responsible for the questions you ask and the repercussions that these questions might have. It can therefore be helpful, depending on the context, to check-in with your interlocutors, gauge their perspectives on the questions you are asking and the directions that your research is taking. This can also provide you with the opportunity to reassure yourself that these participants are still able to continue working with you, or if it might be better to suggest that they step back from the research and help them to seek out relevant avenues of support. A golden rule in ethical research practice is to be clear with research participants about what you can and cannot offer in terms of support. Funding bodies and ethics committees regularly insist that there should be no financial gain for participants taking part in a study. At the same time, I know that I am not alone among colleagues who, upon understanding the desperate circumstances of a research participant have offered money or other forms of material help to support them. It is useful to go into your fieldwork with a concrete idea of what you will be able to contribute beyond your research findings and be willing to share with your participants the ways you hope your research findings might be used in the future.

There is often not sufficient time or funding dedicated by universities to adequately support researchers returning from fieldwork. Instead, this is often confined to a 'post-fieldwork debrief', which, while useful, is not sufficient to address the depth and range of challenges and violent experiences encountered during fieldwork. The following vignette shares my own experience of what happened when I returned from fieldwork, and illustrates a key problem with this approach: namely that it reifies the idea of a hierarchy of challenging fieldwork sites and experiences, leaving some feeling like the challenges they faced are not 'bad enough' to warrant discussion.

EXAMPLE 10.3

'Let's talk about what happened during fieldwork,' said the facilitator, a senior researcher at the university. The participants - a group of doctoral students who had all recently completed fieldwork - sat around in a circle and one by one we began to share our experiences. One had spent the past year in a prison, recording hours of interview material with women who had experienced physical and mental domestic violence. Another had been sexually assaulted by an interviewee. Another had been arrested while attending a protest with interlocutors. Another had spent days on end seeing police and other security forces beating and humiliating migrants. Another had spent months in the archives, reading testimonies of torture. I had experienced armed violence. We all spoke almost flippantly of what had happened: 'My name is x, my fieldwork was in y and was about z, and the worst thing that happened to me was –.' As each of us shared our experiences, the rest of the group nodded compassionately, murmuring expressions of solidarity and of sympathy. Several individuals in the group shared that they too had experienced challenges but they did not want to disclose them to the full group because they were not as severe as the others people had shared: 'My fieldwork was hard but nothing really bad happened – nothing like what you are all talking about.' After one and a half hours of talking one by one in a circle, the session was concluded. We were reassured that 'fieldwork is always hard' and that it was important that we talked about our experiences with one another to process them. Afterwards, everyone went back to work.

The intention of creating a post-fieldwork debriefing space was well meant. Indeed, in my experience it played an important role in creating a community of solidarity among doctoral students who had been through challenging experiences. Yet asking a group of strangers to disclose potentially traumatic experiences in front of one another with no meaningful follow-up is evidently problematic. This is not only because of the vulnerabilities of those involved in the exercise, but also because it feeds into the idea of hierarchies of challenging, violent experiences, silencing some into the belief that their experience was not 'violent enough' to warrant discussion.

Cullen et al. (2021) have promoted the importance of understanding how (inter alia) gender, race, class, age and previous trauma interact with the way that troubling fieldwork experiences can impact individuals. On the question of previous trauma, specifically in relation to research on gender-based violence, Aroussi (2020) has highlighted the lack of academic guidance or support for those who are survivor-researchers (p. 1). Schulz et al. (2022) have powerfully advocated for the role of communities of care in addition to self-care strategies, and particularly in the absence of serious structural support for researchers working on topics related to violence. Alongside that, however, there is a real need to increase awareness among researchers – and, critically, within academic institutions – about the indications of unwellness that might arise in the weeks or months following fieldwork. For instance, you might experience disturbing memories or dreams relating to fieldwork experiences. You might frequently relive experiences from your fieldwork, or feel distressed when engaging with your research material. You could have gaps in your memories of fieldwork, and struggle to engage with your own field notes to fill these. Following my doctoral fieldwork, I spent months being completely unable to engage with my research material. I would relisten to recordings of conversations and interviews, go over notes and transcripts and feel completely paralysed. I did not know what to do with pages and pages of information detailing violent experiences in the lives of my interlocutors. I stayed in close contact with several interlocutors, and followed how their personal histories were developing, but was unable to move forward in anything resembling data analysis. Instead, I took on other projects, threw myself into teaching opportunities, applications for jobs and research grants – all the other 'stuff' of academia that I could justify to myself was still a valid part of 'the job'.

Conclusion

Often the decision to do research on topics of violence, or in contexts of violence, stems from a strong sense of identification with the communities who will become research participants, or out of the hope that research can be used to change a situation of injustice. While a passion for the topic you are working on can be deeply motivating, it must be coupled with the right skill set to do this work safely for yourself and your interlocutors.

Violence can interact with fieldwork in innumerable ways. In response to the many challenges it invokes, it is fundamental that researchers take seriously their responsibility to doing safe and ethical work. Despite an immense peer support network of colleagues working on or in contexts of violence during my own doctoral research, we all shared a feeling that we 'should be able to handle it', and that discussions of the challenges we faced were somehow not welcome in academic spaces.

This must change, and one way of achieving this is to strengthen awareness among researchers surrounding the indications of unwellness as a result of fieldwork. This must be accompanied by an acknowledgement within institutions of the impact that fieldwork in and on contexts of violence and instability can have on researchers; and an action plan to provide researchers undertaking work in the name of that institution with appropriate support. Failure to do so risks grave consequences for both researchers and participants in research.

Recommendations

1 **Think broadly about the ways that violence might interact with your fieldwork.** Challenges related to violence during fieldwork are not limited to researchers working in explicitly violent places. Use the scenarios posed at the start of this chapter to think through the nuanced ways that you might encounter violence in your fieldsite, and how this will affect the direction of your work, the questions you can ask, the sensitivities you will need to navigate and the toll your research might take on you and your participants.
2 **Find out what support is available within your institution.** If your institution does not provide meaningful support to researchers pre-, during and post-fieldwork, find out why not and approach senior members of your department to ask for this to change. There are growing models of good practice in this area, and harnessing support from senior colleagues and supervisors can help to take these discussions to a higher institutional level. If possible, seek this information out before starting fieldwork rather than waiting for something challenging to happen.
3 **Be realistic about what you can work on.** Working in contexts or in subjects of violence is extremely hard. Even if this is a context you know intimately, or a subject matter that you feel passionate about, take seriously the toll that this work can take. University resources for support for researchers are often limited and it is vital to only embark upon this work if you have the personal capabilities and available support networks to do so.

4 **During fieldwork, make time to speak with your participants about the ways the research is affecting them, and do your best to offer avenues of support to those you work with.** Make time for conversations with your participants about the research process. It is vital not to over-promise help to your research participants. At the same time, when working on subjects and in contexts where lives are at risk, to simply state during the consent process that you cannot offer tangible help to those you work with can feel inadequate. Talk to researchers who have previously worked on your topic or in your fieldsite to develop a list of resources and services that might be useful for research participants. Share these lists with your participants and ask for their input to improve them for future research participants you might encounter.

5 **During analysis and writing, separate and manage data that you have but can't use.** In my experience, the easiest way to navigate this is to separate out this data as quickly as possible – decide whether it is safe to store it or better to delete it from your files and not to input this data into any form of analytical software or process – that is, not to be tempted to subsequently use it when you have promised interlocutors that you will not.

Further reading

Abdelnour, S. and Abu Moghli, M. 2021. Researching violent contexts: A call for political reflexivity. *Organization*, July.

This article articulates the goal of political reflexivity for research on violent contexts, drawing from feminist standpoint theory to emphasise the importance of researchers examining their privilege in relation to the geopolitics of the research setting, epistemic privilege of marginalised participants and the political implications of their work.

Enria, L. 2018. Elective affinities: Fragility and injustice in the field. *New Ethnographer* blog post. Available at thenewethnographer.com/the-new-ethnographer/2018/04/25/elective-affinities-fragility-and-injustice-in-the-field (accessed 3 October 2023).

This deeply personal and reflective essay invites researchers to confront the practical, theoretical and political implications of acknowledging their own fragility during fieldwork.

Grimm, J., Koehler, K., Lust-Okar, E., Saliba, I. and Schierenbeck, I. 2020. Safer Field Research in the Social Sciences: A Guide to Human and Digital Security in Hostile Environments. London: Sage.

This book is based on the authors' experiences in conflict settings around the world, and is made up of real-life examples to develop best-practice guidance for conducting research in hostile environments. The book includes a number of tools and templates to help you design and develop a security framework for your research.

Pearlman, L.A. and McKay, L. 2008. Understanding and Addressing Vicarious Trauma: A Reading Course. Headington Institute. Available at mutualaiddisasterrelief.org/wp-content/uploads/2017/05/vtmoduletemplate2_ready_v2_85791.pdf (accessed 3 October 2023).

The Headington Institute provides a variety of literature, studies, training modules and other resources for individuals working in complex and dangerous environments. This reading course offers clear guidance on recognising, managing and addressing vicarious trauma.

Utas, M. 2019. Exploring the backstage: Methodological and ethical issues surrounding the role of research brokers in insecure zones. *Civil Wars*, 21(2), 271–285.

Utas has recently been exploring the role and use of research brokers, intermediaries and assistants in research in and on the context of violence, tackling questions and issues that, as he writes, 'many of us either battle with or consciously ignore – because they are hard' (p. 157–78). This article is part of a broader project looking at the risks researchers expose to assistants and brokers, including, in ethnographic terms, 'key interlocutors' in the field.

References

Abdelnour, S. and Abu Moghli, M. 2021. 'Researching violent contexts: A call for political reflexivity'. *Organization*, July. doi:10.1177/1350508421103064

Aroussi, S. 2020. Survivors are researchers too. *Sexual Violence Research Initiative* (SVRI) blog. Available at www.svri.org/blog/survivors-are-researchers-too (accessed 3 October 2023).

Association of Social Anthropologists (ASA) 2021. *Ethical Guidelines: Additional Resources*. Available at www.theasa.org/downloads/ethics/asa_ethicsgl_resources.pdf (accessed 3 October 2023).

Cronin-Furman, K. and Lake, M. 2018. Ethics abroad: Fieldwork in fragile and violent contexts. *Political Science and Politics*, 51(3), 607–14.

Cullen, P., Dawson, M., Price, J. and Rowlands, J. 2021. Intersectionality and invisible victims: Reflections on data challenges and vicarious trauma in femicide, family and intimate partner homicide research. *Journal of Family Violence*, 36, 619–28.

Grimm, J., Koehler, K., Lust-Okar, E., Saliba, I. and Schierenbeck, I. 2020. *Safer Field Research in the Social Sciences: A Guide to Human and Digital Security in Hostile Environments*. London: Sage.

Markovitz, A. 2019. The better to break and bleed with: Research, violence, and trauma. *Geopolitics*, 26(1), 94–117.

McCann, I.L. and Pearlman, L.A. 1990. Vicarious traumatization: A framework for understanding the psychological effects of working with victims. *Journal of Traumatic Stress*, 3(1), 131–49.

McNeil-Willson, R. 2020. The murky world of extremism research. *New Ethnographer* blog. Available at thenewethnographer.com/the-new-ethnographer/the-murky-world-of-extremism-research (accessed 3 October 2023).

Millar, G. (Ed.) 2019. *Engaging Ethnographic Peace Research*. London: Routledge.

Procter, C., Spector, B. and Freed, M. 2024, forthcoming in Teaching Anthropology. 'Field of screams revisited: Contending with trauma in ethnographic fieldwork'. *Teaching Anthropology*

Rivas, A. and Browne, B. (Eds.) 2019. *Experiences in Researching Conflict and Violence: Fieldwork Interrupted*. Bristol: Bristol University Press.

Schulz, P., Kreft, A., Touquet, H. and Martin, S. 2022. Self-care for gender-based violence researchers: Beyond bubble baths and chocolate pralines. *Qualitative Research*, April. doi:10.1177/14687941221087868

Weiss, N., Grassiani, E. and Green, L. (Eds.) 2023. *The Entanglements of Ethnographic Fieldwork in a Violent World*. London: Routledge.

11

FIELDWORK AND FEELED-WORK: ADDRESSING MENTAL HEALTH IN ETHNOGRAPHY

Emma Louise Backe and Alex Fitzpatrick

Summary

This chapter focuses on the role of mental health in ethnographic fieldwork and training, and proposes steps towards broadening our disciplinary ethos of care. We outline the ubiquity of mental health concerns that still implicitly inform ethnographic fieldwork, as well as the absence of adequate support mechanisms. In order to address these mental health needs, we recommend including mental healthcare modules in methodological training; cultivating conversations that destigmatise mental illness; professional development; improved referral mechanisms, safety planning and support protocols; and adopting orientations towards transformative care and mutual aid.

Table of contents

Introduction 149
The 'heart' of the field: Understanding trauma and mental illness during fieldwork 151
Mental health training and institutional support 154
Improving our head space 157
Conclusion 161
Recommendations 162
Further reading 163
References 164

EXAMPLE 11.1

Before my shift as a rape crisis hotline advocate begins, I run through the breathing exercises I've been trained to employ with clients. Throughout my ethnographic fieldwork at the rape crisis centre, I increasingly drew upon my crisis management training for my own emotional regulation. In occupying the dual roles as ethnographer and advocate, I traversed the delicate spaces of feeling activated around sexual violence, simultaneously affirming the sentiments of pain, guilt and shame voiced by callers, and documenting the intense emotional labour enacted by rape crisis advocates. The longer I bore witness to the suffering articulated on the hotline, the more the thin interface between callers' trauma and my own dissipated. My field notes seemed shot through with despair, my own affect growing more and more numb to maintain my personal composure and emotional boundaries. I started so many sentences with 'How are you doing today?' I forgot to ask the question of myself.

Introduction

The mental health challenges that often accompany fieldwork are a public secret of ethnography. While a utilitarian approach to studying emotion offers opportunities for ethnographic insights, experiences of anxiety, depression, or trauma as part of fieldwork remain highly stigmatised and concealed. Ethnographers with pre-existing mental health issues, or those who develop mental illness complications through research, are immersed in a disciplinary logic of toughness, one in which an individual's affective composure signifies their professionalism and academic preparedness. We are expected to modulate our emotions and manage the psychological costs of mental disorders, as well as the emotional trials that might accompany our fieldsite, lest we signal our illegitimacy or ineptitude as authentic ethnographers. Yet studies have shown that mental illness is on the rise in academia, with research indicating that nearly half of academics demonstrate signs of psychological distress (Fletcher et al., 2022). Depression, sleep issues, eating disorders, substance and alcohol abuse, self-harm and suicidal ideation are all common among PhD students and academic researchers, many of whom are precariously positioned within the job market and have only limited access to mental health services.

This chapter seeks to facilitate a conversation about the role of mental health in ethnographic fieldwork and training and propose steps towards broadening our disciplinary ethos of care. It is informed by a small survey that was circulated globally to practising anthropologists, at various stages of training and professional stability, to understand the contemporary challenges of ethnographic fieldwork. This survey also considered the ways that contemporary ethnographic training has come to account for, or summarily exclude, the role of mental illness and emotional wellbeing throughout the ethnographic process. The results of the survey that we will detail outline the ubiquity of concerns like depression, anxiety, trauma and isolation that still typify the experience of ethnographic fieldwork, as well as the relative absence of support mechanisms for students, practitioners and postgraduates seeking help.[1] The survey is supplemented by a review of the literature[2] (both grey and academic) pertaining to mental health concerns in ethnography. This chapter is indebted to the work of Amy Pollard who, in 2009, conducted similar research among ethnographers in the UK, revealing intense expressions of unpreparedness to handle or address the mental health challenges of ethnography. Finally, in the spirit of feminist praxis, the authors – a medical anthropologist and an archaeologist – draw upon their own experiences with emotional distress throughout fieldwork, including autoethnographic vignettes to illustrate where and how mental health issues and neurodivergence manifest. We highlight the growing visibility of mental illness in ethnography; identify the structural, social and institutional mechanisms that play a role in ethnographers' vulnerability (including the underlying assumptions around what it takes to 'thrive' within academia); and propose a new orientation to emotion in the field.

We recognise the slipperiness of terminology like *mental health* within an ethnographic context. Medical anthropologists in particular have long critiqued Western psychological and psychiatric diagnostic criteria in their tendency to impose pathologised framings of social conditions that occur within a nexus of biology, culture and ecology. Understandings of circumstances like mental health are necessarily mobile and mutable, although the biomedical axis of knowledge and power tends to elevate and reify Western conceptualisations of mental disorders. Despite the contested nature of concepts like mental health in ethnographic enquiry, however, conditions like depression and trauma are nevertheless experientially and materially real for those who suffer from them. While some ethnographers may not identify with diagnoses like anxiety disorder, many report the symptoms typically associated with such a diagnostic claim. Rather than seeking to problematise and complicate these diagnostic categories, the goal of this chapter is to acknowledge the veracity of claims to discomfort, pain and harm, and to chart a path forward, striving to build a thoroughgoing ethos of care in our ethnographic praxis.

The 'heart' of the field: Understanding trauma and mental illness during fieldwork

At the beginning of Ruth Behar's *The Vulnerable Observer*, she cautions her readers, 'This anthropology is not for the softhearted' (1996, p. 24). There is an assumption, then, of the hardness of ethnographic fieldwork, the simultaneous flexibility and rigidity demanded of research. As one respondent to our survey noted, 'I was told that "everyone struggles in the field", but that you just have to figure it out on your own.' Within this ethos of difficulty, however, the mental health outcomes of fieldwork have been largely effaced or ignored. Among the 20 survey respondents, almost half reported experiences of anxiety and depression during their fieldwork. Others conveyed issues of stress, substance use, feelings of isolation and self-doubt, chronic fatigue and trauma.[3] This section will go on to detail the numerous mental health challenges ethnographers experience throughout fieldwork, enumerating the emotional challenges of ethnography and the ways in which mental illness can manifest as a contingency of research.

Isolation and loneliness are not uncommon for fieldwork, even among those who conduct their research closer to 'home'. As ethnographers work to embed themselves in their host communities, establishing rapport and trust, let alone lasting friendships and relationships, can be a challenge. Although the 'remoteness' of the field has been transformed with the introduction of information and communication technologies, fieldwork is still marked by long periods of uncertainty. The self-doubt of what is being 'accomplished' during fieldwork generates its own form of isolation – ethnographers report self-isolation during periods of uncertainty, concerned that their productivity or indecision will be received poorly.

Anecdotes about struggling with anxiety and depression during archaeological fieldwork have been documented through the use of a Twitter hashtag, *#DiggingWhileDepressed*. Originally started as a means of discussing how the isolation and difficult working conditions of excavation can negatively impact mental health, the hashtag was taken up by other archaeologists to discuss their own experiences in the field. Many participants in the discussion shared similar stories of emotional and physical isolation as they worked in demanding environments away from friends and family for prolonged periods of time. Additionally, archaeological fieldwork is often marked by the physical risk associated with excavation – injuries obtained during work can lead to feeling like a burden; an injured archaeologist can easily slip into feelings of depression and self-doubt. Although one participant noted that some commercial companies in the UK are starting to recognise the severity of mental health in the field, it is still accepted by many that physical and mental suffering is simply an occupational hazard that cannot be avoided.

Feelings of anxiety and depression have been similarly cited as commonplace during fieldwork. Mental health conditions that arise during or due to fieldwork impact the ethnographic process; for instance, depression can manifest as disinterest or an inability to care, which renders the ethnographer an unusable tool for research. Indeed, complications elicited in the field do not dissipate upon returning 'home'. Transcribing, coding and analysing field notes, interviews and other ethnographic data can re-trigger or exacerbate latent mental health issues. We cannot plan for everything that may occur during fieldwork, but it is just as difficult to estimate the repercussions that can follow and how entrenched these repercussions can become within our psyche.

EXAMPLE 11.2

'This isn't just hard work,' the Executive Director of the rape crisis centre reminds advocates at a volunteer meeting, 'it's heart work.' Considering the emotional labour necessitated by the advocacy role, 'emotional burnout', as the Executive Director advises the group, 'is very real'. It's difficult not to be invested in the sentiments of clients. You start to feel for and feel with the survivors you talk with daily, even as that emotional vulnerability is expected to remain one-sided. An ethos of self-care infuses the crisis centre's approach to wellbeing. Take care of yourself. But amidst an absence of trauma-informed mental health services for survivors, advocates also struggled to access the support they needed. What do you do when you're on the front-line of a mental health crisis and have no recourse to care at these ethnographic edges?

Trauma in and of the field

Trauma, especially, is not uncommon in ethnographic fieldwork (Reyes-Foster and Lester, 2019). Experiences of trauma can relate to the subject matter and placement of the fieldwork itself. Several survey participants mentioned working in fragile states or conflict zones, where they regularly encountered exposure to violence. Others worked in contexts that elicited strong emotional responses in their interlocutors, such as neonatal intensive care units where babies were born at the edge of viability. Still others interacted with communities that had perpetrated or undergone violence, dispossession and loss of life, thereby interfacing with individuals undergoing their own processes of recovery. The daily encounters with these forms of structural, symbolic and physical violence can take an emotional toll on researchers, signalling the importance of recognising the role of secondary or vicarious trauma among communities working on the frontline. Research among nurses, rape crisis advocates and case workers indicates that trauma can almost operate as a contagion, infecting individuals providing care on a day-to-day basis (Frey et al., 2017). In these circumstances, applied anthropologists might adopt roles that involve care, labour and assistance to those in distress, which can also lead to compassion fatigue or emotional burnout, resulting in a greater likelihood of frustration or limited empathy among those whose affective fuses have begun to wear thin. For ethnographers of colour, and those from the impacted communities, this issue is further exacerbated, as discussed in Chapter 6.

Violence, harassment and assault

Trauma can also emerge as the result of personal experiences of violence or assault. Several survey respondents reported having experienced sexual assault and harassment in the field, a form of gendered and sexual violence that has long gone overlooked in ethnographic training or analysis (Hanson and Richards, 2019). As Eva Moreno (1995, p. 246) writes from her positionality as an ethnographer and survivor of sexual violence,

> As far as the danger of sexual violence is concerned, it may be part of a woman's daily life, but it is not seen to be relevant to the professional part of ourselves – the 'anthropologist' part. 'Anthropologists' don't get harassed or raped. Women do.

The fact that Moreno published her article under a pseudonym is especially telling of the stigma associated with sexual violence, and the additional alienation anthropologists may face disclosing such experiences in a professional setting. In a survey of academic field experiences among biological anthropologists related to harassment and assault, 64 per cent report experiencing sexual harassment in the field and over 20 per cent reported having personally experienced sexual assault while conducting fieldwork (Clancy et al., 2019). Not only were women more likely to report these incidents, but trainees (from undergraduate students to post-docs) were also more frequently targeted for abuse and harassment, indicating the internecine roles of gender, age and professional status in experiences of violence and vulnerability in the field (Clancy et al., 2019). Ethnographers – particularly women, queer folks, and scholars of colour – have endeavoured to break the silence around the vulnerabilities to sexual violence researchers face in the field, noting that the discipline's silence represents its own form of symbolic violence (Berry et al., 2018).

This growing recognition of the intersectional vulnerabilities ethnographers face – cutting across dimensions of race, gender, ethnicity, sexuality, age and physical capability – must be coupled with an understanding of the psychological consequences of sexual violence. Continuous exposure to harassment or incident(s) of sexual assault can result in a panoply of symptoms and sentiments. Ethnographers who experience assault in the field may no longer feel safe conducting research at their chosen site, in addition to concerns that disclosure to their home departments will be met with judgement or reprehension. Trauma associated with rape, sexual assault or violence can also instigate a neurobiological complex in which individuals are 'triggered' by sounds, sights, or smells associated with the traumatising incident(s), triggers that might otherwise disrupt a traditional research day. The psychological symptoms of trauma can also manifest as emotional disruption or dysregulation, spanning from intense mood swings to dissociation. Considering the emotional presence required of interviewing and participant observation, critical tools in any ethnographic research process, these complicated emotional responses elicited by a mental health diagnosis like trauma cannot be treated as separate from what it means to do anthropological work.

Deconstructing the 'imagined default ethnographer'

Discussions of sexual violence and mental health must also occur along a continuum of vulnerabilities often obscured in the ethnographic process. As one survey respondent indicates, 'the imagined grad student is male, cis, white, hetero, no special or curtailed capacities, wealthy, with a large safety net and no dependants'. A similar observation has been made of research positions within academia as a whole – that they were originally structured to accommodate middle-class, able-bodied, hetero, cis single men and have remained as such. This unmarked yet implicit expectation about who an ethnographer is, and how their identity operates in the field, means that we also need to take into account the visible and invisible disabilities that might impact a scholar's work, health and mobility considerations that have only become amplified since the emergence of COVID-19. Individuals with chronic illnesses might find their health exacerbated by conditions at their fieldsite, experiencing bouts of illness that can impact their mental wellbeing. Many ethnographers also enter the field with pre-existing mental health concerns, ones that are rarely accounted for by academic institutions, or the neoliberal presumptions of continuous productivity expected within higher education. Universities may not be equipped to provide the financial or institutional support necessary to manage mental health symptoms and ensure that ethnographers are able to receive adequate treatment in the field. While fieldwork is an immense privilege associated with ethnography, it also presents incredible risks and challenges for those with pre-existing conditions.

Mental health complications associated with fieldwork accordingly impact how, where and in what capacity ethnographic research can be conducted. Respondents to the survey noted that some changed fieldsite locations following an incident of assault or after ongoing feelings of insecurity. Some felt as though they needed to leave their fieldsite on a regular basis in order to get some emotional distance from the labours of their research, or cut short the intended duration of time they'd planned to spend in the field. Issues with anxiety, depression or trauma can also lead to problems of mistrust, difficulty connecting with others, or a retreat from socialising, occurrences that can also impact how ethnographers are able to interact with their interlocutors and community, let alone take care of themselves. In contexts such as these, individuals may feel angry or guilty for not being as productive as they would like, compounding the emotional complications of an already effectively tense situation. Mental health considerations are both a matter of an ethnographer's wellbeing and their ability to conduct the kind of ethnographic fieldwork they set out to accomplish.

Mental health training and institutional support

Perhaps one of the reasons why ethnographers experience mental health crises in the field is due to the comparative absence of methodological training or preparation regarding mental illness in graduate school. This section will be dedicated to tracing the elision of mental illness in undergraduate or graduate guidance for the field; the mental health stigma that prevents disclosure or help-seeking; and the limited psychosocial care options available within traditional universities or research settings.

Departmental preparation and support

Echoing the experiences of Pollard's (2009) research, none of the respondents to our survey felt like they had the pre-fieldwork resources or guidance they needed to recognise and account for mental health issues during their research beyond informal mentions of 'fieldwork blues' or loneliness. 'In my experience,' one participant remarks,

> I had no preparation before going into field research, and I didn't always feel supported during research. I think part of that comes from the fact that people don't talk openly about their negative experiences in the field and, when they do, it's spoken as if those experiences are just part of the game and you have to deal with them to get to the other side.

Ethnographic training in some institutions may be more theoretical in nature, rather than focusing on the practical and applied dimensions of fieldwork. Many anthropology and social science programmes still fail to provide methodological training for their PhD students, focusing instead on the experience-near, improvisational aspects of fieldwork that require self-reflexivity and flexibility. Even considerations like safety planning – ensuring that students have protocols in place in the incident of an emergency – are still largely absent.

Ethnographers rarely feel supported by their academic advisors in discussing feelings of depression, isolation, or anxiety in relation to their fieldwork. Indeed, as Pollard observes,

> A significant number of students expressed feeling silenced when talking about fieldwork with their supervisors. There was a consensus that the need to maintain a 'professional' relationship limited the extent to which they could speak candidly about their experiences. Students reported that they tended to play down difficulties in the field, and wherever possible show how they were going to make difficulties productive in their dissertations.
>
> (2009, p. 15)

Ten years later, the same sentiment is echoed in our own survey – 'I felt like I couldn't discuss it at all. That admitting I was having mental health issues meant I was not meant to be an anthropologist,' said one, while another commented, 'I never felt comfortable speaking about it with advisors or professors. I was worried it would make me look like a bad anthropologist to say that things were upsetting, depressing, lonely.' There is an overwhelming sensibility that issues of emotional hardship are 'unprofessional' or signal the personal ineptitude of the ethnographer's ability to 'get the job done' attitudes that belie deeper prejudices and structural barriers towards neurodivergence and mental health need within the academy.

For students and practitioners who do reach out to their advisors for help, some are dismissed or rebuffed, finding their experiences invalidated or used against them. There might be generational gaps in understandings of mental illness as signs of personal weakness, or institutional issues in terms of how well staff are trained to provide mental health support. It should also be noted that academic staff are rarely compensated for mentorship that occurs outside formal teaching and administrative contexts. Informal emotional support emerges in the intersubjective context of faculty or supervisors going out of their way to support struggling students, even though these personal dimensions of mentorship are not part of the technical responsibilities of the job. Women of colour in academia often bear the disproportionate burden of this type of care for their students (Berry et al., 2018; Navarro et al., 2013). Ethnographers who decide to take time away from the field to undergo treatment or therapy may find their decision belittled, or discover that their funding package is jeopardised by such an 'unproductive' use of time during the dissertation process. Beyond interpersonal mentorship and supervision, mental health services at universities and research institutions are notoriously insufficient.

Coping mechanisms

Rather than risk perceptions of unprofessionalism, many ethnographers turn to peer and family support networks to get them through mental health challenges. It's not uncommon for individuals to establish informal care networks with fellow students or peers, although there might still be concerns of judgement for disclosing feelings of depression or loneliness. While some respondents to our survey were able to access the psychiatric treatment and psychosocial care they needed through their institutional networks, far more relied upon health insurance through family members or spouses. Others had the disposable income necessary to take trips out of their fieldsite, or engage in remote therapy, which served as informal coping mechanisms for psychological difficulties. An ethos of 'self-care' pervades much of the literature on how ethnographers cope with mental illness in the field, laying the responsibility of recovery on the individual. But this ethos is also fundamentally privileged and neoliberal in nature, marking the difficulties of care for individuals without the financial means to pursue alternative options or the community support mechanisms necessary to manage their symptoms effectively. The popularity of self-care practices that require disposable income or free time leads to an unhealthy idealisation that may cause further stress on an individual when said practices do not automatically 'fix' their mental health. In fact, individuals who struggled to access mental healthcare reported turning to substances as an alternative coping mechanism. The use of alcohol and other drugs as a form of 'self-care' represents the toxic cycle of mental health complications that can sometimes lead to a cascading effect. Self-care as a solution is also premised on accommodating what might be considered a fundamentally triggering and discriminatory social environment, rather than transforming the cultural institutions that instigate crisis, or recognising that recovery is rarely linear, prescribed or permanent.

Universities and institutions have, unfortunately, taken a similarly perfunctory approach to mental health for their students, faculty members and staff, prioritising publicity-friendly events over meaningful care or systematic change. For instance, many universities and colleges still employ a short-term, crisis-oriented approach to counselling and therapy. This type of limited counselling model was initially conceived to help students with a narrow set of psychological issues such as homesickness or school-related stress, providing crisis relief services that address a narrow vision of transition from emergency to stabilisation. This crisis-oriented approach, however, presumes that psychological issues can be dealt with in three to six counselling sessions and then referred elsewhere. For students whose psychosocial needs fall outside the strict parameters of a crisis paradigm, or those who don't have the health insurance to cover out-of-school referrals, the university offers few solutions. The limited psychological resources available to students, post-docs and faculty members are not only constrained by time, but also space. Considering that many ethnographers conduct their fieldwork in remote locations, digital or mobile mental health services by phone or internet could serve as a useful recourse or bridge during the months or years away. Such platforms, however, have yet to be scaled up in any meaningful way at universities, and still require digital resources like a strong Wi-Fi connection or smartphones with enough data to sustain long-distance conversations.

Ultimately, ethnographers who experience or develop mental health complications through the process of the fieldwork report feeling abandoned by the very discipline they've chosen to pursue; by their professors, supervisors and mentors; and by the institutions that profit from their theoretical and intellectual interventions but remain either unwilling or incapable of intervening to provide comprehensive, holistic and trauma-informed mental healthcare support. Ethnographers may be warned that fieldwork can be a challenging and isolating experience, but rarely are they cautioned about the isolation they might suffer from within their own departments.

━━━━━━━━━ EXAMPLE 11.3 ━━━━━━━━━

I am standing on the metro, the same song playing on a loop in my earbuds. I've learned that the sway of the train helps to ground me in my body, especially on days when I'm prone to dissociation. I've been given lately to fits of floating, detached from my body to observe from a distance. I have become a participant-observer of myself. Sometimes the numbing serves as a protective factor. Other times I fear the absence of feeling. I haven't learned yet how to hold the stories I hear on the hotline. To dismiss or forget the narratives told to me feels like an abdication of my ability to care – all I have to do is hold space for them. But that act of holding is both generative and multiplicative – a cascading effect of disclosure and trauma. Caring is transitive, with the interior and the exterior pushing against one another. Among the stories I hold are also my own. This act of witnessing is never politically or emotionally neutral.

Improving our head space

Ethnography excels in the vulnerability of experience-near methodologies, calling upon modes of embodiment that position the researcher within the lived experiences and affective landscapes of their fieldsite. Yet the emotional dimensions of fieldwork also tend to be taken up in academic literature through a functionalist perspective, urging anthropologists to consider how emotions allow them to sense and experience the same things as their interlocutors, reinforcing an emphasis on emotions having to be 'productive' or theory-building in the field. The same could be said of the mental health consequences that necessarily accompany this state of emotion – in the postmodern turn, and the increasing adoption of applied methods in fieldwork, we cannot ignore the personal stakes and psychological crises that can accompany this research. The personal aspects of an individual's identity, medical history, or mental health status are not evacuated by this new positionality in the field. Indeed, in many cases the process of ethnographic exploration exacerbates old wounds or affects new internal conditions. Vicarious trauma due to the nature of the field, the subject matter of the fieldwork and the extent to which the ethnographer comes to interface with stories and experiences that stretch personal coping strategies can no longer be overlooked or deemed as diagnoses of 'weakness'. We do ourselves and our communities a disservice the more we treat issues like depression, bipolar disorder and trauma as problems of the 'Other,' or systematically elide experiences of injury or hardship to elevate the myth of the fieldworker as intrepid hero. This collective responsibility can be taken up within the ethnographic community in a number of ways, including: mental healthcare modules in methodological training; cultivating conversations that destigmatise mental illness; professional development; improved referral mechanisms, safety planning and support protocols during crisis; and adopting orientations towards transformative care and mutual aid.

Ethnographic training

First and foremost, mental health considerations must be integrated into *ethnographic training for researchers throughout their careers*. Preparatory field methods courses can include modules on mental health. These modules could reference existing literature on the emotional toll of fieldwork and allow instructors to speak more openly about the 'toughness' of their own ethnographic research. As one survey respondent notes,

> the difference I felt when I finally heard somebody say, 'Yes, I know how that feels. I went through something like that. It was awful and I felt like shit,' was huge. It validated my experience and made me stop doubting myself. I had been telling myself for years that I was a bad anthropologist for letting my anxiety get to me. That's the first thing that needs to change – acknowledge that these challenges are real, and that your feelings are real and valid.

Open conversations about the possibilities of mental health issues throughout fieldwork will help to reduce the secrecy and stigma surrounding mental illness in ethnography. Greater transparency by instructors will also help to break down the myth of individualism and self-sufficiency in field research, recognise both vulnerability and fallibility and affirm that care itself must remain central to our training pedagogies.

Whether in the context of formal field courses or professional development workshops, methodological attention to mental health should also equip students and researchers with the tools to address mental health challenges. This preparation can include *departmental protocols for safety planning* if conflict or violence breaks out, if the individual experiences a physical attack or sexual assault at their site, or if the researcher no longer feels safe conducting fieldwork at their chosen location. Prior to departing for the field, researchers should be made aware of their mental healthcare resources and options available through their university or affiliated research institution, especially if remote or digital therapy options are available, or if the researcher anticipates issues accessing pharmaceutical medication they need during their fieldwork. Coordinating conversations within the classroom, or encouraging informal discussion to occur outside a professional setting, regarding personal coping mechanisms and self-care techniques will also prepare students to consider their own forms of self-efficacy and share resources and practices they employ during mental health crises. It is vital that institutional support is balanced with giving students the ability to exercise their own agency with regards to their individual care and wellbeing.

Professional development

Instructors, researchers and academics may not necessarily be trained or equipped to address considerations of mental health in the classroom. Ethnographic organisations like the American Anthropological Association (AAA) should invest in *professional development* to ensure that professors possess the knowledge, skills and resources they need to speak to the role of mental health in ethnographic fieldwork. This professional development can draw upon the institutional resources already in existence at many universities, like the dynamics of trauma-informed care provided by Title IX Offices in American institutions or counselling centres. Departments can work to establish relationships and referral mechanisms with trained and designated mental health practitioners at their universities so that they can better connect students and other scholars with the resources they need without taking on additional labour.

Universities and institutions must also commit towards systematic change in the way that they approach mental health on an establishment-wide level (Fletcher et al., 2022). To properly accommodate those with mental health issues, universities and institutions must first allocate proper funding specifically for mental healthcare. With funding secured, programmes and policies will need to be developed that address the various mental health issues and conditions that appear among their students and faculty. We suggest creating a committee dedicated to this task, enlisting staff members, student representatives and mental health specialists as members. This would allow for the necessary expertise required to handle these issues while including the voices of those who are most affected. Additionally, suggestions from staff and students alike would allow for the scope of mental healthcare to broaden beyond specific programmes. As problems such as precarious employment, difficult workloads and financial anxieties can exacerbate mental health issues, it will be necessary for a potential mental health committee to also support and lobby for better conditions within academia.

Transformative care

On a larger scale, we must inevitably address the overarching elements that create such precarious and harmful environments for ethnographers. One possible way to accomplish this is through *transformative care*. Within the conceptual framework of transformative justice, injustice is not just resolved, but transformed into constructive and tangible change. With transformative care, we are not only concerned with finding solutions, but also in dismantling the structures that allow these problems to flourish, and prohibit our own individual and collective flourishing. Transformative care recognises that systematic oppression – stimulated by capitalism and differentially inflected through the various identities and subject positions that ethnographers occupy – creates the sociocultural context that can cultivate and further exacerbate mental health issues. By eliminating these oppressive structures and replacing them with ones that encourage healthier, more equitable environments, transformative care can produce treatments that actively heal, rather than replicate unhealthy dynamics.

To set transformative care into action, the ethnographic community may benefit from adapting collective strategies used within activist circles. Activists practise solidarity by maintaining support networks at a grassroots level and building communities of *mutual aid*. Mutual aid has long been practised as a means of using the strength of a collective to subvert systems with unequal power dynamics; for example, as current healthcare systems are often influenced by governmental bodies or the pharmaceutical industry, medical networks centred around mutual aid can allow patients to bypass a corrupt system that actively harms and marginalises others. Mutual aid examines these institutional and structural factors with a critical eye and resists the urge towards individualism, using in its stead a praxis of communal support and active communication to collectively organise and provide aid to others.

For ethnographers, mutual aid can be employed through *peer support groups and unions*. These communities place emphasis on combating isolation through group support and inclusion. It should be noted that peer support groups are *not* led by an external specialist like a psychiatrist or physician; instead, the entire group consists of people who share a common issue (such as mental illness) and rely on chosen facilitators or communal trust within the group to allow meetings to progress smoothly. This non-hierarchical, peer-based approach has been noted in studies to be rather successful in a variety of groups. Student unions within and across university settings are similarly critical to collecting data on the needs of ethnographers in the academy, formulating a shared set of goals within intellectual collectives and holding institutions accountable for gaps in the continuum of care.

These recommendations should be taken as an incitement to action, rather than a comprehensive protocol for ethnography writ large. Transitions need to occur simultaneously from the top down and from the bottom up, beginning, first and foremost, with anthropology departments committing to the emotional, as well as the intellectual needs of their scholars and staff members. Mobilisation will likely need to begin from within, turning the gaze inward as so often happens in the self-reflexive turn. Yet the labour of transformation cannot only fall on the junior scholars – it must be a collective manifesto, one in which we are all invested in building one another up.

Conclusion

Ethnographers who enter the field are encouraged to radically shift their mental landscapes, a cognitive and affective move which allows them to feel with and alongside the places and people that populate their research. Our mode of ethnographic inhabitation is meant to destabilize and unsettle, especially as the exposed nerves of inquiry, intellect and emotion become activated. Yet graduate students from all disciplines find themselves in increasingly precarious situations. Not only are they faced with the uncertainty of what lies beyond graduation, but also a world beset by competing crises: of the environment, of the economy, of public health, of attacks against autonomy and existence. As such, it should come as no surprise that their mental health is at great risk. While a comprehensive study of ethnographers in graduate programmes, or those who have graduated from universities and are currently working in ethnographic settings, has yet to be conducted, our survey, the growing body of autoethnographic literature and informal conversations on anthropology blogs, digital forums and online platforms signal a similar oversaturation of psychological concerns within the ethnographic community.

As anthropology continues to diversify and ethnography is increasingly taken up in other academic disciplines and professional settings, we must strive to ensure that our ethos of inclusion, respect and care is modelled in the ways that we acknowledge and attend to mental illness. Let us therefore remain attentive to the practices of care we carry into our work. We must bring a sense of responsibility to our academic coalitions and those who have chosen to dedicate themselves to the labour of ethnographic work. Let us look, then, towards the possibilities such emotional attentiveness can enact among ethnographers, and the futures such encounters with mental illness can anticipate.

EXAMPLE 11.4

'Would you like to co-author a chapter on mental health?' I pause before I answer and think about the difficult year I've just had. Only months ago, I was at my lowest point since my nervous breakdown at the start of 2017. Fieldwork that year had been difficult; a traumatic accident left me physically and mentally unable to return to our work-site. For three weeks, I worked indoors while the rest of my team was out, confronting terrible weather conditions and doing back-breaking labour in caves. They were doing the 'real' archaeology – while I, on the other hand, sat alone doing analytical work. I felt guilty and cowardly. How could I call myself an archaeologist? Some days, I would take brief walks in the woods and think about never going back. I always returned, of course, but it got increasingly harder. Finally, one emotionally draining evening, I turned to Twitter. #DiggingWhileDepressed: what started as a single hashtag became a virtual therapy group, where archaeologists from around the world shared their experiences with mental illness during fieldwork. I thought about how that solidarity made me feel. It didn't cure my depression, of course, but knowing that I wasn't alone at least helped light up those last few days of excavation. I still struggle with talking about mental health, and I knew that writing about something that affected me so intimately would be like walking through a minefield of triggers. But I also knew how important this work would be. So, finally, I replied, 'Yes.'

Recommendations

1. **Integrate mental health considerations into ethnographic training and departmental policies.** This will help to reduce the invisibility and stigma of mental illness. Departmental policies should consider what additional supports and institutional leverage and networks can be drawn upon to ensure that students can speak openly about their struggles, and receive flexible and sensitive assistance if mental health issues arise.
2. **Institutionalise departmental protocols for safety planning.** Every department should have a protocol in place for safety planning if conflict, violence or other forms of disruption (political, climactic, or personal) arise in the context of fieldwork. These protocols should ensure that if practitioners experience a mental health crisis, they are not left by themselves to navigate accessing logistics and support, or will experience penalties as a result of potential delays.
3. **Invest in professional development and mentorship around mental health.** Ethnographic organisations, communities and departments should embark on training and professionalisation around mental health with the goal of increasing sensitivity, awareness, responsiveness and understanding of the resources available to students and practitioners. Departments should take the time to educate themselves on the accommodations that can be made within their community, and cultivate opportunities for mentorship.
4. **Advocate for more robust mental health support and institutional transformation within departments and facilities of higher learning.** Universities and institutions must commit towards systematic change in how they approach mental health on an establishment-wide level, including sufficient funding for mental healthcare; flexible packages and funding options for individuals who might need to take a break from their studies to seek care; and foster support systems that don't punish individuals with chronic psychological disorders or health issues. These structural interventions will work against ableist understandings of ethnography and promote more systemic change within academic institutions.
5. **Promote opportunities for mutual aid, peer support groups and unions.** Ethnographic communities can adapt collective and transformative care strategies to build more peer-to-peer support structures for students and practitioners. These can include operationalising principles from mutual aid, bringing together peer support groups and supporting unions, all of which will help to sustain more holistic forms of psychosocial support.

Notes

1. The authors want to acknowledge the limitations of the survey. We recognise that a survey about emotional wellbeing is likely to experience respondent bias, with participants already likely interested and engaged with issues of mental health in ethnographic fieldwork. Our survey responses may not be a representative sample of all early and mid-career ethnographers working in the field, but do echo many of the same concerns and complaints collected by Amy Pollard. These constraints also gesture at the limited research we do have on mental health among ethnographers, and the necessity of continuing to turn our analytical lens inward.
2. Our review of the literature included in our works cited unfortunately had to be cut down due to the constraints offered by the book publishers. We wish that we could have done more to honor the rich body of texts of ethnographers reflecting on their mental health challenges, including their experiences of joy despite hardships, especially to demonstrate the importance of citation. For a more robust list of the literatures we consulted, please consider reading "Policy Statement: Mental Well-being among Anthropologists at Universities: A Call for System Transformation" in Medical Anthropology Quarterly which the authors helped to co-write."
3. Although this chapter is organised around the different ways that mental illness can manifest, none of these conditions should be treated as separate or discrete from one another. Overlapping, co-occurring symptoms are not uncommon.

Further reading

Brown, N. and Leigh, J. 2020. *Ableism in Academia: Theorising Experiences of Disabilities and Chronic Illnesses in Higher Education*. London: UCL Press.
This edited volume represents a variety of theoretical approaches to the subject matter, including feminist and poststructuralist perspectives. More importantly, it contextualises much of the current discourse on ableism within the confines of the neoliberal academy and provides groundwork for academics wanting to push for further disability justice in higher education.

Davies, J. and Spencer, D. 2010. *Emotions in the Field: The Psychology and Anthropology of Fieldwork Experience*. Stanford, CA: Stanford University Press.
Emotions in the Field is a critical volume of essays by anthropologists considering how emotion must necessarily inform our methods and forms of writing and representation as ethnographers. Contributors like Vincent Crapanzano, Arthur Kleinman, Ghassan Hage and Michael D. Jackson illustrate the friction between analytical, political and personal emotions, the moments of clarity and complication that emotions have in field-based data collection.

Kafer, A. 2013. *Feminist, Queer, Crip*. Bloomington: Indiana University Press.
One of the key texts for discussing disability, Kafer's *Feminist, Queer, Crip* approaches the subject from an intersectional perspective, directly connecting disability with sexuality and gender. Kafer creates a framework that challenges ableist norms by imagining an accessible future that encompasses all disabilities and identities.

Lakshmi Piepzna-Samarasinha, L. 2018. *Care Work: Dreaming Disability Justice*. Vancouver: Arsenal Pulp Press.

Piepzna-Samarasinha and the other authors and activists featured in *Care Work* ask what it would mean to make space for scholarship from the sick bed. To do so involves engaging with the imaginative and practical dimensions of care work and collective access, a form of communitarian liberation academics, practitioners and fieldworkers can centre in the scholarship we cultivate, the bodies we make space for and the ways we might crip conceptions of productivity and creativity.

The Care Collective 2020. *The Care Manifesto: The Politics of Interdependence*. London: Verso.

The Care Collective's powerful text reimagines a world in which both personal and communal care is of utmost importance. Although it uses a broad definition of care work throughout, *The Care Manifesto* is widely applicable to many spheres of life, and this flexibility will make it a highly useful text.

References

Behar, R. 1996. *The Vulnerable Observer: Anthropology That Breaks Your Heart*. Boston: Beacon.

Berry, M.J., Argüelles, C.C., Cordis, S., Imhoud, S. and Velásquez Estrada, E. 2018. Toward a fugitive anthropology: Gender, race and violence in the field. *Current Anthropology*, 32, 537–65.

Clancy, K.B.H., Nelson, R.G., Rutherford, J.N. and Hinde, K. 2019. Survey of Academic Field Experiences (SAFE): Trainees report harassment and assault. *PLOS One*, 9, e102172.

Fletcher, E.H., Backe, E.L, Brykalski, T., Fitzpatrick, A., González, M., Ginzburg, S.L., Meeker, R., Riendeau, R.P, Thies-Sauder, M. and Reyes-Foster, B. 2022. Policy statement. Mental well-being among anthropologists at universities: A call for system transformation. *Medical Anthropology Quarterly*, 36, 155–72.

Frey, L.L., Beesley, D., Abbott, D. and Kendrick, E. 2017. Vicarious resilience in sexual assault and domestic violence advocates. *Psychological Trauma: Theory, Research, Practice, and Policy*, 9, 44–51.

Hanson, R. and Richards, P. 2019. *Harassed: Gender, Bodies, and Ethnographic Research*. Berkeley, CA: University of California Press.

Moreno, E. 1995. Rape in the field: Reflections from a survivor. In Kulick, D. and Wilson, M. (Eds.), *Taboo: Sex, Identity, and Erotic Subjectivity in Fieldwork*. London: Routledge. pp. 219–49.

Navarro, T., Williams, B. and Ahmad, A. 2013. Sitting at the kitchen table: Fieldnotes from women of color in anthropology. *Cultural Anthropology*, 28, 443–63.

Pollard, A. 2009. Field of screams: Difficulty and ethnographic work. *Anthropology Matters*, 11.

Reyes-Foster, B. and Lester, R. 2019. Trauma and resilience in ethnographic fieldwork. *anthrodendum*. Available at anthrodendum.org/2019/06/18/trauma-and-resilience-in-ethnographic-fieldwork/ (accessed 3 October 2023).

PART 4

INCLUSIVITY IN ETHNOGRAPHIC WRITING

12

PARTICIPATORY ETHNOGRAPHIC METHODS: COLLABORATIVE DATA PRODUCTION, ANALYSIS AND ETHNOGRAPHIC REPRESENTATION

Anne E. Pfister

Summary

This chapter presents creative approaches to ethnographic methods that involve participants as research partners who produce and analyse data, co-theorise and contribute to ethnographic representation. It highlights epistemological approaches and multimodal methods for making ethnographic production and representation a more collaborative, inclusive endeavour. The author uses examples from research at a deaf, signing school in Mexico City as a case study.

Table of contents

Introduction 167
Epistemology and community-based research approaches 168
What is epistemology? And why is it important? 169
What is community-based research? 170
Doing participatory analysis 172
    Photovoice for analysing themes 173
    Co-theorising using photovoice 175
    Personal history timelines 176
Conclusion 179
Recommendations 180
Further reading 180
References 181

Introduction

This chapter describes ideas for involving participants as collaborators throughout the research process to push our work beyond the confines of singular ethnographic perspectives, specifically in analysis and representation. I write from the understanding that inclusive ethnography means moving towards more parity between researcher and participants and suggest that our participants should inspire our methodological choices and participate in the use of those methods with a goal of renovating ethnographic production. I provide specific ideas for collaboratively involving participants at various stages of community-based research (CBR) and explain how epistemology connects the interrelated processes of identifying research themes and questions, as well as data production, analysis and ethnographic representation. I describe a process called *participatory analysis*, drawing on long-term ethnographic research among deaf youth and their families. Throughout the chapter, I use my research as a case study for how participatory methods can help anthropologists dissolve the limitations of more 'traditional' ethnographic methods, while being attentive to context and community-specific strengths and needs – including language and language modalities. I describe photovoice and personal history timelines briefly, highlighting these as 'methodological innovations' that tap specialised 'insider knowledge' among participants and produce often-unexpected outcomes. Participatory analysis is a cornerstone justification for multimodal methods like photovoice and personal history timelines because the triangulation of methods, as described here, yields complex meanings and rich ethnographic detail that cannot be gleaned from one methodological strategy alone. Through creating, organising and analysing data, the participants can amplify our scope of investigation – by bringing in themes we would not have generated without participant input – or narrow our scope by identifying what is most contextually important.

I write with the aim of broadening what has traditionally been a narrow conceptualisation of who creates and presents ethnographic research, adding methodological discussion to what is conceived as 'inclusive ethnography'. Participatory analysis helps researchers extend beyond the traditional realm of how and where research takes place, and shakes up how data becomes codified, theorised and presented. The methods discussed here are two of many potential 'methodological innovations' that can be inspired by the epistemologies we wish to incorporate, the research contexts we explore and the strengths and perspectives our participants themselves offer. Above all, this chapter encourages you to explore how multimodal ethnographic approaches and participatory analysis might reveal novel anthropological insights in your own research contexts and move our field towards more inclusive ethnographic production at all stages of the process.

Epistemology and community-based research approaches

Data collection and analysis are interwoven throughout the ethnographic research design, and each deliberate decision made by researchers (as well as chance encounters and various coincidences!) are steps towards building our ethnographies. But how do we know what questions to ask? What data to pay attention to? What perspectives do we prioritise or exclude because of the methods we employ? The 'lone ethnographer' in anthropological research has traditionally been seen as a relatively autonomous individual who steers a research project from start to finish. Yet, there is increasing awareness that the detached ethnographic observer – reminiscent of authoritative, historical ethnographies – can be patronising and risks paternalistic and otherwise harmful consequences contrary to anthropology's ethics. Questions for us to consider include: do we risk reproducing the very colonialist attitudes and classist hierarchies we (rightly) problematise if we do not invite the people we recruit as participants to also make ethnographic observations? How can we encourage participants to take an ethnographic stance, to go from participants to participant-observers and analysts? This chapter invites you to think through ways research participants might become more critical observers of the very same phenomena we study. Methodological approaches can involve participants in positions that Freire (1982 [1972]) refers to as *co-investigators*, and by reinventing traditionally separated roles (i.e., 'researcher' and 'informant'), we can make ethnography a more inclusive endeavour.

While this approach is not new, participatory methods and community-based research approaches are not always part of the anthropology students' training. Similarly, most research participants are not trained as ethnographers. So, this chapter offers perspectives on careful epistemological consideration and methodological choices to blur 'the distinction between researcher and researched, subject and object, bringing all parties together as equal partners in the process of generating and interpreting data' (LeCompte and Schensul, 1999, p. 50). This chapter invites you to imagine the possibilities when participants are cultural theorists alongside anthropologists and suggests that collaborative, participatory ethnography is a way to decolonise anthropology while also improving our craft and making anthropological outcomes more practical, accessible and dynamic. An approach that advocates for research that shares outcomes, theories and analyses in various ways is often referred to as the 'participatory turn' in anthropology (Jessee et al., 2015). This chapter provides field-based examples of how to conceptualise and utilise participatory methods towards one of ethnography's primary goals: cultural theorising. Using examples from my own research, I make the case that participatory analysis is an exciting endeavour because it integrates questions, data and conclusions that a 'lone ethnographer' may never arrive at – or imagine – on her own.

What is epistemology? And why is it important?

The goal of inclusive ethnography is the incorporation of different emic viewpoints, so epistemology is a central concept we need to understand. But what is epistemology? Underpinning epistemology is a complex question: *how do we know what we know?* The word 'epistemology' refers to the dynamic theory of knowledge that people use to interpret phenomena, reality and experiences. I am a hearing researcher with the goal of understanding and authentically relaying the emic perspectives of my deaf participants and the people closest to them. To do this, I must acknowledge how my own hearing status affects my conclusions about deaf lifeways and how my own epistemological approach to research (and other things) may be different to that of my deaf friends and participants. In many anthropological research contexts, the lived experience of participants – and their epistemologies – are very different from our own.

To illustrate how epistemology shapes enquiry, knowledge and experience, consider an ethnographic example from my research among families of deaf youth in Mexico City. During ethnographic interviews, I often ask parents to describe how they discovered their children's deafness. Mandatory newborn hearing screening was not consistently implemented in Mexico at the time, so most participants brought their newborn babies home unaware of their hearing status (i.e., if they were born hearing, deaf, hard-of-hearing). Deaf parents, who were more attuned to the possibility of deaf offspring than hearing counterparts, gathered and interpreted early 'data' differently than hearing parents. For example, when their babies slept through loud noises, many deaf parents, or parents with deaf family members, might have wondered earlier, or more readily, if this was a sign the baby might be deaf. One deaf mother claimed she knew her son was deaf early on because, from the earliest days, as she signed to and around him she remembered him 'communicating with his little hands'. In fact, many deaf parents I work with claimed they 'knew' their own children were deaf without seeking an official medical diagnosis. However, many hearing parents who experienced similar circumstances either did not pick up on these early indicators, or, when they did (typically much later), they relied on audiometric testing and diagnoses to 'know' their child was deaf. Individual families' stories differed in important ways, of course, but data from interviews help illustrate the epistemological differences between how deaf and hearing parents 'knew' how to look for signs of deafness, or how/when they 'knew' their child was deaf.

As the example above illustrates, epistemology is rooted in experience and experience shapes every part of what we think and do. As such, epistemology affects *what we know, how we know it* and *when we know it* in both subtle and profound ways. The lived experiences, or 'knowledge', among deaf and hearing parents influenced the questions they asked (or didn't) about their newborns (i.e., could she be deaf?); how and when they looked for data (i.e., specific attention to the baby's response to different stimuli); and how they interpreted that data (i.e., deaf parents' experience-based knowledge and intuitions vs hearing parents' reliance on medical expertise and testing). Both groups of parents in the example (coarsely parsed as 'hearing' and 'deaf' for this example), eventually came to similar conclusions about their children's hearing status. However, their differing epistemologies shaped when and where they looked for information, impacted their perceptions of influence (lived experience vs medical authority), how and when they reached conclusions (when they 'knew' their child was deaf) and, of course, how these realisations were interpreted and experienced (which varied, but tended to cluster appreciatively between the two groups).

Returning our focus to the role of epistemology in anthropological research, we are reminded that data collection and analysis are parallel processes in ethnography. In any fieldwork situation, the ethnographer is witness to a potentially overwhelming array of stimuli because human activity is constant and complex. Human behaviours and phenomena are often obvious but are just as often elusive. Epistemology is an important consideration in methodological discussions because it is a primary filter – it shapes the work of 'interpreting what is seen; and deciding which of the things seen by researchers are real, valid, and important to document' (LeCompte and Schensul, 1999, p. 41). Participants in research most certainly have opinions on what is important, and keen insights into what is real and valid in the contexts with which they are familiar. Recognising how unwieldy ethnographic fieldwork might become is reason to suggest that participants themselves can – and should – help guide the process of what we pay attention to and *how* we know what we know.

What is community-based research?

When inclusive ethnography is the goal, an inclusive approach must be integrated and planned at the start of the research process. For example, I take seriously my responsibilities as a hearing researcher to purposefully select research methods that actively involve deaf participants, to make a commitment to ongoing reflexivity and to be attentive to the language needs and communicative preferences of deaf participants. I purposefully choose visual research methods because the visual sense is an important component of deaf epistemologies (Kusters and De Meulder, 2013). Deaf studies scholars Dai O'Brien and Annelies Kusters (together with Maartje De Meulder) refer to the visual orientation of deaf people who can see as 'visucentrism' or 'a unique corporeality in their experience of the world' (2017, p. 265). I use *Lengua de Señas Mexicana* (Mexican Sign Language, or LSM), but I am not a fluent signer, so I use LSM interpreters when communicating with deaf youth and adults. Finally, I take a community-based research (CBR) approach to centre participants at all stages of the research design. I count myself among many contemporary ethnographers inspired by the power of CBR to invite discourse among diverse people within – and outside – academia, especially towards advocacy and social justice. In my own research, this means working to reverse the stigma associated with 'hearing loss' and critiquing associated deficit models by incorporating the unique perspectives and abilities that are 'gained' with deafness, what is known as 'deaf gain' (Bauman and Murray, 2014).

'Community' is a term that may mean different things in different contexts, so researchers must consider what 'community' might mean in their own research contexts. In my own research, I underscore the considerable variation in how deaf children and adults experience deafness while also attempting to distil some of the values, shared experiences and cultural features (including language needs, modality and use) that impact, shape and define deaf networks. Many readers have likely heard the term 'd/Deaf community', yet anthropologists understand that conceptualising a singular 'Deaf community' – or any community – as an essentialised experience or homogeneous group is problematic and to be avoided. In fact, it is difficult to find a working definition of 'community' within anthropology, despite our liberal use of the term.

While not the focus of this chapter, the idea of a 'd/Deaf community' helps us understand how 'community' often needs to be broken down to be meaningful in the selection of ethnographic methods. Deaf communities are sometimes understood as groupings of people who subscribe to 'deaf culture', which might be described as a solidarity formed around shared identities, languages and experiences of deaf signers. But not all deaf people use sign language or identify as culturally deaf. And while some countries, including the United States and the United Kingdom, boast well-defined deaf culture concepts, deaf networks in Mexico, Cambodia and elsewhere, form in different socio-political contexts, face different challenges, and may or may not have strongly formed ideas about deaf culture as a unifying concept. Just as importantly, many deaf individuals may or may not affiliate themselves with a 'deaf community'. Like any group of humans, deaf networks are also internally diverse, and many factors, including varying degrees of auditory input and varying life histories, influence an individual's experience of deafness. So, thinking through the 'communities' in our CBR projects is an important starting point, but is also something that needs to be addressed throughout fieldwork. As inclusive ethnographers, we must trace the defining characteristics of the communities with whom we work, while also maintaining appreciation for – and underscoring the richness of – the inevitable homogeneity and individuality within those communities.

My primary research site, Instituto Pedagógico para Problemas del Lenguaje (the Pedagogical Institute for Language Problems, or IPPLIAP), is in a residential neighbourhood southwest of Mexico City's historical centre. IPPLIAP is one of very few specialised Mexican deaf schools providing instruction in LSM through a bilingual model (Spanish and LSM). As mentioned earlier, medical professionals advise most families with deaf children, and many warn hearing parents against sign language. In the predominantly hearing environment of urban Mexico City, this is one of the reasons so many students at IPPLIAP learned LSM relatively late in life. I chose IPPLIAP as my primary research site because I wanted to research families that purposefully chose LSM for their deaf children. I wanted to understand how and why they came to IPPLIAP and how LSM (and the absence of it, where applicable) impacts their lives. IPPLIAP as a 'community' creates a unit of study for the purposes of my research because it is a physical and ideological place where many members of a particular deaf Mexican community congregate. IPPLIAP creates a defined, but permeable, perimeter for 'community', one that refers to a network of families, educators, administrators, interpreters, alumni and other deaf and hearing adults radiating from IPPLIAP.

Yet, each subset within IPPLIAP must also be considered a 'community' with distinct perspectives, motivations, experience and interests. So, to inclusively involve each of the groups within the larger network of participants, my methodological approaches to working with each group differed. For example, I sent surveys to all parents upon arrival at IPPLIAP to inform them of my research, give them the option to contribute data and recruit them for follow-up interviews. I then set up focus groups and conducted semi-structured interviews to meet with family participants. I conducted participant observation and interviews with teachers and administrators at IPPLIAP and at community and social events. This research project spans more than a decade, so, during an extended research stay in 2018, my children were old enough to attend school at IPPLIAP as temporary guests, providing me the chance to be a participant-observer as an IPPLIAP parent. Throughout this project, I worked most closely with a handful of key participants to devise different aspects of the research design, and I consulted with them regularly about research goals, themes and outcomes. These IPPLIAP insiders – who each, at times, occupied *co-investigator* roles – included the director of the school (Mercedes), as well as the sixth-grade teacher of the cohort of students I worked with (Marcela), the school psychologist (Fabiola) and a school-employed interpreter (Alberto). Furthermore, parents regularly told me they desired more information on deafness, so their interests and participation also take on co-investigative roles as they shape the research process.

Many of the key principles of CBR resonate with anthropologists aiming for a more inclusive practice because CBR is a collaborative, integrative and iterative process. As the name implies, the concept of community is a guiding principle of CBR, so research participants are central to the research design at all stages. Many point to the democratisation of research as a primary goal of CBR, one in which knowledge is co-constructed and horizontal dialogue occurs between researcher and participants. Another guiding concept of CBR is bolstering the strengths of communities, which requires first acknowledging their unique features. Students and practitioners interested in this approach might involve participants in defining 'community' and in tracing the contours of their communities. Researchers should allow for the identification of communities-within-communities and work with participants on best approaches to collaboration. Researchers can ask participants to identify community strengths, and they should be prepared to periodically revisit how participants understand these ideas, recognising that subsets exist within larger communities and that the desires, strengths and goals of these groups change through time.

Doing participatory analysis

Ethnographies are typically written, most ethnographic research methods are language-based and researchers tend to use and value the modalities they are most comfortable with. Yet there are many reasons why a researcher might consider incorporating multimodal methodologies into a variety of aspects of their research. The learning and language modalities of deaf youth participants inspired 'methodological innovation' as I prepared for my research and while in the field. I use participatory visual and multimodal research methods with deaf youth, including photovoice, digital storytelling and a method I call personal history timelines.

One of the greatest advantages of using participatory methodology and CBR is the opportunity to contextualise data alongside the participants creating and collecting them. Participatory analysis is an iterative process of analysing data with participants to co-construct knowledge about various topics, a process that is continually developed and justified within a context of rigorous, scientific research. 'Participatory analysis' was first developed by Wang and Burris (1997) through photovoice methodology as they asked research participants to select, contextualise and code participant-created photographic images. I advocate for applying the spirit and methodology of participatory analysis to various research components throughout the ethnographic research process, as discussed here. Below, I describe how participatory, multimodal methods can be employed creatively to establish research themes and questions, towards data generation and in collaborative ethnographic representation.

BOX 12.1

Ethnographers and scholars tend to produce knowledge based on the ways they learn and communicate best. Ask yourself: what are the ways you are accustomed to learning and communicating? Are these different from your participants? What modalities are more and less inclusive in your research context? What kinds of methods and modalities might encourage participants to co-construct knowledge? What are the most inclusive options for ethnographic representation?

Photovoice for analysing themes

Participants in *Proyecto Fotovoz* (Project Photovoice) spent a week or two taking photographs in response to our themes and presented their images to our workshop group of ten people, using LSM to explain how their images related to the research themes we provided. These workshops provided an entrée into participants' social worlds, giving us a chance to follow up on themes and a variety of topics that might not have otherwise occurred to us. I learned about hobbies and how participants spent their free time, prompting friendly conversation, about pets or fashion for example, and this allowed us to build rapport more quickly than we might have in a typical interview setting. Participatory analysis through photovoice provides opportunities to include participants in the generation of research topics and questions, and it also gives them control over what they want to share with participants, researchers and other potential audiences.

Marcela and I followed up with participants individually about photographic images and, through this discourse, we learned about things that might have been awkward to ask about directly. For example, we learned about family dynamics and home life, who participants lived and spent time with and other topics without direct questioning. Discussions about photos made it easier to learn about who was using sign language in participants' lives, and this was something I was keenly interested in. For example, when people in an image appeared to be using an LSM sign, I could ask about it casually, without having to directly ask who signed fluently and who did not. Asking 'Is this person signing something?' might lead to an explanation of what that person was doing (signing or doing something else), or a conversation about how much or how little LSM that sibling, parent, or friend knew. Images created a springboard for conversation, and this increased the odds for spontaneous discussions more than asking isolated or one-dimensional interview questions. Furthermore, a question like 'Does your father sign?' might produce a one-word answer, and 'yes' or 'no' to answers like this likely do not describe complex language practices in the home. Furthermore, I may not have asked about extended family dynamics (aunts, cousins, in-laws) without knowing about them through the broader context provided by the images they appeared in. This illustrates how images quite literally bring topics into the research domain. The one-on-one process of discussing photographs is a rich form of data generation and participant analysis.

BOX 12.2

Photovoice is a method wherein participants are asked to respond to research questions and themes using digital photography. I worked with the entire sixth-grade cohort at IPPLIAP and their teacher, Marcela, to create two semester-long workshops and a culminating exposition called Proyecto Fotovoz (Project Photovoice). Participants were given digital 'point-and-shoot' cameras and Marcela and I introduced weekly photography lessons and research themes. We began with familiar topics, like 'Family' and 'Mexico and the City', and, after practising together for several weeks, moved on to more complex topics like 'Mexican Sign Language' and 'Dreams and the Future'.

Photovoice projects generate a large amount of data, sometimes in the form of hundreds (or even thousands!) of images, and the conversations about them are also important data. The drawback to lots of data, of course, is the time it takes to code and analyse them, a task that can quickly become unwieldy or overwhelming. Yet, the process of participatory analysis allows researchers and participants to collaboratively code images into themes in several ways. For example, shared experiences can be gleaned quickly when discussing images in a workshop setting, which functions as a kind of focus group. Youth participants often photographed similar topics or would collaboratively discuss an experience or theme. The images were engaging and there was a sense of excitement viewing images that facilitated comment and discussion. For example, though the participants went to school together and many of them had known each other for years, they may not have visited one another's homes because many travelled hours to get to IPPLIAP from different parts of Mexico City and surrounding areas.

Co-theorising using photovoice

Another example illustrating participatory analysis of images is one that frustrated me at first, but that eventually became an important reminder of how – and why – participants can help guide interpretation of data. Across many of the weekly themes, including the week LSM was the specific theme, many youth participants took images of themselves making hand gestures that were not LSM signs. Some of these gestures are familiar and recognisable to many people, like the formation of a heart shape using both hands, two fingers extended in a peace sign, or a handshape with only the first and pinkie finger pointing up, like the 'rock on' emoji (see Figure 12.1). Another image photographed by many participants was the American Sign Language (ASL) sign for 'I love you'.

As I looked through dozens of images with gestures like this, I admit to feeling disappointed; I wondered how to interpret them and wondered if participants misunderstood the directions or the theme. I finally realised (or admitted to myself) that the source of my frustration was my own preconceived ideas of what I hoped the participants would capture, that I was subconsciously trying to get them to respond a certain way. So, I self-corrected by going back to the participants to ask about their gestures, bringing me back in better alignment with Wang and Burris's idea that participatory analysis as 'an approach avoids the distortion of fitting data into a predetermined paradigm' (1997, p. 382). When I went to youth participants to ask them more about why they took the image of 'rock on' or their hands in the heart shape, they responded by explaining that these were gestures many people recognised.

The use of the ASL sign for 'I love you' by LSM signers in Mexico City initially confused me. Yet, as I settled into long-term participatory analysis, I slowly learned this sign was indeed

Figure 12.1 Ricardo took an image of himself making the 'rock on' handshape, which is not an LSM sign, but is widely recognisable in many contexts, including to many hearing and deaf Mexicans. When we asked Ricardo about why he chose this gesture and image, he explained simply that it is cool and represents a *'rockero'* (rocker) style. He answered our questions in a way that communicated 'Everyone knows that!' underscoring that recognisability was a factor in his choice of this communication.

recognisable to many deaf Mexicans. The iconicity of the ASL sign made it popular among LSM signers and showed up in photos and elsewhere far more than a corresponding local Mexican sign (the LSM sign for *'te quiero'*, for example, is very different and did not appear in participants' photos). My research at IPPLIAP began before the 'selfie' was as popular as it would soon become, and most of the sixth-grade participants did not have mobile phones during the project (in 2012–13). Indeed, the popularity of selfies and social media potentially increased the circulation of the ASL sign 'I love you' among LSM users. It is common now to see LSM users on Facebook, Instagram and other social media smiling and holding up an ASL 'I love you', for example. These images are not intended to profess love to a particular person but may signal solidarity with a generalised audience of LSM signers, and perhaps an 'imagined community' of signers beyond Mexico (see also Pfister, 2020).

Two important themes emerged from this group of images, both illuminated through participatory analysis. First, these images and explanations confirmed what I suspected: most young LSM users knew the difference between LSM and gestures or non-LSM signs and they employed both as part of a sophisticated communicative repertoire. Second, as participants explained that they used non-LSM for recognisability, they were also describing a communicative strategy they regularly employ. For example, when we asked Ricardo about the image in Figure 12.1, he answered our questions in a way that communicated: 'That's the sign for "rock on"; everyone knows that!' This underscores how deaf youth were acutely aware of different modalities because they regularly navigated signing *and* non-signing environments. They were accustomed to improvising to make themselves understood because many of the people in their lives did not use LSM fluently (or at all). Photovoice provided an outlet for them to articulate their awareness of their linguistic improvisation and the different language and communicative skills they regularly employed. Photovoice also encouraged them, more than 'traditional' ethnographic methods might have, to think about and explain why they chose different language practices in different circumstances. This process exemplifies collaborative meaning-making, underscoring a particular deaf youth perspective on their multilayered language landscapes (hearing and deaf) and modalities (signing and non-signing).

Personal history timelines

Most of the deaf youth I worked with were born to hearing families, so most did not begin learning LSM until they entered school at IPPLIAP. Hearing children typically exhibit command of their home languages before entering pre-school, so deaf children often arrive at accessible language and proficiency at later ages than their hearing counterparts. A confluence of factors contributes to this delay in language acquisition, including the fact that most hearing families do not use or know LSM; they receive recommendations from medical doctors advising them against exposing their children to sign language; and they have limited access to deaf, signing networks. I wanted to understand how and when IPPLIAP families encountered and learned sign language and I was able to investigate this using participant observation and interviews with parents. But, just as important and intriguing are children's perspectives on what life was like before learning LSM, and how that time compared to their lives after sign language.

I sensed that traditional ethnographic interviews might not be the best approach to learning about these two life stages. First, when ethnographers sit down with participants to conduct semi-structured interviews, the researcher typically asks a question and expects an immediate and spontaneous response. Yet, we talk less in methodological training about the times when our research and practice may benefit from participants working with ideas for longer stretches, and researchers iteratively revisiting complex themes with participants. I was asking deaf youth to think about memories and times when they may have felt confused, which may have sparked curiosity and emotion about the past. So, I wanted them to be able to reflect on the questions, recall memories, talk to their families if they wished, and think through what they were willing to share with us, without feeling surprised, rushed or pressured.

I heard many detailed accounts of the transformative power of sign language from parents and deaf adults within the community. So, I wanted to understand youths' perceptions and memories of that experience while they were still young. In other words, I wanted to see how learning LSM factored into their life histories. So, I worked with Marcela and Fabiola to create a project that asked youth participants to create a timeline illustrating chronological high and low points in their lives and other important personal events, including when they came to IPPLIAP. Participants were free to use the communicative mode most comfortable for them, and they used a combination of written Spanish, illustrations and/or photographs to document significant life events. Participants described these to us in LSM and the timelines were used as guides and visual cues to augment interviews with youth participants, creating a multimodal communicative practice through participatory analysis. Personal history timelines helped focus attention on participants' experiences before and after coming to IPPLIAP, which usually coincided with their first contact with LSM and a signing community.

Methods like the one I develop as personal history timelines appear in qualitative research under different names and prioritise different aspects of experience in current social science literature. So, while timelining may not be new or my invention, I was not familiar with timelining as methodology during fieldwork because I had very little training on collaborative and participatory methods. Furthermore, I believe anthropologists should continually make 'methodological innovations' by adapting or inventing methods to suit their participants and contexts while they are in the field, tailoring them as they learn more about the participants and the context. However, some academic advisors and institutional review boards may not always agree, so researchers should anticipate their need to be flexible and clarify these expectations.

The creation of personal history timelines helped elucidate the role of language in participants' lives. For example, using his timeline as a guide, Leonardo described his inability to understand hearing teachers and peers at the Centro de Atención Múltiple (Centre for Disabilities, or

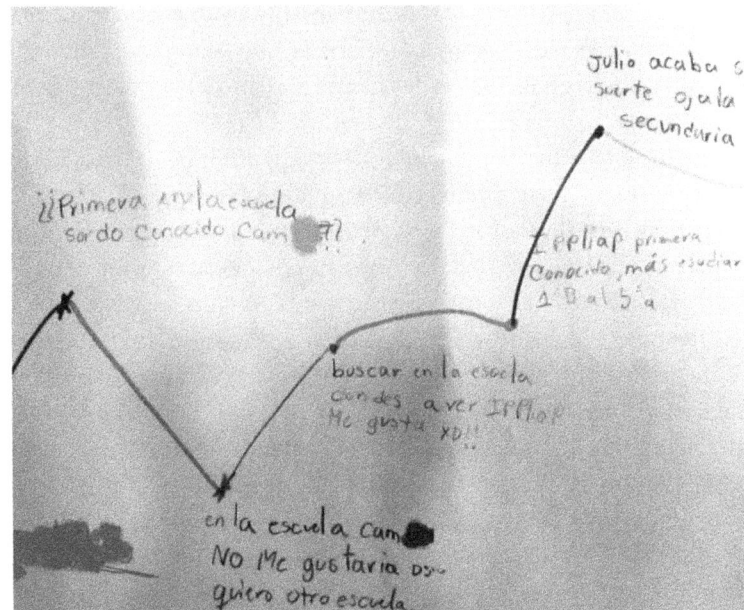

Figure 12.2 Leo's personal history timeline describing his school experiences. English translations (left to right) 1) First grade in the deaf school CAM (redacted to protect the school identity); 2) I didn't like the school CAM, I want another school; 3) Looking to find a school, let's see, I like IPPLIAP!! 4) IPPLIAP first grade, I know more people and study more (first grade to fifth grade); 5) July, with luck I'll finish 6th grade and hopefully go to middle school (see also Pfister et al., 2014).

CAM) that he attended prior to transferring to IPPLIAP. Leonardo used the expression 'mente negra' (black mind) to describe the state of confusion and uncertainty he experienced among teachers and peers who did not use LSM proficiently.

Leonardo's limited access to spoken Spanish made it difficult for him to participate in the predominately hearing environment of the CAM. He contrasted this dark time with his experience at IPPLIAP. When teachers and students communicated in LSM, his ability to understand became 'más claro' (clearer). Leonardo was nine years old when he transferred to IPPLIAP where he learned LSM, began to understand and communicate more, made friends and was happier. He remembered and described this time as a symbolic mental darkness clearing because he experienced language socialisation and became a part of the IPPLIAP community he and his friends cherished for the support and togetherness they felt there.

Personal history timelines allow the researcher and participants to focus on a particular issue, timeframe, or question. They then use participatory analysis to work together towards a fundamental aspect of the ethnographic endeavour: creating experience-based narratives. The graphic nature of personal history timelines allows the researcher and participants to revisit (or even showcase) these narratives so they can discuss and think through similarities in participants' stories as well as the ways their experiences diverge. This process can take place in a focus group or individually, depending on the nature of the content and the familiarity of the community.

Conclusion

There are many benefits to using a variety of methodological approaches in long-term ethnographic research, like those I describe here. First, methods allow the researcher to engage with groups within the community differently and establish different levels of rapport. When working in large communities, it is natural and necessary to connect with participants differently because we cannot be everywhere all at once. Furthermore, researchers may need to strategise about where to put their emotional and social energies in the field, both to meet research goals (i.e., focusing on different perspectives and working within time and funding limitations) and for the health and safety of the researcher and participants (i.e., avoiding burnout, protecting mental and physical health and avoiding sensitive situations). Importantly, incorporating many different methods within one project increases opportunities to triangulate data, or compare findings, as described here. Finally, there is growing awareness that research with children and youth calls for – and benefits from – approaches that go beyond 'traditional methods' commonly used with adult participants, and deaf researchers call our attention to ethics and methods specific to researching among deaf networks.

This chapter contributes to literature presenting creative approaches to methods that involve participants as research planners, data collectors, analysts, consultants and ethnographers. I outlined how different groups of participants were involved in various components of the ethnographic research process from the generation of research themes and questions to ethnographic representation. Deaf youth produced and collected data in the form of photographic images, personal history timelines and narratives and summaries of and about those data. Discourse around their work, including their informal workshop presentations to their peers, created the generation of themes and theories. Later in the workshop, they sorted, analysed and categorised data by prioritising what they wanted shared more broadly, and by creating titles and descriptions of those images for an exposition. Each iterative step was participatory analysis that helped shape the project and resulting ethnography.

Through participatory analysis of the experience-based narratives in personal timelines and images in photovoice, researchers and participants identify patterns in human behaviour and theorise about them. In other words, they are working collaboratively towards one of the ultimate goals of ethnography: cultural theorising! Working with our participants can distil explanatory reasoning when they are involved in theories of – and about – culture(s). As we saw, deaf youth were more than capable of doing this when given the tools and the opportunity. The epistemological orientations of participants, in collaboration with the epistemological orientations of the researcher, add validity to the interpretations that constitute ethnographies. That is, the participants themselves can – and should! – lead us to the anthropological insights we seek.

Recommendations

1. **Budget the time and resources necessary for participatory approaches.** Methods like photovoice, with multiple stages of collaborative effort and vast amounts of data, may take more time than traditional methods because participatory analysis is an iterative process. Budget for equipment and materials for expositions, displays, or productions to showcase collaborative work.
2. **Consider the different roles participants can play as co-researchers.** These might take many forms, ideally throughout the project. Think through the ways you can incorporate participatory analysis most effectively, with consideration of language and language modality since effective communication is a crucial factor in collaboration and inclusivity.
3. **Be prepared to recognise and challenge your own feelings in response to participant contributions.** Working through your feelings, both privately (through field notes, for example) and collaboratively, by engaging participants to understand what they wish to communicate, to produce richer and more authentically inclusive analyses and representation.
4. **Build in opportunities for reciprocity and advocacy, while building rapport**. Photovoice is a powerful tool for advocacy because participants can tell their stories in different modalities and to diverse audiences. Images and expositions can be used creatively and practically as reciprocity with participants and this can help build rapport with communities while drawing attention to the issues most important to them.
5. **Be aware of – and honest about – potential risks and ethical obligations.** Consider issues surrounding privacy and anonymity of individual participants and institutions, especially when using visual methods. Researchers and participants can lose 'control' over images that circulate digitally, and images can be altered by third parties without researcher or participant consent. These potentialities should be addressed candidly in recruitment, in informed consent processes, in research proposals and with institutional review boards and local permission-granting agencies.

Further reading

Baines, K. and Costa, V. (Eds.) 2022. *Cool Anthropology: How to Engage the Public with Academic Research.* Toronto: University of Toronto Press.
Cool Anthropology is an edited volume that aims to be a 'how-to' guide for researchers interested in public, applied, engaged or community-driven anthropology. The editors divide the volume into four parts: Imperatives, or anthropological responses to current issues; the use of online platforms to reach greater audiences; Reimaging public spaces, about student-led projects within and outside university settings; and Creatives, showcasing artistic approaches and collaborations with anthropologists or anthropological research.

Gubrium, A. and Harper, K. 2013. *Participatory and Digital Methods*. Walnut Creek, CA: Left Coast.
Participatory and Digital Methods is a foundational and comprehensive guide to theory and practice surrounding participatory methods to 'produce rich multimodal and narrative data guided by participant interests and priorities ... for greater access to social research knowledge beyond the academy' (p. 13). This book is a resource for students and researchers interested in theories and practice of participatory visual methods, as well as specific methods like photovoice, digital storytelling, story mapping and participatory film and videomaking.

Kusters, A., De Meulder, M. and O'Brien, D. (Eds.) 2017. *Innovations in Deaf Studies: The Role of Deaf Scholars*. Oxford: Oxford University Press.
Innovations in Deaf Studies is an important example of dedicated focus on the impact of ontologies (defined within the book as 'deaf ways of being') on research by problemetising thinking about communities from top-down perspectives and calling for the creation of 'bottom-up' accounts of epistemologies. Though this volume is specific to Deaf Studies (notably, all contributors to the volume are deaf), there are important take-aways that apply to many research contexts.

References

Bauman, H.-D. L. and Murray, J.J. 2014. *Deaf Gain: Raising the Stakes for Human Diversity*. Minneapolis: University of Minnesota Press.

Freire, P. 1982 [1972]. Creating alternative research methods: Learning to do it by doing it. In Hall, B. (Ed.), *Creating Knowledge: A Monopoly? Participatory Research in Development*. New Dehli: Society for Participatory Research in Asia, 29–37.

Jessee, N., Collum, K.K. and Schulterbrandt Gragg, R.D. 2015. Community-based participatory research: Challenging 'lone ethnographer' anthropology in the community and the classroom. *Practicing Anthropology*, 37(4), 9–13.

Kusters, A. and De Meulder, M. 2013. Understanding deafhood: In search of its meanings. *American Annals of the Deaf*, 157(5), 428–38.

LeCompte, M.D. and Schensul, J.J. 1999. *Designing and Conducting Ethnographic Research*. Walnut Creek, CA: AltaMira.

O'Brien, D. and Kusters, A. 2017. Visual methods in Deaf Studies: Using photography and filmmaking in research with deaf people. In Kusters, A., De Meulder, M. and O'Brien, D. (Eds.), *Innovations in Deaf Studies: The Role of Deaf Scholars*. Oxford: Oxford University Press, 265–296.

Pfister, A.E. 2020. En Mi Casa Quiero Señas: Photovoice as language advocacy. *Visual Anthropology Review*, 36(2), 255–74.

Pfister, A.E., Vindrola-Padros, C., Johnson, G.A. 2014. Together, we can show you: Participant-generated visual data in collaborative research. *Collaborative Anthropologies*, 7(1), 26–49.

Wang, C.C. and Burris, M.A. 1997. Photovoice: Concept, methodology and use for participatory needs assessment. *Health Education and Behavior*, 24(3), 369–87.

13

GOING AGAINST THE GRAIN IN WRITING ETHNOGRAPHY

Ezgi Güler

Summary

Some institutional and disciplinary pressures placed on early career ethnographers conflict with authoring ethically and politically committed works. Drawing on the author's personal experience in writing an ethnographic dissertation, the chapter illustrates the tension between pondering the ethics and politics of ethnographic representation and neoliberal and objectivist expectations. It then explains how these unfitting structural demands impact ethnographic writing and describes a number of alternative writing practices. They include ethical and critical self-reflexivity, personally and politically engaged writing, representation of complexity of social worlds and formation of supportive writing communities. These strategies not only ethically and politically responsible representation, but also inspire critical analysis.

Table of contents

Introduction	183
Ethical and political commitments	185
Partial representations	185
Representational dilemmas	187
Representing complexity and diversity	188
Incompatible institutional and disciplinary expectations	190
Neutral ethnographic writing	190
Producing faster and more	192
Conclusion	193
Recommendations	193
Further reading	194
References	195

Introduction

This chapter discusses some of the difficulties that may accompany the writing of new ethnographies and provides us with some ideas and tools to address them. The collection of essays in *Writing Culture: The Poetics and Politics of Ethnography* (Clifford and Marcus, 1986) proposed new modes of ethnographic writing that acknowledge the partial and incomplete nature of ethnographic knowledge and that consider the implications of power in ethnographic representation and language. In the 21st century, these ideas on representation have been expanded and refined. At the same time, ethnographic writing has taken new directions, such as an increased engagement with ethnography's political potentials and responsibilities (McGranahan, 2014). As ethnographers of today, we strive for a critical and transparent writing that is respectful of research participants and concerned with local issues. Yet, an ethnographic writing practice that takes on explicit ethical and political responsibilities involves complexities, especially given the structural pressures we face in academia today.

After having carried out a committed fieldwork comes the phase of generating ethnographic stories and accounts. Sherry Ortner (2006, p. 42) broadly describes ethnography as 'the attempt to understand another life world using the self – as much of it as possible – as the instrument of knowing'. Then writing, through which we construct and express this intimate, embodied and experiential knowledge, is a vital stage of ethnographic research. The process of writing a self-reflexive ethnography takes us on a beautiful journey. We recall what prompted us to pursue our research, generate stories, engage with the meanings of a social practice and construct our 'voice' and ethnographic accounts. Writing self-reflexively can also provide healing through the process of acknowledging and reflecting on the difficult emotions that may accompany the entire research process – especially for those of us with a challenging fieldwork experience. For all these reasons, writing ethnography is as much an introspection as it is the enquiry of the other. What stories we choose to tell and how we interpret social worlds are inevitably personal in some ways. Contemplating these decisions in our written work helps us to self-explore, through which we build intimacy with ourselves, too. By so doing, we learn better where we, as researchers and humans, are positioned today and grasp the socially situated nature of the knowledges that we produce.

While stimulating, writing ethnography also tends to be a long and complex process. After collecting a rich set of materials through an extended field engagement, many of us, especially first-time ethnographers, may expect the writing phase to be less demanding – both practically and emotionally. On the contrary to such expectations, prior ethical and political preoccupations remain, and novel dilemmas emerge at this stage. In order to promote a safer and more ethical fieldwork practice, recent social scientific literature is indeed paying increasing attention to the challenges ethnographers face in the field. With a few remarkable exceptions, however, there is not much published material and institutional guidance to support us through the complexities of writing an ethnography. In this chapter, I will draw on my own research as a doctoral student to discuss some of the obstacles that early career ethnographers may face in the writing phase and to offer some suggestions for addressing them. Although writing permeates every stage of ethnographic research, this chapter focuses exclusively on the practice of crafting ethnographic texts.

EXAMPLE 13.1

As a doctoral student, I experienced a great deal of anxiety in the process of writing an ethnography of a community of transfeminine sex workers. First, I was preoccupied with my representation of an already stigmatised group, which caused me to constantly rethink the arguments I had constructed, the language I had chosen, and the descriptions I had drawn. Second, the emotional difficulties that came with re-engaging with my field materials impacted my writing routine. Having listened to numerous stories of violence and abuse directed at my interlocutors, I sometimes felt a strong urge to distance myself from my research, which evoked feelings of guilt towards both my interlocutors and supervisors. Writing about violence also involved ethical complexities. I received little institutional support in navigating these challenges.

As in my experience, in addition to the practical challenges like organising and making sense of a large volume of notes and information, we might also grapple with the ethical and political questions that persist at the stage of writing. What piece of information should be omitted? Which aspects of interlocutors and research locations should be anonymised? How should research participants be portrayed? To what extent should the researcher be visible in their writing? Will the research outputs make a difference in the lives and struggles of the communities we write about? In this chapter I unpack the dilemmas that such questions entail and explain my approach to navigating them.

Certain institutional and disciplinary expectations placed on ethnographers can limit our capacity to contemplate these questions and come into conflict with writing ethically and politically engaged texts. For instance, an increasingly neoliberal academia requires rapid production of research 'outputs', which is particularly incompatible with the nature of ethnographic knowledge production. For those of us in social sciences outside anthropology, the quality of our research is assessed by the contribution of our findings to generalisable models and, the legitimacy of our work can be questioned if we refuse the detached and neutral writer model. While these concerns vary depending on the academic environments and traditions we are part of, many of us are familiar with such pressures and accusations, making it difficult for beginning ethnographers to find their own voice and pace.

Ethical and political commitments

Many new ethnographers – but especially those who work with underprivileged groups – feel a sense of responsibility to their research participants, which also manifests itself in the writing phase. The ethical and political considerations that guide our writing are manifold, though this section focuses primarily on those related to the representational choices and reflections in ethnographic writing. Such considerations bring about particular care regarding how arguments, descriptions and language in ethnographic texts depict the lives and experiences of others. What are the ways to ensure that our descriptions of the lived experince do justice to the social and political realities of research participants? These kinds of enquiries, which all ethnographers working in distinct domains may face at some time during the writing process, do not always have simple, straightforward answers. Instead, the dilemmas that they entail could be addressed through self-reflexive writing and engaging with the complexity and variety of social worlds in our representations. These commitments do not jeopardise scientific rigour; on the contrary, a thorough and nuanced representation of research participants' lives and cultures and a self-reflexive reasoning enrich our texts analytically.

Partial representations

Ethnography has historically been used to research cultures and places that are particularly 'other' or 'unknown'. Nowadays, ethnographers from different fields are increasingly working with their own cultures or communities and in their native languages. This type of ethnography has sparked a lively debate, not just because it establishes a less hierarchical relationship between researcher and participant. Relatedly, researchers' personal connection with the communities and deep understanding of the cultures they study are reflected in their writing, diversifying and complicating representation of the lived experience in ethnographic texts (Jacobs-Huey, 2002).

While it is not possible to draw a firm line between the insider and outsider status, this dichotomy nevertheless guides discussions on positionality in ethnographic literature. Ethnographers studying familiar or 'home' contexts are typically described as insiders, regardless of what research participants think of them. Panourgiá (1994, p. 46), however, argues that 'simply by being of the country/ culture/ group/ family, one is not automatically guaranteed infinite and non-terminable knowledge of the culture'. It is because researchers simultaneously experience multiple positionings in the field, which may also be situation-specific (Narayan, 1993). Furthermore, a variety of experiences among members of a social group or a community challenge homogeneous, universal constructions of identity and illustrate the complexities of positionality during the research process. In fact, a lot of ethnographers who worked in familiar environments reported feeling both insiders and outsiders over the course of their research (Jacobs-Huey, 2002). Even when there are a number of shared identifications, the inequality between ethnographer and participants persists in some cases. Taken together, these reflections imply that insider status does not resolve all dilemmas regarding representation that researchers face in ethnographic enquiry. Conversely, although representational concerns are manifold when lived experience is conveyed by a predominantly outsider researcher, being an outsider does not preclude one from producing analytically sound, morally aware and politically engaged ethnographies.

EXAMPLE 13.2

My multiple and layered position in my doctoral research can be defined as 'betweenness'. In addition to bringing a deeper awareness of the enormous privileges I had compared to my research participants in a cisnormative society, fieldwork became a process through which our commonalities were also explored. I frequently joined a group of trans women watching the evening news in a neighbourhood café, where we discussed rising femicides and the increasing cost of living in the country. We were all concerned about these issues. I then attempted to understand the specific consequences of both our distinct and shared experiences and preoccupations in my research.

No representation of social reality can be as complex, comprehensive and radically diverse as reality itself (Goodall, 2000, p. 55). The questions we ask, the reactions we elicit, the accounts we give priority to and the explanations we provide are shaped by our own lived experience and result in 'partial' representations. Therefore, ethnographic writing both as insiders and outsiders necessitates a thorough reflection on positionalities and the power imbalances they may imply in the research process. However, how such reflections are conducted is decisive.

Though there is an increasing dedication to honest, transparent and critically reflexive writing among ethnographers (see Koning and Ooi, 2013; Verbuyst and Galazka, 2023), ethnographic texts do sometimes engage in discussions on positionality in superficial and self-serving ways. Feeling performance anxieties under neoliberal academia, researchers are motivated to camouflage failures, awkwardness, anxieties and tensions experienced during the research process, which cause the methodological reflections employing self-reflexivity to be 'self-censured, sanitized and overtly persuasive' (Verbuyst and Galazka, 2023, p. 63).

Similarly, when discussions on self-reflexivity are built on fixed and homogenising identity categories without further articulation, they risk obscuring the complex and varying character of human experience and, echoing Jennifer Robertson (2002), stereotyping both self and the other. Especially as junior ethnographers, we may feel more preoccupied with our performance and self-representation, so we may exhibit these tendencies in our writings more frequently. While our personal histories undoubtedly influence how we conduct and write about fieldwork, positionality does not automatically and completely enable or inhibit knowledges. Rather than leaving positionalities as self-evident in an ethnographic narrative, we should investigate the specific meanings they take in the settings where we work and reveal their effects and limitations on our research. As a result, we become more critical of our own assumptions and ideas, which is an invaluable learning opportunity provided by ethnography.

There is no such thing as a complete ethnography. Yet, critical self-reflexivity allows us to account for the ways in which our experiences, knowledge and assumptions shape the construction of ethnographic accounts and narratives. Another useful implication of writing self-reflexively is that we pay attention to how our presence might have changed the course of events and interactions in the field. A reflexive writer then intentionally shares with their readers how their lived experience interacts with field experience, making certain knowledges available, while concealing others. Such transparent reflections are vital not just for a deeper level of comprehension, but also for the ethically and politically responsible ethnographic practice.

Representational dilemmas

It is critical to acknowledge that our ethnographic representation of social reality is profoundly influenced by our own social positionings. However, we are also responsible for the effects of our words. As contemporary ethnographers with explicit ethical and political commitments, we feel especially accountable for what we write to those who entrust their stories in us. What to include and exclude in our written work and how our texts represent the lives, practices, feelings, beliefs and values of our research participants are critical considerations that emerge during the writing phase. Some of the challenges I encountered while writing my own dissertation were directly related to these questions.

EXAMPLE 13.3

For a long time, I debated whether to write about community tensions caused by structural pressures in my research context. These analyses were relevant to my larger research question and would help me draw a more thorough portrayal of the relationship between politico-legal structures and the everyday experiences of my research participants, yet this brought a representational dilemma to the fore. On the one hand, I was worried that parts of my dissertation could be used to validate the widespread stereotypes about trans sex workers. On the other hand, omitting this subject would risk creating an idealised and paternalistic depiction of my research participants' community life and struggle. My decision was informed by the insights of feminist anthropologists who faced comparable challenges, as well as conversations I had with my key interlocutors. I eventually came to agree with Ortner (1995) that the incomplete description of the lives of interlocutors and their local realities is a romanticising tendency and denies those we study their full humanity and subjectivity. Navigating through these two ethically risky terrains was like walking a tightrope since I had to find the appropriate words and approaches to discuss such delicate subjects. Rather than picturing these dynamics as community characteristics, I focused on the processes by which hostile conditions induced tension and competition among my research participants, whose lives are so precariously situated at the margins of urban Turkey.

While some early career ethnographers, particularly those working with marginalised or disadvantaged groups, may be able to connect to the issue raised above, others encounter distinct representational dilemmas based on their research topics and contexts and their own political sensibilities. Regardless, what is essential in navigating representational challenges is ethical self-reflexivity, which makes ethnographic writing attentive to the everyday material and discursive circumstances of research participants. Ethical self-reflexivity urges ethnographers to evaluate both the possible consequences of their written work for all people involved and the larger social and political implications of their research.

Ethical self-reflexivity calls for case-by-case consideration of the numerous complexities we may encounter along the writing of an ethnography, which takes time and effort to read, elaborate and debate with others. Therefore, institutional demands to write more quickly and in greater quantities, as we will see later in the chapter, contradict profoundly the careful reflection that such morally and politically complex judgements demand.

Representing complexity and diversity

Ethnography acknowledges the messiness of life. It enables attention to the complex, dynamic and varied nature of lived experience by its close touch with the everyday. It can provide a coherent narrative of the social world, while at the same time convey as much of its complexity as possible. By representing the complexity of social reality, rather than reducing it to smaller and mutually exclusive categories, ethnographic practice potentially brings about a more ethically and politically responsible conduct of research, and is also a crucial way to offer unique insights into theory.

Manifesting the varieties of lived experience and cultural meaning in communities about which we write is one of the methods to remain faithful to complexity in ethnographic writing. Our narratives and arguments should be informed and enriched by the diverse – and 'deviant' – voices and experiences of research participants. For instance, in my research, I tried to depict the multiplicity of trans subjectivities and presentations that coexisted among my interlocutors. I also incorporated into my ethnographic narrative a range of perspectives on their involvement in sex work. It was crucial to me that no personal opinions or experiences be excluded in favour of simplified arguments or flattened theories.

In addition to voice, it is vital to engage with participants' silences, though in some cases we may instead choose to respect what is left unsaid. Silence, a widespread phenomenon in all human interactions, may occur in ethnographic interviews or conversations for a variety of reasons. It may simply be a mode of communication; signify withholding or resistance; point to what is taken for granted; or conceal certain knowledges that cannot be vocalised or are too risky to reveal (Poland and Pederson, 1998). In ethnographic research, silences can be traced by paying attention to not only the words spoken, but also pauses, non-responses, hesitancies, whispers, facial expressions and body language during an interaction. These could be recorded by taking extensive field notes that would include verbal and non-verbal cues as well as the context in which they occur. Silences can be analyzed in light of the power structures that surround them. Tracing silences may also necessitate allowing for ambiguity and unintelligibility in their interpretations.

Along with interpersonal diversity, accounting for the element of change also contributes to a more thorough representation in ethnographic narrative. It is very plausible to witness fluctuating circumstances and shifting personal accounts over the course of fieldwork. Engaging with the changing conditions of day-to-day lives and the evolving practices and subjectivities result in constructing the social scientific concepts of interest more dynamically in our analyses and writing. In sum, focusing on variety across individuals and time goes against the propensity to generate a fixed and monolithic understanding of social reality and an essentialising construction of social groups. This approach to writing instead reflects the varied and ever-changing character of human experience.

An ethnographic narrative that addresses contradictions and ambiguities encountered in the field is another way to attend to the complexities of the social worlds we study. Several writing methods may be useful in this attempt. Incorporating voices in all their messiness helps to expose the depth and richness of research participants' experiences, thoughts and feelings. It also reveals doubts, uncertainties and ambivalences embedded in personal accounts. This could be accomplished by including full accounts and exact wordings from research participants, rather than plucking an example or a justification out of context to support a specific thesis. In a similar vein, thick descriptions provide in-depth and contextualised understanding of social practices and help expose their paradoxes and multiple meanings.

The writing practices covered in this subsection, result in greater contemplation, detailed description and therefore lengthier texts. But scholarly journals, which have become the most common means of publishing research, tend to impose one-size-fits-all word limitations (Gerring and Cojocaru, 2020). Journals' stringent space constraints sometimes only allow for short quotations and quick descriptions rather than longer textual representation, limiting the space authors need to articulate ethnographic material and argument. There are a number of scientific journals that have flexible word limitations, which might be more appropriate for the nature of ethnographic publication. Also, despite its declining popularity, the fieldwork monograph still provides a conducive vehicle for communicating the breadth and nuances of ethnographic research.

Incompatible institutional and disciplinary expectations

A variety of institutional and disciplinary constraints make it difficult for us to uphold the stated ethical and political commitments regarding ethnographic representation. In this section, I will specifically focus on the demand to produce research outputs quicker and in greater numbers, as well as to retain a distanced and impartial posture in our writings. What specific pressures might these expectations create on our texts? I address this question by examining the influence of the neoliberal academia and the objectivist pressures on ethnographic writing, which early career researchers encounter to varied degrees depending on the disciplines and academic cultures they are part of. I will also discuss the alternative practices that are more suited to the nature of ethnographic writing.

Neutral ethnographic writing

Some early career ethnographers are grappling with the expectation to write neutral ethnographies. The authority of a 'neutral ethnographer' has historically been reinforced by the notion of scientific objectivity in social science research. Post-colonial, indigenous, feminist and critical social science, however, has challenged the field of anthropology in recent decades, pointing to the entanglement of the so-called neutral observer and writer role with wider colonial, exploitative systems of power. This interrogation has been transformational, and what has emerged as a result is an approach to anthropology that is concerned with the social and political implications of research; that embraces participatory and collaborative methodologies; and that is committed to human liberation. Nevertheless, the notion of neutral ethnography is still very much alive in other branches of social sciences.

As a doctoral researcher, my academic writing was often criticised for being too intimate and political, therefore lacking scientific rigour. I was advised to maintain a friendly detachment from my research participants and to use non-political language. A distant writing both personally from research participants and politically from their struggles contradicted the kind of ethnography to which I aspired. However, as a would-be ethnographer, it took me some time to develop the skills required to construct and defend my writing.

As in my experience, some junior researchers are encouraged to adopt a distant position towards research participants because personal engagement is seen to unavoidably compromise the scientific credibility. In this approach, there is no valid space for writing about the various ways in which meaningful relationships with study participants help us comprehend their experiences in more profound ways. Although there may be different levels of engagement between ethnographers and their research participants, ethnography is fundamentally a relational work. While we must be mindful of the ethical dilemmas that might arise from such involvement and prioritise transparency in our relationships, the truth is that developing close ties, especially with key interlocutors, is highly possible. Dropping the academic armour, according to Kari Lerum (2001, p. 481), 'helps move one from dry, detached writing and analysis to passionate writing that ultimately inspires critical analysis'. That is, reflections informed by personal engagement with research participants have the ability to disturb power dynamics and give deeper and more intimate insights into others' experiences in ethnographic research. Transgressing impersonalising tendencies, autoethnographic writing is a striking illustration of how reflecting on one's own personal experience can be the key approach for creating knowledge (Denshire, 2014).

'Scientific' writing also tends to restrict references to authors' emotions and vulnerabilities that surface during the research process (Goodall, 2000, p. 190–1). However, it is unlikely that we can separate emotions from how we write about the field process in ethnography. There is indeed an ethnographic tradition that explicitly acknowledges that emotions can be usefully integrated in our reflections and analyses. Emotional reflexivity, as McQueeney and Lavelle (2017) explain, can contribute to the generation of critical knowledge by contextualising emotions, using emotions to uncover power in the research process and connecting emotions to personal biographies. This reasoning has significantly influenced my methodological approach. Rather than being a barrier to my analysis, my emotions and embodied experience offered a deeper insight into the lives of my interlocutors and the research process, as the following vignette illustrates.

EXAMPLE 13.4

It is a summer night in 2018. At the end of a long day I am leaving the hair salon to catch the last train home. Part of the side street where I am walking is pitch black. As always, I hurry to reach the railway station, which is within a short walking distance. When I arrive at the crossroads, a car unexpectedly stops on my side of the street. The driver wolf-whistles to catch my attention and asks me to get into the car. I notice the gazes of four men in the car looking me over. For a brief moment, I fear being forced into the car. Terrified, I indicate my refusal with a hand gesture, which also vaguely communicates my outrage, and continue walking. I immediately regret the gesture and hope that they will not retaliate. My heart is racing, my palms are sweating, my knees are shaking. I speed up my step and walk away until I blend in with the crowds at the railway station. As I ride the train, I feel guilty for being so relieved to be finally leaving the 'field', which reminds me of how privileged I am in comparison to my research participants. I remember that for trans women who sell sex on the streets of Turkey, violence is not a scary exception, but a commonplace, everyday experience. As in this case, reflecting on my emotional experiences allowed me to develop a deeper grasp of the conditions under which my interlocutors live and work, as well as the vast power disparities that exist between us.

The pressure for neutral social sciences also calls the legitimacy of politically engaged ethnographic writing into question. Rather than solely focusing on a scientific puzzle or a gap in the literature, political ethnography is motivated by an impulse to alleviate human suffering caused by the structural processes of violence, exclusion and exploitation. The politically impartial and detached approach to social science, however, operates based on the researcher-activist and science-politics dichotomies. Ethnographies with social justice goals are discredited as lacking critical focus on these bases. But by explicitly engaging with the tension between the two, ethnographies can productively incorporate political commitments and critical analysis. In fact, a growing number of perceptive ethnographies with explicit political commitments and solidarity with research participants "create knowledge that is at once empirically grounded, theoretically valuable, and contributes to the ongoing struggle for greater social justice" (Speed, 2006, p. 75).

Producing faster and more

The fast-paced, metric-driven neoliberal academy puts researchers under pressure to rapidly generate marketable research outputs (Gill, 2016). To enhance their institutional productivity statistics, universities employ productivity measures, which quantify and compare 'progress'. Finding ourselves in an increasingly precarious position, early career researchers feel compelled to produce as much as possible under time constraints. These efforts, in addition to deteriorating mental health and increasing competitiveness within universities, disrupt academic knowledge generation processes. A shift of focus from substance to quantity of outputs alters the nature of our writings.

While such trends pertain to the contemporary academia as a whole, the demand to produce more, and quicker, has a particularly severe effect on ethnographic research and writing. The invisible productive time spent to reflect on the experiences of the field without publishing, which is crucial for ethnographers, is not considered productive in neoliberal terms (Giri, 2000, p. 179). Short-term contracts limit the time and energy that early career ethnographers may devote to developing a self-reflexive voice and experimenting with writing. Likewise, some PhD programmes in social science are not set up in a way that aids students in honing their ethnographic writing abilities. An increasing competitiveness and pressure for individual success in academia discourages ethnographers from reflecting on what went wrong and the challenges faced in the field, preventing them from collectively learning from their 'failures' (Verbuyst and Galazka, 2023).

As a response, we can consider how we can refuse the demands of this exploitative system and take responsibility for developing alternative research and teaching models. For instance, based on feminist ethics of care and politics of resistance, scholars have long urged for collaborative efforts to slow down scholarship (see Mountz et al., 2015). Slowing down in this context would not only assist us to protect ourselves and one another from the competitive and individualising demands of neoliberal academia; it would also mean a stronger commitment to thorough and ethical scholarship practices. As ethnographers too, we can try to collectively slow down, and create spaces and communities where credible and critical forms of scholarship can flourish. Slowing down in the process of ethnographic writing would help us to find much needed time, supportive writing communities and creativity. Additionally, we can openly and critically discuss in our writing the ubiquitous but uncomfortable aspects of the fieldwork, such as, anxieties, challenges and mistakes. By doing so, we can expose the ambiguities of the field experience and challenge the unequivocally 'successful' fieldwork narrative endorsed by the neoliberal logic.

Conclusion

In this chapter I have argued that in addition to the practical challenges of writing ethnography, a number of structural pressures placed on early career researchers can potentially compromise their ability to write ethically sensitive and politically engaged ethnographies. Among these are the pressures to produce faster and more and to take a neutral and distanced ethnographic stance both personally and politically. These multilayered demands affect various aspects of ethnographic research, as they have troubling impact on writing. I also discussed alternative writing practices that enable a deeper ethnographic understanding of and respect for the social and political realities of research participants.

This is not to argue that all guiding principles or support systems within the field and institutions of social sciences are hostile to ethnographers. Yet, we frequently find ourselves having to operate around or against the institutional requirements that are incompatible with the main methodology that we employ. It is also crucial to emphasise that not all ethnographers are affected by these pressures in the same way. Anthropology, in particular, has effectively refused the impartial writer position and the pressure for parsimonious and generalisable explanations. Because I drew on my own experience, some of the obstacles described in this chapter may be more similar to those encountered by ethnographers training in political science or sociology departments. Nonetheless, given the overall evolution of social science and an increasingly neoliberal academic climate, as new ethnographers, we are all writing against the grain in some respects.

One of the chapter's practical suggestions is to resist the competitive and individualising pressures of neoliberal academia, for example, by building writing communities in which we take the time to support and critique one another. While there are no quick fixes for the complex and deeply rooted issues that we face in the social sciences today, this may provide us with the space and tools we need to craft critical ethnographies that address the ethics and politics of textual representation.

In fact, ethnographic alternatives are thriving today. Seasoned ethnographers have created a variety of writing genres and provided us with tools to deepen and enrich our analysis and representation. Among these tools are self-reflexivity, emotionally engaged reflections, complex, dynamic and varied depictions of lived experience, and the incorporation of political commitments and critical analysis in ethnographic writing. By delving into each of them, this chapter has explained that while a complex and laborious craft, ethnographic writing is also a resource capable of bringing together empathetically, politically and critically situated insights.

Recommendations

1 **Self-reflexive writing.** Through critical self-reflexivity, we can interrogate how our positionings and situatedness impact our accounts and narratives. Ethical self-reflexivity also encourages us to take into account the political and ethical implications of the representations and knowledge we produce about others' lives and cultures.

2 **Representation of complexity and diversity.** An ethnographic narrative that integrates silences and divergent voices; changing circumstances and personal accounts; and ambiguities and inconsistencies of practices and subjectivities all contribute to depicting the complexity and diversity of social worlds we study.
3 **Personally and politically engaged writing.** Personal engagements with research participants and political engagements with their struggles do not necessarily jeopardise the scientific integrity of our work. While we must carefully assess the ethical hazards in such engagements and avoid causing harm to our participants, the reflections deepened by our personal and political involvements can provide critical knowledge that is also theoretically valuable.
4 **Collective defiance.** We can explicitly call into question or quietly defy the norms and expectations that do not fit the nature of ethnographic writing, endanger our mental health and compromise the credibility of our written work. We can collectively engage in slow and self-reflexive scholarship. Writing in periods and taking breaks when needed are especially important for those of us who have had emotionally challenging fieldwork experiences.
5 **Writing groups.** Creating alternative spaces and communities, such as writers' groups that read and react to each other's texts, can enhance the clarity and coherence of ideas and encourage authors to experiment with writing, to display vulnerability and to seek advice in a safe setting, in addition to helping build a continuous writing routine. A supportive writing group can also act as a forum for discussing the implications of our language, stories and arguments as we develop ethnographic works.

Further reading

Emerson, R.M., Fretz, R.I. and Shaw, L.L. 2011. *Writing Ethnographic Fieldnotes*. Chicago: University of Chicago Press.
An excellent resource for those who want to advance their abilities to turn fieldwork experiences and observations into a polished ethnography, as well as generate and organise field notes. The authors believe that taking field notes is a skill that can be developed and refined via study and practice.

Goldstein, D. 2003. *Laughter Out of Place: Race, Class, Violence, and Sexuality in a Rio Shantytown*. Berkeley: University of California Press.
An outstanding example of a specific ethnographic genre, with its novel-like and accessible language and lively and moving storytelling centred on a main character. As a cultural outsider writing about the humor of women in a Rio de Janeiro shantytown, Goldstein navigates complex ethical commitments, from which readers may learn a great deal.

Goodall, H.L., Jr 2000. *Writing the New Ethnography*. Walnut Creek, CA: Alta Mira.
This text provides students with a fundamental grasp of the creative writing process, offering advice, examples and exercises for each stage. The book covers the construction of personal voice, the development of self-reflexivity, representing ethnographic experiences and the ethics of

writing ethnography. It is like a good mentor – it's enjoyable to read, encouraging on the journey and instructive when faced with difficulties.

McGranahan, C. (Ed.) 2020. *Writing Anthropology: Essays on Craft and Commitment*. Durham, NC: Duke University Press.

This text serves as a comprehensive resource for ethnographers at all stages of their careers and addresses a wide range of topics, including storytelling, scholarly responsibility, ethnographic genres and authorship, describing the many struggles and joys of ethnographic/anthropological writing.

Narayan, K. 2012. *Alive in the Writing: Crafting Ethnography in the Company of Chekhov*. Chicago: University of Chicago Press.

Narayan uses the life and writings of Chekhov, a Russian short story writer and playwright, to inspire her new directions in writing ethnography and creative non-fiction, providing recommendations and helpful exercises on story, theory, scene, embodiment, biography, voice and narrator.

References

Clifford, J. and Marcus, G.E. (Eds.) 1986. *Writing Culture: The Poetics and Politics of Ethnography*. Berkeley: University of California Press.

Denshire, S. 2014. On auto-ethnography. *Current Sociology*, 62(6), 831–50.

Gill, R. 2016. Breaking the silence: The hidden injuries of neo-liberal academia. *Feministische Studien*, 34(1), 39–55.

Giri, A. 2000. Audited accountability and the imperative of responsibility: Beyond the primacy of the politica. In Strathern, M. (Ed.), *Audit Cultures: Anthropological Studies in Accountability, Ethics and the Academy*. London: Routledge. pp. 173–95.

Gerring, J. and Cojocaru, L. 2020. Length limits. In Elman, C., Gerring, J. and Mahoney, J. (Eds.), *The Production of Knowledge: Enhancing Progress in Social Science*. Cambridge: Cambridge University Press. pp. 98–126.

Goodall, H.L., Jr 2000. *Writing the New Ethnography*. Walnut Creek, CA: Alta Mira.

Jacobs-Huey, L. 2002. The natives are gazing and talking back: Reviewing the problematics of positionality, voice, and accountability among 'native' anthropologists. *American Anthropologist*, 104(3), 791–804.

Koning, J. and Ooi, C.S. 2013. Awkward encounters and ethnography. *Qualitative Research in Organizations and Management: An International Journal*, 8(1), 16–32.

Lerum, K. 2001. Subjects of desire: Academic armor, intimate ethnography, and the production of critical knowledge. *Qualitative Inquiry*, 7(4), 466–83.

McGranahan, C. 2014. What is ethnography? Teaching ethnographic sensibilities without fieldwork. *Teaching Anthropology*, 4, 23–36.

McQueeney, K. and Lavelle, K.M. 2017. Emotional labor in critical ethnographic work: In the field and behind the desk. *Journal of Contemporary Ethnography*, 46(1), 81–107.

Mountz, A., Bonds, A., Mansfield, B., Loyd, J., Hyndman, J., Walton-Roberts, M., Basu, R., Whitson, R., Hawkins, R., Hamilton, T. and Curran, W. 2015. For slow scholarship: A feminist politics of resistance through collective action in the neoliberal university. *ACME: An International E-Journal for Critical Geographies*, 14(4), 1235–59.

Narayan, K. 1993. How native is a 'native' anthropologist? *American Anthropologist*, 95, 671–85.

Ortner, S. 1995. Resistance and the problem of ethnographic refusal. *Comparative Studies in Society and History*, 37(1), 173–93.

Ortner, S. 2006. *Anthropology and Social Theory: Culture, Power, and the Acting Subject.* Durham, NC: Duke University Press.

Panourgiá, N. 1994. A native narrative. *Anthropology and Humanism*, 19(1), 40–51.

Poland, B. and Pederson, A. 1998. Reading between the lines: Interpreting silences in qualitative research. *Qualitative Inquiry*, 4(2), 293–312.

Robertson, J. 2002. Reflexivity redux: A pithy polemic on 'positionality'. *Anthropological Quarterly*, 75(4), 785–92.

Verbuyst, R. and Galazka, A.M. 2023. Introducing 'navigating failure in ethnography': A forum about failure in ethnographic research. *Journal of Organizational Ethnography*, 12(1), 61–75.

CONCLUDING RECOMMENDATIONS FOR EDUCATORS

Branwen Spector and Caitlin Procter

The chapters of this textbook have argued that working together towards an inclusive ethnography requires the compassion, collaboration and allyship of students and university staff together. Change can only come by resisting the ways that the neoliberal university institution aims to move us away from working as a collective. As such, we propose the following interrelated actions and attitudes.

Compassionate and inclusive supervisory practices. A researcher's engagement with their supervisor is often their gateway to interacting with the institution as a whole (including the adminsistration, ethics bords, funding bodies, etc). It can also result in the overburdening and overwork of supervisors, who themselves can feel isolated or unqualified to manage the emotional, psychological and physical impacts of ethnographic research. Supervisors can practise inclusivity by maintaining an awareness of the multiple directions in which researchers are pulled, and centring care in the relationship. This can involve establishing a clear and reasonable agreement of mutual expectation of the supervisory relationship, and by encouraging universities to provide a code of conduct or relationship of care agreement to which the supervisory practice is accountable.

Help students to see that pre-empting challenges is part of their professional responsibility. Because so few educators in positions of authority in institutions speak up about the challenges they faced in their own work, the perception filters down that this is something that academics do not (or should not) talk about. A culture shift is needed to create an environment in which honest discussions about the complex realities of fieldwork become the norm. It is important to encourage students to see this as part of 'the job', and to take the potential for fieldwork challenges as a professional responsibility.

Creation of diverse spaces. Ethnographic and other qualitative research methods courses should make space in curricula and the classroom to specifically focus on challenges in ethnographic research. This helps those in training to understand that research is a nuanced and non-linear process. It also normalises the experience of challenges, and allows a community of support to be developed both within student cohorts and between staff and students. Building this kind of community allows those conducting research to be vulnerable and avoid the isolating experiences common among first-time researchers. It also cements a sense of compassionate support for those needing it. Creating space for deeper reflection on the kinds of challenges that fieldwork can involve is critical. This can be done, for instance, by asking students to write an essay on what they imagine to be the biggest challenges they will face in their research. Often the first time students think about the challenges they will face is when they do an ethics or risk assessment, in which they feel a need to write defensively in order to have their research approved. Encouraging deep thinking about fieldwork challenges at an earlier stage is vital.

Re-thinking ethical review procedures. Many universities teach and present ethical approval for research as a box-ticking exercise in avoiding liability rather than responding to notions of ethics as an ongoing process. There is often an emphasis on ethics as an administrative hurdle, or as a document through which the university can avoid claims of malpractice. This is particularly irresponsible when research ethics forms a part of most graduate methodological training. Where possible, ethics review procedures should also ask questions in relation to the wellbeing of the researcher and how this might be impacted by their work.

Advocating for the provision of mental health support for those conducting fieldwork. Some universities now offer substantive mental health support to social scientists before, during and after fieldwork – but unfortunately this remains the exception rather than the rule. In institutions where this kind of support is not available, it is important to understand where and why there is resistance to mental health provision in connection to fieldwork. Evidence from universities who are conducting this work suggests that these interventions do not need to be costly, and lead to healthier researchers who are better equipped to do their work.

Index

Pages followed by "*f*" refer to figures.

Abdelnour, S., 141
ableism, xxii, 49–50
academic pressure, 19–21
Advancing Research on Conflict doctoral training workshop, xviiii
Alphabet, 38
American Anthropological Association (ASA), 159
American Sign Language (ASL), 175, 175*f*, 176
Apple, 38
Aroussi, S., 144
attention deficit hyperactivity disorder (ADHD), 13
autism, 13

Backe, E. L., xxiii, 12
Baird, A., 20, 23
Behar, R., 151
Berry, M., 79, 80, 83, 84, 86, 87
biometric recognition, 39
Blumer, H., 55
borderline personality disorder (BPD), 13
Bredenbröker, I., xxii, 49, 61n1
Burris, M.A., 173
Butina, M., 37

Campbell, F. K., 50
Canadian NGO Citizen Lab, 34
Centro de Atención Múltiple (CAM), 39, 177, 178*f*
Cerwonka, A., 4, 6
Clarke, A., 74
cloud, 40–41
coded-as-Black woman
  anti-sexual harassment, 81
  counterparts thinking, 84–86
  exit strategies, 86–87
  harmless, 83–84
  past skin colour, 84
  perceptions of race and gender, 80–81
  privileges, 87–88
  suiting your fieldsite, 81–83

community-based research (CBR), 167, 170–173
COVID-19 pandemic, xviii
  conferencing, 42
  emergence of, 154
  home-schooling, 74
Crenshaw, K., 49
Critical disability theory, 51
Crypto-parties, 44
Cullen, P., 144
cybersecurity
  data protection, 40–41
  digital identity, 39
  internet access, 42–44
  overview, 34–35
  secure communication, 41–42
  threats to ethnographers, 35–38
  threats to human security, 35

'dangerous' work, xix
data anxiety, 19–21
data protection
  cloud, 40–41
  encryption, 40
  restriction, 40
Davies, J., 8
Deibert, R., 35
Devereux, G., 9
digital identity
  biometric recognition, 39
  multifactor authentication, 39
  passwords, 39
disability
  academic discourse, 51
  anthropological methods, 50
  classificatory category, 51
  fieldwork in India, 52–56
  interlocutors, 50, 55
  intersectional approach, 52
  medical and social model, 54
  multiple sclerosis, 56–59
  overview, 49–50
  SEND system, 69

divyang, 54
Donnelly, M.K., 26
Driessen, H., 11
Driscoll, C., 127
Dwight, A., 36

Egyptian Interior Ministry's National Security Agency, 34
ethical dilemmas
  balancing empathy and distance, 27
  case study, 25
  participant observation, 26–28
  power imbalances, 28–29
  research focus, 26
  speaking and writing practice, 29
ethical feminist
  blurring and re-forming boundaries, 106–107
  familiarity, friendship and trust, 108–109
  fragility of relationships, 106
  interview challenges, 112–113
  methodological insights, 110–111
  observing relationships, 111–112
  overview, 105–106
  reconciling conflicting narratives, 112–113
  relationships power, 110
  suspicion, betrayal and distrust, 109–110
ethnographers
  academic identities, 36
  cybersecurity issues, 37
  female ethnographers, 98
  LGBTQ+, 100
  sexual and social field, 94
ethnography, xvii–xviii
  analysis and writing, xxiv
  equality, diversity and inclusion, xvi
  fieldwork skills, 4–5
  fragility of relationships, 106
  future of, 11–14
  inclusivity, xx–xxi
  mental health, 11–14
  sexuality, 94–96
  time and space, 73
  training, 158–159
  wellbeing, 12

Facebook, 38, 41, 119, 120–127, 129, 130, 176
Fernandez, S., xxiii
fieldwork
  ableist conceptions, 49
  coded-as-Black woman, 78–90
  disability in India, 52–56
  doctoral research, 65
  fatigue, 19–21
  managing relationships, 129–130
  motherhood and power imbalances, 70–71
  multiple sclerosis, 56–59
  refugee communities, 136
  seeing sexuality, 93–94
fieldworkers
  attention, 7–8
  improvisation, 5–7
  resilience, 8–10
  social skills, 10–11
Fitzpatrick, A., xxiii, 12
Foley, D. E., xxi
Freire, P., 168

Google Android, 38
Google Maps, 119, 122
The Great British Bake Off, 127
Gregg, M., 127
Guler, E., xxiv

Hall, M. C., 51
Hanson, R., 22, 24
Haraway, D., 113
Hedges, M., 34, 37
heteronormativity, 96, 97
hidden discourses, 3
Hochschild, A., 108
Howell, N., 12
human-centred cybersecurity, 35, 37, 43

inclusive ethnography, xx–xxi
  compassionate and inclusive supervisory practices, 197
  creation of diverse spaces, 197–198
  culture shift, 197
  mental health support, 198
  re-thinking ethical review, 198
  structural inequalities, xxi
Indian Rights of People with Disabilities Act, 54
Instagram, 120, 121, 122, 127, 128, 130, 176
internet access
  Tor protocol, 42–43
  virtual machines (VM), 43
  virtual private networks (VPNs), 42
Irwin, K., 29

Jansen, W., 11
Jones, G.A., 26
Joseph, J., 26

Kaur, T., xxii, 49, 52, 57, 59, 60
Khan, H., xxiii
Khashoggi, J., 34
Kobayashi, A., 83
Kovats-Bernat, J. C., 23
Kusters, A., 170

Lavelle, K.M., 191
Lecocq, B., 3
Lerum, K., 190
LinkedIn, 43
Lorimer, F., 9

Malkki, L., 4, 6
The Managed Heart, 108
Martin, E., 13
Massey, D., 100
McCann, L., 142
McGranahan, C., 106
McQueeney, K., 191
mental health
    anxiety and depression, 151
    complications, 154
    coping mechanisms, 156–157
    departmental preparation and support, 155–156
    ethnographic training, 158–159
    imagined default ethnographer, 153–154
    improve head space, 157–160
    isolation and loneliness, 151
    overview, 149–150
    professional development, 159
    sexual violence, 153
    training and institutional support, 154–157
    transformative care, 160
    trauma, 152–153
    violence, harassment and assault, 152–153
methods training, xix, xv, xvi, xxi, 4
Microsoft, 38
Moghli, M.A., 141
Moreno, E., 153
motherhood and care responsibilities, 67–68
multifactor authentication, 39
Murstein, M., 49, 50

neurodiversity, 13, 15
New Ethnographer, xix, xv, xvi, xviii, xx, 3
New Ethnographer blog, 3

O'Brien, D., 170
Ochs, E., 13
Oliver, M., 54
O'Rourke, M., 57
Ortner, S., 183, 187

participatory analysis
    ASL sign, 175, 176
    community-based research approach, 170–172
    description, 167
    epistemology, 168–170
    experience-based narratives, 179
    inclusive ethnography, 168
    IPPLIAP families, 176

    iterative process, 173
    learning and language modalities, 172
    LSM signs, 175
    methodological innovations, 167
    personal history timelines, 176–179
    photovoice projects, 173–174
Pearlman, L., 142
Pfister, A. E., xxiv
Philip, S., xxiii
phishing emails, 36
Pollard, A., xix, 12, 150, 155
Prince, D. E., 14
Procter, C., xxiii

reflexive ethnography
    care and relationality, 67–70
    entanglements and embodiment, 70–72
    ethics of care, 64
    feminist approach, 66–67
    institutional challenges, 72–74
    intellectual and emotional challenges, 64
    messy trajectories, 72–74
    motherhood and care work, 72
    motherhood and power imbalances, personal experiences, 70–71
    personal challenges, 71–72
Regini, G., 34, 37
Reid-Cunningham, A. R., 56
Richards, P., 22, 24
Robertson, J., 187
Rodgers, D., 26, 27

safety dilemmas
    case study, 20–21
    context-related risks, 22–23
    positionality-related risks, 24–25
    topic-related risks, 23–24
    unwanted suspicion, 23
Salman, M. B., 34
Schulz, P., 144
Scott, S., 10
secure communication
    email, 41
    messaging apps, 41
    online conferencing, 42
sensibility, 4, 56, 155
sexuality
    before, during and after fieldwork, 93–94
    ethnography, 94–96
    of participants, 96–97
    politics, 99–100
    of researcher, 97–99
Smith, K. L., 9
Smith, S., xxii, 63, 64, 65, 68–70, 71–72, 74
Snapchat, 121, 127

social media
    acquaintances, friends, lovers, 127–129
    ambient presence, 127
    communication, 121–122
    digital armchair anthropologists, 124–125
    digital identity, 119–120
    digital technology, 129
    location tags, 122–123
    managing relationships, 129–130
    on- and offline network, 120–121
    overview, 119
    own identity, 123–124
    participant observation, 125–126
    post-field research, 129–130
    pre-field research, 121–124
    safety and online research, 126
social science disciplines, 3, 12
Solomon, O., 13
special educational needs and disability (SEND), 69
Spector, B., xxiii, 81, 119, 120, 122–125, 127–129
Stanford Encyclopedia of Philosophy, 51
Summers, F., 74
Sutton, T., xxiii, 81, 119, 120, 121, 122, 123, 125–130

Theidon, K., 27
time-consuming process, 19
Tor protocol, 42–43
Townsend-Bell, E., 87
transformative care, 148, 158, 160
Twitter, 43, 120, 126, 130, 151, 161

UAE National Day, 34
UK High Court, 34
UK institution social science department, xvii
UK National Cybersecurity Centre, 44
United Nations Convention on the Rights of Persons, 54

Vanderstaay, S. L., 28
Van Osch, E., xxii, 63, 64, 65, 67–71, 73
violence and instability
    build trust, 138–141
    context of violence, 137
    fatigue and exhaustion, 143
    overview, 135–136
    post-fieldwork debrief, 143
    privileges, 141–142
    thinking, 136–138
    vicarious trauma, 142
    warrant discussion, 144
    yourself and your interlocutors, 143–144
virtual machines (VM), 43–44
virtual private networks (VPNs), 42
Visweswaran, K., 110
The Vulnerable Observer, 151

Walton, S., 124
Wang, C.C., 173
Washington Post, 34
Wengle, J. L., 8
Wikipedia, 42
Wolcott, H. F., 6
Wolseth, J., 29
Woodland Park Zoo, 14
World Health Organization, 51
Writing Culture: The Poetics and Politics of Ethnography, 183
writing ethnography
    complexity and diversity, 188–189
    institutional and disciplinary expectations, 184
    institutional productivity statistics, 192
    neutral ethnographic writing, 190–192
    overview, 183–184
    partial representations, 185–187
    representational dilemmas, 187–188
    spaces and communities, 192

www.ingramcontent.com/pod-product-compliance
Lightning Source LLC
Chambersburg PA
CBHW080214040426
42333CB00044B/2666